D1564237

THE GREEK UPHEAVAL
Kings, Demagogues and Bayonets

THE GREEK UPHEAVAL

Kings, Demagogues, and Bayonets

Taki Theodoracopulos

CARATZAS BROTHERS, PUBLISHERS
New Rochelle, New York
1978

First published in England by Stacey International.

U.S. edition published by
CARATZAS BROTHERS, PUBLISHERS
246 Pelham Road, New Rochelle, N.Y. 10805

ISBN 0-89241-080-9
Library of Congress Card
Catalog Number 77-91601

Contents

The author wishes to express his gratitude to two friends who assisted with the creation of this work. To shield them from the bellicosity of sections of the Greek press only their Christian names will be mentioned: Cristos M. and John B. I also want to thank Beth Rigos for her expert help in editing and typing the manuscript, as well as Anthony Lejeune. Last, but not least, my profound gratitude to Mr. William F. Buckley, Jr, for his encouragement and help throughout the project.

FOR MY PARENTS

Chapter 1

Karamanlis and Democracy
Return to their Birthplace

THE incessant blare of martial music on the government-controlled radio was suddenly interrupted by a brief, terse statement. 'President Phaidon Gizikis,' said an emotionless voice, 'has had discussions with a number of Greek politicians with a view to forming a new coalition government. The armed forces have decided to turn the governing of the country over to a civilian government.'

The time was 7 p.m. on Tuesday, July 23rd, 1974. And with that simple statement, which ended a seven-and-one-half-year dictatorship, democracy was restored to the land of its birth.

In the mood of despair which had increasingly prevailed, the Greeks could scarcely believe their ears at first. Yet rumours had been sweeping the ancient city throughout that fateful day, one of the hottest in memory. John Rigos, the U.P.I. bureau chief in Athens, had been one of the first to hear them. A portly, bald, avuncular man, Rigos is the dean of the foreign press corps. A kindly soul, who somehow always finds time to help foreign correspondents lost in the labyrinth of Greek political manoeuvres, he is, nevertheless, one of the ablest newsmen around. An ever-present sixth sense told him to follow the rumours of the street; so he set out for the presidential palace located in the centre of downtown Athens facing Constitution Square.

Once there the newsman was struck by the unlikely sight of ex-politicians entering the gates of the palace. Some were being chauffeured in government limousines; other were driving their own cars. One of them, ex-premier Athanasiades Novas, a septuagenarian, just walked through, wearing an ordinary shirt and trousers. Although unable to get past the gate himself, Rigos had seen enough. He raced back to his office in Valaoritou Street and filed a report that startling new developments were about to break in Greece.

The time was 1:30 p.m. As the stifling afternoon wore on the rumours multiplied. By 5 p.m. a medium-sized crowd had gathered outside the pink, neo-Hellenic presidential palace which served as the parliament building before the coup of April 21st, 1967. Throughout the city clusters of people were congregating around cafés which provided television sets or radios.

Athens is a city which thrives on rumours. The Athenians have always loved gossip and politics. So it was natural that this secret meeting of politicians instantly roused the old Greek political animal from its seven years of hibernation.

But abruptly the euphoria and excitement subsided. An announcement over the radio declared that 'certain rumours which are circulating are totally baseless and put out by enemies of the state.' As darkness, matching the people's mood, descended, the crowds slowly broke up.

Then came the 7 a.m. announcement signalling the junta's collapse and, in a matter of minutes, the good news had swept the city.

A small knot of people who had waited across from the old palace in the huge, centrally-located Constitution Square soon built up to 500, then 5,000, later still to an incredible 50,000. Hesitantly at first, they raised their fingers in the sign of a V and began shouting, 'Victory for the people.' More and more people swarmed over the square, exploding into cheers and chants of hysterical celebration.

Soon the sea of humanity—which by now had passed the 100,000 mark—overflowed into the streets, paralyzing traffic. Blue and white Greek flags appeared out of nowhere and a brisk business was done by anyone who could furnish the hysterical crowd with flags or pictures of political leaders. As the joyful procession passed the Metropolis, the city's cathedral, an enterprising priest came out selling candles. Then, as night enveloped the scene, the flickering of thousands of candles danced among the crowd.

For many Greeks this was an unforgettable moment. It could only be compared in its intensity with that of the liberation of Greece in September 1944, when the German invaders were driven out by the Allied armies. Then, as now, people had spontaneously spilled out into the streets in paroxysms of joy over their sudden freedom.

The delirious crowds were not aware of the intense drama taking place inside the President's office. An hour after the announcement of the junta's collapse there was still no final decision as to who would succeed the fallen puppet government. Two urgent calls to American Secretary of State Henry Kissinger resolved nothing as far as the Cyprus question was concerned. Nicosia was rumoured to be again under attack and about to fall, while Greek commanders in the north were having trouble restraining their tank crews and junior officers from crossing the Evros River and striking at the Turkish mainland.

At 8:30 p.m. news filtered out of the President's office that ex-Premier Constantine Karamanlis had been summoned from his self-exile in Paris to lead the nation. An even greater wave of enthusiasm engulfed the crowds as rhythmic chants of 'Ka-ra-man-lis' filled the air.

'On to the airport' came the cry and the sea of humanity flowed toward the outskirts of the city as if by remote control. Buses, taxis and private cars were commandeered. Most people simply walked, and a long chain of celebrants, carrying flags, candles, flowers and pictures of the sixty-seven-year-old leader, snaked toward the airport ten miles to the east.

Since the outbreak of hostilities five days before, the airport had been closed. Camped inside the white stone and glass, Saarinen-designed terminal were some hundred tourists, mostly Americans, who had either been left stranded by the sudden closure of the airport or wished to make sure of a plane out of the troubled country the moment flights were resumed. Not one hotel bed was available in Athens, as it was the height of the tourist season. These would-be travellers looked on in horror as the crowd rushed the strong police contingent guarding the arrival building. But they were quickly assured that, for once, this was not an anti-American demonstration.

The waiting lounges and V.I.P. rooms rapidly filled with a smattering of Athenian personalities. The 'do you know who I am?' way of handling authority is nowhere more prevalent— or more successful—than in Greece. Rules are to be applied, but with exceptions. And there were about two thousand exceptions that night as all the beautiful people talked themselves through the police cordon and pushed inside.

Shipowners, industrialists, movie actors and actresses, night-club singers, football players and two of the best known madams in Athens—one wearing a large picture of Karamanlis on her front, a second on her back, and little else—mingled with the sweating newsmen and overworked police.

Lambros Eftaxias, the elegant and cultured former Minister in the Karamanlis government, had struggled through the confusion with his dignity intact but his beautiful silk suit rumpled beyond recognition. 'I've never seen so many ghosts assembled in one place,' he remarked to a newsman, eyeing politicians who had been put away in mothballs for seven years.

The Greek crowd, being highly emotional, started embracing each other and cheering as each new personality appeared on the scene. Some of these arrivals, like industrialist-banker-shipowner George Andreadis, who had been among the most vigorous supporters of the colonels, did raise a few eyebrows.

But the stars of the evening were the former politicians. They were fawned over by everyone who had ignored them— by police, by capitalists and journalists alike. Speculation about who would get what ministry helped pass the long hours as the vigil which had begun at 9 p.m. continued past midnight.

Fortunately there was no air traffic. Only two military transports landed in the adjacent American base, causing some confusion among the surging, expectant crowd.

Finally the interminable wait came to an end. At precisely 2:02 a.m. the Mystere 20, lent for the occasion by French President Valery Giscard d'Estaing, touched down on the landing strip; Karamanlis was on Greek soil again.

The plane taxied slowly towards the apron until the crowd broke the police barriers and rushed the whining jet. The cool French pilot quickly shut off the engines and motioned to the ground signaller, by throwing up his hands, that his responsibilities were over.

As the newsreel floodlights zeroed in, the plane's door was lowered and out stepped the man on whose shoulders rode the hopes of nine million Greeks. It was exactly ten years, seven months and seventeen days since he had left his native country clandestinely, under false accusations, to a self-imposed exile in Paris.

Although sixty-seven years of age, he was still a very handsome man; in fact, according to John Rigos, he had improved with age, like a vintage wine. The famous black beetle-brows toned down now by touches of grey, the Grecian profile and imposing stature still intact, he seemed even more distinguished when one compared him with the faceless, grey men he was replacing.

The frenzied crowd surged forward once again in an attempt to lift him on to their shoulders. Karamanlis looked bewildered, almost afraid, but quickly regained his composure while the police slowly, painfully, opened the way towards a waiting limousine. Engulfed by the throng, his three brothers tried in vain to reach him. Old friends, close associates of the past, important personalities were all swept aside as unknown men and women—some young, mostly middle-aged—fought past the guards in order to touch him or to kiss his hand in the traditional Greek way of showing respect.

No one had thought of installing a loudspeaker; thus the few words with which he addressed the people went unnoticed although thunderously received. Then the black Mercedes crept away through the cheering multitudes and led the ten-thousand-car procession towards the capital.

Arriving at the presidential palace, Karamanlis was immediately ushered into the wood-panelled office where President Gizikis, Archbishop of Athens Seraphim, and former politicians were gathered and waiting to greet him.

The time was 3:00 a.m. but yet another hour was to go by before Karamanlis would agree to be sworn in. The heated discussion came to an end when Petros Garoufalias—a man who had played a pivotal role in the fall of Papandreou and in the eventual collapse of the monarchy—reminded everyone that the country could not stand any more bickering. At 4:15 a.m. Archbishop Seraphim, wearing a gold-braided cassock, swore in Constantine Karamanlis, the peasant boy from Macedonia, in the presence of General Gizikis, the chief of the armed forces and eight political figures. Greece had a government at last.

Chapter 2

The Two Protagonists and Their Inevitable Collision

THE simple voluntary surrender of the Colonels to the civilian government of Karamanlis, without a popular uprising or yet another countercoup, will eventually prove to be as controversial an issue for future historians as the attempt to assassinate Makarios; all the more so since these officers were to be tried for insurrection and high treason—crimes which carry the death penalty—by the very people to whom they had yielded so easily.

Ioannides and his colleagues were hardly the type to panic or collapse. What, then, forced them to surrender their power and seal their own doom?

Why had the super-hawk Greek junta sat idly by while its arch-enemies, the Turks, invaded an island considered to be part of the sacred motherland, napalmed and strafed Greek-Cypriot civilians and caused hundreds of thousands to flee their homes and become refugees, without firing even a symbolic round in anger?

What role did the United States and the Central Intelligence Agency play in the drama? And what about the Soviet Union's meddling in Cypriot affairs and implied threat of naval intervention?

The answers to these questions fall into place when the fateful fortnight of July 10th to 24th is reconstructed. But first the background must be sketched in.

Since April 21st, 1967, Greece had been ruled by a military-backed government. Its strongman, ex-Colonel George Papadopoulos, was overthrown in a countercoup led by Brigadier Demetrios Ioannides in November of 1973. The young officers who overthrew Papadopoulos felt that his liberalization programme—which had turned the government over to historian-politician Spyros Markezinis and had set a timetable for free elections—would mean a reversion to the chaos that prevailed before 1967. They accused Papadopoulos and his ministers of deviating from the goals of the revolution. They further promised that, after a thorough house-cleaning, the army would lead the way toward a healthy democracy.

Demetrios Ioannides, the fifty-three-year-old Brigadier who overthrew his old comrade-in-arms and fellow-conspirator Papadopoulos, was born—like the majority of Greek officers—in extreme poverty. He came from that bleak part of north-western Greece known as Epirus, a land that throughout the centuries has had to endure the wars between Greece and her traditional Balkan enemies.

Ioannides's opportunity to escape from his harsh environment—plus his first square meal—came when he entered the Military Academy in 1940. The Italian invasion of Greece occurred while he was still a cadet. When the country was occupied by the Axis powers, he joined the E.D.E.S. partisans in the mountains. (E.D.E.S. was a non-communist guerrilla organization.)

In 1951 Ioannides was involved in an unsuccessful attempt to compel the late king, Paul I, to accept Field Marshal Alexander Papagos as Prime Minister. When the Field Marshal himself intervened by asking the young officers to 'stop all this nonsense,' Ioannides was one of the last to surrender. After that he barely managed to stay in the army—his bravery and good record helped—and he wrecked several promotions by his unbending stance against corrupt politicians and élitist officers.

A man who would pass by unnoticed, Ioannides possessed none of the charisma in looks or personality needed for advancement. Many young officers received quick promotion and influential positions through the royal palace and parliamentary cocktail circuit: but not this young provincial with his traditional peasant dislike of anything smacking of élitism. He was once described as a walking definition of the word 'dour.'

Ioannides believed that patriotism and honesty were the

only ingredients needed for individual perfection. Among his convictions there was also a fundamentalist and all-embracing anti-communism, fired by religion, and allied to a passionate faith in the civilizing mission of Hellenism.

Tough and brave, he had few close friends. He never moved out of the family home and cared for his widowed mother, his younger sister, and a flock of relatives. Living an exemplary, almost ascetic, private life, he remained a bachelor and devoted his spare time to reading the classics—mostly Aristotle and Plato—and attending church.

While other more flexible and ambitious officers accepted the shortcomings of Greek political life, Ioannides never wavered. From an early age he was convinced that all politicians were corrupt and Greek parliamentary life a disgrace and a national danger. He was first exposed to this dishonesty when he found politicians rigging elections. He once said that he would follow any party, except the Communists, which was honest. But this proved difficult, if not impossible. All political parties cheated in Greece, thereby undermining democracy in order to serve personal and petty interests.

In 1965, as an ageing Major, Ioannides was posted to Cyprus. He served as an operations officer with the Greek contingent and was able to get a first-hand impression of what he was to call later on 'the treacherous ways of the Red Bishop'.

The Cypriot Republic was then only five years old, but to worried Greek officers it was already clear that President Makarios was committed to a policy of independence, rather than to the sacred cause of 'Enosis,' or union with Greece. To Ioannides this was betrayal of the highest order. Too much blood had been spilled and too many battles fought throughout the centuries in the name of 'Enosis'. The cause had to be put right and anyone standing in the way must be eliminated.

Upon Ioannides's return to Greece in 1967 he was promoted to Lieutenant-Colonel and made battalion commander at the Greek officer cadet school. He was one of Papadopoulos's fellow putschists in the 1967 takeover, and was then appointed head of the military police with extraordinary powers under the existing martial law. Refusing promotion during Papadopoulos's seven-year reign, he developed the military police

(E.S.A.) into a highly effective paramilitary force of almost 20,000 men.

Continuing to live without fanfare, Ioannides looked upon Papadopoulos's liberalization experiments with a jaundiced eye. He was also opposed to the life style of some ex-officers turned ministers, who, he felt, were being slowly seduced by Athenian society into the political world's old sins. Taking advantage of the student riots in November 1973, he decided to step in.

Cracking down brutally on all forms of dissent, he and his fellow hard-liners picked a civilian puppet government and also appointed an old friend—the shy, humble and impeccably honest General, Phaidon Gizikis—as President.

Ioannides remained, as always, behind the scenes, working out of his office in the E.S.A. building adjacent to the American Embassy. Eight months later his turn would come. Some of the people closest to him believe that if Ioannides had not had a tour of duty in Cyprus things would have turned out differently. However, that is a matter of conjecture.

Cyprus has always been a thorn in the psyche of men like Ioannides and, sooner or later, the pain would probably have become unbearable anyway. Cyprus was, and is, Greece's Achilles' heel, the inspiration for heroism, the excuse for abominable crimes.

Cyprus has been described as having 'all the ingredients for conflict'. Geography has played a greater role in its history than alliances and treaties. Situated in the southeastern part of the Mediterranean, Cyprus lies an equal distance from the Turkish and Syrian coasts. It has always been considered, however, as the easternmost appendage of Hellenism. From the earliest times the island has been inhabited by Greeks. In the Middle Ages it was part of the Greek Byzantine Empire; like the rest of Greece, it was invaded and occupied by the Ottoman Turks. During Ottoman rule (1571-1878), the island's inhabitants preserved their national identity and religion intact. It was during this period that the first Ottoman settlers arrived in Cyprus; but the newcomers never became a significant part of the population. During the nineteenth century Turkey tried to get rid of Cyprus in exchange for

European assistance in her fight against the Egyptians. When England embarked on an imperial policy under Disraeli and Salisbury, in the latter part of that century, the island passed over to her on lease.

As rich archeological remains testify, the Greeks have been there for three thousand years, and thus consider the island to be theirs, and theirs alone. When Britain annexed Cyprus in 1914, after Turkey entered the War on the side of Germany, it was thought natural enough to offer the island to King Constantine I of Greece, if he would agree to make common cause with the Allies. (The king refused, giving an early indication of the Greek monarchy's political acumen.) In 1923, under the terms of the Treaty of Lausanne, Turkey officially ceded all her rights regarding Cyprus. As a result, Cyprus became a Crown Colony in 1925.

With a population of approximately 650,000—of which 530,000 were Greeks and 120,000 Turks—Cyprus has been a divided community ever since. Demands by Greek Cypriot nationalists for independence from British rule and unification with Greece erupted into armed conflict on April 1st, 1955. The political leader of the nationalists was Archbishop Makarios. The military campaign was led by Colonel George Grivas, a former officer of the Greek army and a Cypriot by birth, who formed the National Organization of Cypriot Fighters, to become known as E.O.K.A. from the initials of its name in Greek. Grivas's E.O.K.A. guerrilla movement successfully resisted British counter-insurgency operations. The level of violence was considerable but mainly confined to the two principal antagonists—the Greek-Cypriot supporters of E.O.K.A. and the British security forces. Although remaining aloof from the fighting, the Turks were, nevertheless, determined that there should be no new base for Hellenism. During the struggle for 'Enosis' Grivas made it clear that the enemy was the British government. But from June to early August 1958 the anti-colonial struggle spilled over into a wider intercommunal strife. The atrocities committed during the brief period were gruesome and the savage blood-bath has never been forgotten by either side.

The most important point about E.O.K.A., which explains

the frustration of the Greek officers, is that it failed to achieve its objective—union with Greece. The struggle ended with the Zurich and London agreements of 1959, which made Cyprus an independent state.

But that proved only the beginning of the Cyprus tragedy. With less than 20 per cent of the population and only 12 per cent of the land, the Turkish community was accorded 30 per cent of the seats in parliament and the same proportion of positions in the civil service. Three of the seven ministers in the government were to be Turks and the army was to recruit 40 per cent of its strength from the Turkish side. Most important of all, the Turkish Vice-President was accorded a veto on all major decisions.

On December 13th, 1959, Makarios became the first President of the Republic of Cyprus, a position he has held ever since. President Archbishop Makarios has proved himself a Houdini of political and physical survival. Before the July coup against him be boasted that he had survived fifteen Greek Governments. He was destined to live through the fall of a sixteenth—the one that tried to oust and kill him.

Several students of Greek and Cypriot history believe that his resilience can be attributed to his origins. Makarios was born Michalis Mouskos on August 13th, 1913, in the village of Panaghia in western Cyprus, the son of a local shepherd. At the age of thirteen he entered Kykko Monastery and eventually became a monk. As a clergyman he took the name of Makarios, which means 'the blessed one,' and exchanged the shepherd's staff for the study of theology and, later, law at Athens University. In 1946, after being ordained an archimandrite, he went to the University of Boston, where he studied religion and sociology. In 1950 he was elected Archbishop of Cyprus and Ethnarch (leader of the nation), a dual title reflecting the spiritual and temporal leadership which the Cypriot Primates offered to their people.

The reasons behind the Greek surrender in Zurich were many, but the most important factor was that the Greek Prime Minister at the time, Constantine Karamanlis, was anxious to get on with his economic development programme for Greece and therefore to get the Cyprus problem out of the way.

Although the Greeks accepted the terms with great reluctance, it was the indiscriminate use of the veto by the Turks which swiftly led to a paralysis of the political and fiscal life of the island. This impasse led Makarios to seek revision of some clauses of the Constitution. The ensuing Turkish-Cypriot reaction resulted in riots in December 1963 and in the setting up of a Turkish-Cypriot administration in their sectors of the island. Faced with the danger of a spreading conflict, the United Nations sent an emergency peace-keeping force to the island for three months. Thirteen years later the troops were still there. Since 1964 a *de facto* partition has found Greeks and Turks living side-by-side, but avoiding each other.

Although inter-communal talks began in 1968 no real progress was made. The Turks lived mostly in landlocked enclaves and travelled through Greek territory when they wanted to take a ship or a plane. The Greeks provided them with water and electricity, which the Turks were unable to furnish for themselves.

Twice in the last thirteen years—in 1964 and 1967—relations between Greece and Turkey have reached breaking-point over Cyprus. Both times American mediation preserved peace. (The brinkmanship practiced by both sides, and the timely American arbitration which helped each Government save face, was to have disastrous results for Greece in 1974. Greece then miscalculated Turkish threats and overestimated America's influence on Turkey.)

Although it is hard to get objective opinions from anyone involved in the Cyprus problem, it is fair to assume that the Turkish claims were not only unreasonable, but unrealistic. There are countless sovereign nations which include minorities larger than the Turkish minority in Cyprus as part of their indigenous population. No claims for a state within a state are expressed by these minorities while their rights are guaranteed. The rights of Turkish-Cypriots had been observed, apart from a few isolated incidents by the extremist fringe. But the Turks— both in Cyprus and on the Turkish mainland—pressed their unrealistic proposals because of the disunity among Greek-Cypriots over the cause of 'Enosis'. This issue, has been as divisive a factor as the atavistic differences between Moslem

Turks and Christian Greeks.

Makarios's policy of aiming for independence, rather than union, inevitably brought conflict. The die-hards of 'Enosis' were led once again by the hero of the struggle for independence, General Grivas. The Cypriot army, which goes under the name of 'National Guard,' had been directed since its inception by mainland Greek officers. (There are 1,800 officers commanding a force of roughly 20,000 men. The Turkish counterpart, also directed by mainland officers, has a strength of about 15,000 men.) It was natural for the pro-union E.O.K.A. to infiltrate the National Guard. Grivas, who died of natural causes in 1973, had formed his second guerrilla army which he named E.O.K.A.-B.

Makarios also took steps to ensure his position. He encouraged the formation of a private army by his personal physician, Dr. Vassos Lyssarides, a left-wing politician who had close relations with Palestinian guerrilla organizations. He also equipped an élite Praetorian guard, the 'Epikouriki,' with weapons from Communist-bloc countries.

A period of bombings and assassinations between the pro-Enosis and the pro-Makarios factions undermined any solution to the more important Greco-Turkish impasse. Makarios himself was the target of many assassination attempts by pro-Enosis elements. But he gave as good as he got. He was accused of turning a blind eye to murder squads which systematically got rid of his opponents, although concrete proof of this was never established. What has been confirmed, however, was his great reliance upon the Cypriot Communist Party (A.K.E.L.) in order to survive. A.K.E.L. has long been the most cohesive and integrated group on the island. It has always followed the Moscow line to the letter, never appeared to be short of funds, and has been most effective in the labour union movement. The Communists, who were violently opposed to 'Enosis', had throughout the years backed Makarios to the hilt in his resistance to pressures from Athens and Ankara. They were suspected, nevertheless, of having underground contacts and a tacit understanding with the Turks—in fact, an alliance pledged to keep Cyprus independent. After all, Makarios's line that 'Enosis' was desirable, but not feasible, suited both the Communists and the Turks.

The ideological conflict between Makarios and the Greek junta of Ioannides was an obvious one. Makarios's trips to Moscow and Peking did no more than raise eyebrows among narrow-minded, super-nationalistic, Greek officers. And his open resistance to the influence of Athens was coming to a head as Ioannides came to power. (Whatever charges may be levelled against the Papadopoulos administration after the suspension of parliamentary life in 1967, its policies toward Cyprus were restrained and constructive. 'Enosis' had often been used as a political football by the squabbling politicians, who threw away numerous opportunities for a just and final settlement, but this no longer happened after Papadopoulos took charge. Immune from criticism by parliamentary opponents, Papadopoulos decided that good relations with Turkey were more important than the romantic dream of 'Enosis.')

Thus the stage was set for the final collision between the Rasputin-like Makarios and the super-patriot Ioannides. That Cyprus now lies in ruins—economically, as well as physically— is even more heart-rending when one considers what it was like before the Turkish invasion. Blessed with an ideal climate of mild winters and cool, dry summers, with an abundance of raw materials, metals and agricultural products, her inhabitants were fully employed and enjoyed the highest standard of living among the Mediterranean peoples.

All this was to come to an end on July 20th, 1974, as the Turkish troops poured into the island, leaving death and destruction in their wake. The crucial letter from Makarios to General Gizikis played a pivotal role. It was delivered on Saturday, July 6th, and Greece and Cyprus are still reverberating from its effects.

Chapter 3

Why Makarios Had To Go

O N Saturday, July 6th, 1974, President Phaidon Gizikis was, as usual, staying late in his office in the Old Palace. His inner sanctum, situated in the southeastern corner of the huge building, was well protected from the city's bustling noises. The high-ceilinged office, redecorated during the presidency of George Papadopoulos, combined simplicity with elegance and comfort. A desk, two armchairs, and a conference table for eight were the only furniture in the room. Gizikis found that here he could escape from the urban noises he hated—the palace is surrounded by the city's only large green belt—as well as from the painful memories of a young and beautiful wife who had recently passed away.

Although a once charming and beautiful city, Athens has become, like most overpopulated urban centres, a noisy, smoky jungle of concrete. The Athenian work schedule is split in two, in an effort to escape the high afternoon temperatures. Offices open early in the morning, close at 1:30 p.m., re-open around five in the afternoon, and close for the day at nine in the evening. On that particular Saturday afternoon most people had already left the city for the beaches to take advantage of the half-day holiday.

A tall, distinguished-looking man, Gizikis was probably the only member of Ioannides's hated regime to command any respect from the Greek people. He was not considered brilliant, but his honesty and bravery were known to everyone. And his simple, taciturn ways—coming as they did after Papadopoulos's inflated grandiosity—helped endear him to the man in the street. He disliked being the titular head of the kind of

26

dictatorship which Ioannides had imposed, and had agreed only after he was assured by the junta that its role would be a transitional one. This gullibility was to have enormous repercussions later on, but at that particular moment Gizikis was convinced that an eventual change toward normality would be forthcoming.

Nevertheless, Gizikis possessed a rare quality for a military man, and particularly for a Greek. He recognized his limitations, and never assumed himself to be right when things pointed to the contrary.

On that evening, as he was about to leave for home, a secretary brought him an official letter, addressed to him personally, from his Cypriot counterpart, Archbishop Makarios. When Gizikis first read the letter his reaction was that of annoyance, not much more. He rang Brigadier Ioannides at the E.S.A. building a mile away. Over the phone he explained the main points of Makarios's message. Ioannides wasted no time. In less than five minutes he was entering Gizikis's inner sanctum.

Makarios, in this critical letter, accused the Athens government of plotting to overthrow him; of trying to kill him; of fomenting revolution; and he stated unequivocally that 'the root of the evil is very deep and extends as far as Athens.' More important, he demanded that the Greek officers of the Cypriot National Guard be recalled to Greece because the Guard 'had become a centre of conspiracy against the State.' He ended the letter by expressing his distaste for the non-democratic Greek regime in no uncertain terms.

Although by now seriously troubled by this provocative letter, Gizikis began immediately to seek a compromise solution. He had no love for Makarios. Few are the Greek officers, or politicians for that matter, who harbour any fond thoughts of the 'priest.' Yet, in the cause of peace, Gizikis favoured a cooling-off period for reflection, and an eventual compromise.

Ioannides was not of the same mind. He cursed the 'treacherous priest,' called him a communist at heart, 'who would sacrifice Cyprus to the Turks in order to keep absolute power for himself.' Feeling humiliated, he opted for immediate action. Gizikis argued that, as they were the only two people in Athens who knew the contents of the letter, humiliation hardly entered into it. Reluctantly, Ioannides agreed to wait until Monday morning before convening a meeting of the chiefs of staff and the government.

But on Sunday morning, July 7th, Cypriot newspapers published the Archbishop's letter under banner headlines. Makarios had deliberately given it to the press, thus making sure that no compromise would be possible. To the officers stationed in Cyprus, the letter came as a bombshell. To those completing their two years of duty it meant they would be going home early. To others, recently arrived, it meant the loss of financial benefits. To them all it was an act of extreme provocation. In the officers' club in Nicosia there was open talk of treason by Makarios. There were also cries of 'let's get rid of the priest,' until a senior officer finally intervened.

Back in Athens, the censored press carried no news of the letter. However, Cypriot newspapers, as well as travellers from Nicosia, spread the word. The immediate reaction of most Greeks was that Makarios was asking for a showdown, although no one could explain why he had chosen that moment for it.

In Vouliagmeni, the seaside resort ten miles from the city, Christo Mavrogeorgios's first thought was that disaster has struck. A former officer, educated at Berkeley and later a Professor of Political Science at the University of California, Los Angeles, he had returned after 1967 and became one of Papadopoulos's presidential advisers. Being familiar with the junta's way of thinking, Mavrogeorgios gauged the situation correctly. 'Why in hell is the Bishop openly provoking people who are tough . . . and unimaginative?' he asked. 'And who is going to defend the island after the officers leave? His paramilitary organizations?'

There was no question that, by allowing the military regime in Athens no face-saving option, Makarios had crossed the Rubicon. Later events would prove that, although he might have been caught somewhat off guard by the Colonels, he had already made contingency plans for any eventuality. Makarios's excellent grapevine had not failed to report that the

Archbishop's open flirtation with the Communist bloc countries was pushing the Athens-Nicosia relationship towards breaking point. His recent crackdown on pro-Enosis elements had forced the opposition into a corner. Furthermore, he sensed that the Ioannides regime was floundering. Its popularity, both on the domestic and international fronts, had reached its lowest point. The country's economic recession had most Greeks grumbling and blaming the government's ineptitude, while the stories of torture which leaked out had western public opinion up in arms.

Makarios thus saw his chance to kill two birds with one stone. If Ioannides backed down and withdrew the Greek officers from Cyprus, Makarios would have eliminated the most powerful pro-union element from his realm. If Ioannides refused, or tried something foolish, his plan was to call on the super powers for support, knowing full well that Athens would have trouble finding any great power to back her cause.

Beyond all that, there was something else, perhaps as romantic a dream as 'Enosis,' but probably much more realistic. Makarios saw himself as a possible compromise leader of all the Greeks. He entertained thoughts of sitting one day in the pastel neo-classical palace facing Constitution Square. And why not? If he were to be the one to tweak Ioannides's nose, or force him into a catastrophic blunder, to whom would the grateful Greeks turn? Who had the international exposure and the prestige with both power blocs? Who had stayed away from inter-party squabbling in Greece? Who had resisted the junta all along and yet had not taken part in the pre-1967 feuds among the politicians? The only other candidate, Constantine Karamanlis, was dismissed by Makarios as a man of the Right, unacceptable to the rest of the politicians in Athens, themselves leaderless and hopelessly split.

So Makarios decided to send the fateful letter. The benefits to be reaped were immeasurable; the possible damage seemed negligible, and certainly not irreversible. After dispatching his letter, which was dated July 2nd, Makarios put his praetorian guard on the alert, notified the secret police to be ready for any eventuality, and took off for his annual summer holiday in his chalet in the Troodos Mountains.

In addition to being a public slap in the face to the Colonels, the letter had arrived at a most inopportune moment in Greek-Turkish relations. A new Turkish government headed by Bulent Ecevit was trying to use the weakness of the Greek regime to challenge the theory that the Aegean is a 'Greek lake'. On November 1st, 1973, several weeks before an American oil company had sunk a drill off the Greek island of Thassos in the north Aegean, the Turkish Government awarded oil exploration concessions in an area west of the Greek islands of Lesbos and Chios—outside the six-mile territorial limit around the islands. But the Greeks pointed out in a protest on February 7th that the concession was given on the continental shelf which Greece claimed belonged to her. The Turks rejected that argument and sent two bombers on target-practice over the central Aegean without permission from Greece or from N.A.T.O. In retaliation the Greeks pulled their ships out of a N.A.T.O. naval exercise.

The dispute heated up in the spring of 1974, after oil was found near Thassos, and promised to be a long drawn out affair. Both sides placed orders for weapons and put their armies on the alert.

Pouring oil on the 'oil-fires' was a danger that seems to have escaped Makarios. He always believed that Turkey's foreign policy was based more on bluff than on action. And on that point the Greek junta agreed with him. Thus the setting for a blunder with a chain of repercussions was completed.

On Monday morning, July 8th, the Greek people had still not been informed by the media of Makarios's request. However, it was being openly discussed by journalists and political observers around the Ministries and in the adjoining cafés. Diplomatic and political life is centred around the palace and most civil servants, journalists, and ex-politicians use 'Pinci's,' the coffee shop near the Ministry of Information, as a meeting place. On that Monday morning the habitués of 'Pinci's' could hardly restrain their glee. Evangelos Averoff, the patrician ex-Foreign Minister under Karamanlis, was there, along with Byron Stamatopoulos, Papadopoulos's ex-Minister of Information. So was the ubiquitous U.P.I. head, John Rigos. The consensus of opinion was that Makarios had done a brave thing, although nobody went as far as to predict that the outcome would be anything more than an embarrassment for Ioannides and company.

Greek life in general, and Greek politics in particular, have one thing in common: compromise. Situations are never allowed to go to extremes, and when they do—as in 1922, when one general and five politicians were executed for the Asia Minor disaster, or in 1944, when civil war broke out—the consequences are felt for generations to come.

Given this attitude, most political observers restricted themselves to speculating about what, if anything, Ioannides would do, and left it at that. After all, both rivals were Greek and the matter was a political one. A peaceful solution with an all-important face-saving clause was certain to be found.

While all the speculating was going on at 'Pinci's', back at the old palace the government had convened. For the embattled Prime Minister, Adamandios Androutsopoulos, this was one more problem to add to the already mounting crises engendered by the sluggish economy and the Turkish demands in the Aegean. Androutsopoulos was educated in the United States, where he had worked as an accountant. His law degree from the University of Chicago had later been challenged by a fellow Greek, but nothing was proved. After his return to Greece, he had served as Economic Minister in the Papadopoulos government. When Ioannides took over, he was named Prime Minister. A rather innocuous-looking man with a sad countenance, he was the epitome of what is commonly called a puppet. Nevertheless, he was an honest man, had dabbled in economics, and, for want of a more likely candidate, was chosen to be Prime Minister. Those people who would even consider collaborating with Ioanides's Government were very scarce indeed.

The rest of Androutsopoulos's Ministers were also nonentities, with the exception of Professor Elias Balopoulos, Minister of Co-ordination; General Vassilios Tsoumbas, Minister of the Interior; and Constantine Rallis, Minister to the Prime Minister and an ex-Minister under Karamanlis.

The Foreign Minister, Constantine Kypreos, was perhaps the worst example of ineptitude. A Greek who had lived most of his adult life in Egypt and a chemist by profession, he was appointed Minister of Industry during the early days of the Papadopoulos regime. He was ousted, but became Minister of Industry again when Ioannides took over. Then on July 4th, when the Foreign Minister, Spyros Tetenes, an able career diplomat, resigned over the Androutsopoulos Government's handling of the Cyprus question, Kypreos was given the job.

The act of naming Kypreos Foreign Minister was indicative at best, of the regime's naiveté, and, at worst, of downright bungling. Although a successful businessman, he had absolutely no knowledge of the geopolitical problems involved. He had never even attended a diplomatic meeting at any higher level than a cocktail party, and was totally unprepared to face such wizards of circumlocution and subterfuge as the Turk, Bulent Ecevit, and of course, Makarios.

During the ministerial meeting Balopoulos and the Minister of Culture, Professor Demetrios Tsakonas, insisted on a compromise. They were able to convince the rest of the Government, and the decision was taken to recall the Greek Ambassador in Cyprus, Efstathios Lagakos, for consultations and that Kypreos should eventually meet Makarios in Nicosia.

The Greek Government's plan was to gain time by stalling Makarios, while replacing, at the most, half of the 650 officers whose withdrawal he was demanding. This would bolster their defences in the eventuality of war with Turkey. For all its faults, the Androutsopoulos administration had tried valiantly to replenish the armed forces' arsenal, which had been left almost criminally depleted by Papadopoulos.

In undertaking this task, Greece had placed orders with France, worth £100 million, for forty Mirage planes and 125 AMX-30 tanks. Four more gunboats equipped with Exocet surface-to-surface missiles had been ordered, to create a fast-moving naval strike force. Greece was also in the process of taking delivery of thirty-eight Phantoms, ordered from the United States.

So time was of the essence, and the naive ministers went about trying to outwit the wily Makarios, while Ambassador Lagakos flew back and forth continuously between Athens and Nicosia.

By the time the Council of Ministers had reached a decision, however, Makarios's fate had already been sealed. At an earlier meeting in the President's office the same morning Ioannides and the chiefs of staff had decided to overthrow Makarios and install a man of their own choice.

Present at that meeting were General Phaidon Gizikis, the President; General Gregorios Bonanos, Commander-in-Chief of the Armed Forces; Lieutenant-General Demetrios Galatsanos, Commander-in-Chief of the Army; Vice-Admiral Petros Arapakis, Commander of the Navy; Lieutenant-General Alexander Papanikolaou, Commander-in-Chief of the Air Force; and, of course, Brigadier Ioannides.

Among the six men present, Ioannides was the hawk, arguing for an extreme solution. Gizikis remained the most opposed to him—though calling him 'son,' the traditional Greek form of endearment. Throughout the whole crisis Gizikis was the only one in the higher echelons of government to exhibit wisdom and good sense. Although the President agreed about the necessity of getting rid of Makarios, he was afraid of the international consequences that would result. The commanders of the armed forces agreed, typically, with both men: but they were the ones—ironically—who swayed Gizikis to go along with the plan. They assured him that any Turkish intervention could be easily contained by the submarines lying off the northern coast of Cyprus and the Phantoms based on the nearby island of Crete.

The decision to overthrow Makarios was taken unanimously and was signed by everyone present. This lack of foresight by the highest echelons of the Greek Armed Forces was not surprising. Without exception all of the men who took that crucial decision had reached their positions, not through merit, but through surviving a purge of abler officers during the Ioannides countercoup. General Bonanos had become Commander-in-Chief of the Armed Forces from being commander of the Third Army. A good commander and staff officer, he badly lacked the qualities of leadership and political acumen that his new position required.

General Bonanos's immediate predecessors were two highly respected and brilliant Generals: General Anghelis and

33

General Zagorianakos. Their equally able deputies, General Brumas and General Mourikis, had resigned in protest when Bonanos was named Commander-in-Chief by Ioannides. One cannot help but wonder how things would have turned out if stronger willed and more courageous officers had been at the helm.

The Commander-in-Chief of the Army, Lieutenant-General Galatsanos, was a good field commander but a failure as a staff officer. A protégé of Brigadier Pattakos—whose armoured units rolled into Athens in the original coup of 1967—Galatsanos had, nevertheless, gone over to Ioannides during the countercoup six year later. He was given the top post in the army as a reward.

Vice-Admiral Arapakis had been a trusted Papadopoulos man in the generally monarchist navy. It was he who alerted Papadopoulos that certain officers were plotting the return of the King and were in contact with the right-wing politicians, Evangelos Averoff and Petros Garoufalias. After the mutiny had been squashed and the mutineers dishonourably discharged, Arapakis replaced Admiral Margaritis as head of the Navy. He managed to keep his post by joining Ioannides against his old friend. Arapakis surprisingly was a very able officer, but over-ambitious and sadly lacking in moral character. His rocketing career was achieved mainly as a result of conspiracies and disloyalty.

The Commander-in-Chief of the Air Force, Lieutenant-General Papanikolaou, had been appointed during the Papadopoulos regime. He also was an able officer, although weak in character. Afraid of Ioannides, he did not dare to contradict him for fear of losing his top post. In the spring of 1974 Papanicolaou had gone to the United States to receive the first batch of Phantom jets ordered by Greece. During his stay there he had talks with military and State Department officials, who sounded him out on Ioannides. A reliable source within K.Y.P.—the Greek Central Intelligence Agency —reported afterwards that Papanikolaou had been told by these American officials that the Ioannides regime would have to go. Further, that he had reached a tacit understanding of cooperation in case unforeseeable events should arise. As things turned out, the K.Y.P. report proved very reliable indeed.

Among the reasons behind Ioannides's decision to overthrow Makarios, the revenge motive scarcely features. It was more a futile effort to play a grand geo-political game. Ioannides and his colleagues knew that they controlled the Cypriot National Guard. They could also count on the support of E.O.K.A.-B and the Greek contingent based in Cyprus. This contingent, numbering 950 men, had been sent to the island in accordance with the Zurich agreement of 1959. These were all pluses.

On the minus side, primarily, would be the outcry of international public opinion. England was sure to howl at the overthrow of the head of a Commonwealth nation. So would—though in lower tones—the Soviet Union, which associated its interests in the area with Makarios and his warm attitude toward the Cypriot Communists. All the Western, Eastern, and Third World countries would also deplore the act.

But in Ioannides's rather elementary thinking, that was all that could happen. The United Nations would pass a resolution deploring the fall of Makarios and demanding his immediate reinstatement. If Makarios could not be reinstated, the whole thing would blow over. The powerless United Nations had not, after all, been able to stop aggression anywhere else. Why should it be different now? Particularly since the problem could be interpreted as concerning only Greeks.

The 'creation of facts'—so admirably practised by the Turks a few days later—therefore became paramount. Makarios would be got rid of, a Greek-Cypriot installed in his place, and the way opened for a possible third front in case of a war with Turkey.

This, then, was the overriding thought behind Ioannides's action. The heating up of the 'oil war' between Greece and Turkey, and the possibility of an armed conflict between them, had both countries drawing up contingency plans. The obvious battleground would be their short northern frontier on the Evros River and the islands of the Aegean. But if a third front could be opened, only forty miles from the Anatolian coast, it would be an enormous thorn in Turkey's side, diverting Turkish strength away from the main battlefields.

Therefore the potential third front had to be made secure. This having been done, Greece could arm the island's garrison without difficulty and even base an expeditionary force there. All this could obviously not take place while Makarios insisted on a policy of non-alignment and continued his anti-junta actions.

Furthermore, there were other reasons for such diversionary tactics. Ioannides knew that the rising economic crisis was making the people fidgety and dissatisfied. Confrontation with Turkey could mean the end of his regime through the intervention of external forces. In his simple mind he saw a rallying point for all Greeks in the possible union of Cyprus and Greece, as well as in a strong Greek challenge to the Turkish claims on Aegean oil.

In this he seems to have been misled—purposely or otherwise—by American C.I.A. agent Peter Koromilas, who had been in contact with Ioannides throughout the years, and let it be known that, if Makarios were removed, the American marines would not be landing in Cyprus to reinstate him. Another C.I.A. agent, whose name must be withheld, but who like Koromilas, is of Greek parentage, also encouraged Ioannides during the crucial week following the delivery of Makarios's letter.

This is not to say that these agents spoke for the American government. But in Ioannides's mind it was enough, for it is customary in this part of the world to leave things unsaid. Let meanings be interpreted as they may; let them give the impression that what was said was not what was meant. It has been like this since ancient times. The Delphic oracle was never wrong.

The intelligence agents who advised Ioannides must have taken lessons from that analogous oracle. They never gave him anything of substance, nor did they tell him that so-and-so would like him to act in such-and-such a way. They just dropped hints and let him take it from there. Being a natural plotter, Ioannides listened and wondered if the American government might not really be thinking along the same lines as he was. He had risen through the ranks in the army during the cold war, and had learned to trust the Americans as anti-communists.

Finally, there was the fact of America's disenchantment with Papadopoulos after he refused landing rights to American cargo planes during the Yom Kippur War of 1973. Thus Ioannides felt that, if he could take Cyprus away from the 'Red Bishop,' his position would be enormously strengthened, as he could then negotiate a base for American ships, planes, and even missiles close to the volatile Middle East.

All of which convinced Ioannides that it was now or never, as far as Makarios was concerned. And after all, he had no choice. He had been allowed none by the Archbishop's ultimatum. Therefore orders were given for the assassination of Makarios to take place on Monday July 15th.

Chapter 4
The Coup

THROUGHOUT the week of July 8th to 14th only a small number of officers learned of the intended coup against Makarios. Colonel John Bravakos, assistant to President Gizikis, and Lieutenant-Colonel Michael Pylihos, Ioannides's adjutant, were among them. They began issuing specific assignments. The actual attack was to be carried out by members of the Cypriot National Guard and led by the acting head of the Guard, Brigadier General Georgitsis.

The head of the National Guard, General Denisis, had been called to Athens for consultations with the Government. He flew from Nicosia on July 12th, accompanied by Greek Ambassador Lagakos. His trip was accorded banner headlines by the Greek press, which has as yet published nothing concerning Makarios's letter. An all-important meeting to discuss the Cyprus situation was scheduled for Monday July 15th, and Denisis, Lagakos, the Chiefs of Staff and the entire Cabinet were to attend. (This, more than anything, must have made Makarios lower his guard, because even the wily Archbishop thought that any decision as final as the violent overthrow of a head of state would be discussed and argued at length by all the persons involved.)

Thus, by chance, the leadership of the coup fell to the acting head of the Guard, Georgitsis. As he was to remark ironically afterwards, 'I got my plum assignment through default.'

In Nicosia the anti-Makarios segment of the press had started asking the Archbishop embarrassing questions about the timing of his letter. 'Why now, your Beatitude,' said one headline, 'when the mother country needs us most?' Another newspaper pointed out that Greece and Turkey could go to war over Aegean oil rights at any moment, and Turkey was bound to use any weakening of the Greek forces on the island to her advantage. Still another paper said that Makarios had had fourteen years to train Cypriot officers if he did not wish to rely on the Greek ones, and had only decided now that the Greeks were not good enough because it suited his never-ending machinations.

The pro-Makarios press had not been idle either. A lively campaign was started against the Greek officers and Greek contingent stationed on the island. Adding fuel to the fire was an announcement from the Archbishop's office reducing military service from twenty-four to twelve months.

Simultaneously, what could fairly be described as a state of terrorism against Greek officers and men went into effect. This was conducted by the so-called 'auxiliaries,' who were euphemistically known as policemen but were in fact Makarios's élite guard. In this they were assisted by 'armed groups of citizens', who were, in reality, mostly Lyssarides's Communist shock troops.

On July 9th a sailor of the National Guard, known for his pro-Enosis sympathies, was arrested by the 'epikouriki' and thrown from a speeding car. As a result he suffered a broken back. On the evening of the 10th a soldier was mortally wounded because he failed to stop when challenged at an 'epikouriki' check-point.

The presidential palace, as well as the Archbishopric and the Kykkou Monastery—a stronghold of Makarios's élite troops, were closely guarded by his men. During the last tension-building week, all roads leading to these areas were totally controlled.

Quite naturally, this state of affairs had the officers of the National Guard in an uproar. Embittered and feeling betrayed, they were ready for anything. If nothing else, it was a perfect psychological moment for a kill.

All this does not indicate that Makarios's policies and subsequent letter to Gizikis lacked popular support. On the contrary. He spoke for the majority of the Greek electorate

39

and—most important—for the 35 per cent of the electorate which regularly voted pro-communist.

Within this popular mandate, it is fair to say that Makarios stretched his powers to the limit. It is an undeniable fact that his strongarm squads tortured and arrested E.O.K.A.-B elements with impunity; the latter, of course, were not strangers to violence and civil disobedience themselves. Who was to blame seems a classic 'chicken or the egg' problem. Thus, as the weekend approached, Nicosia resembled a powder keg about to explode.

To sum the situation up and the various warring parties, here is a list of the military groups, with a rough estimate of their strengths:

(a) The National Guard. It consisted of 10,000 Greek-Cypriots and was led by 650 Greek officers. (Although loyalties among the men were split between pro- and anti-Makarios elements, it was fair to assume that orders by their officers would be obeyed without incident.) Within the National Guard were included thirty-five air force officers who commanded and supervised the two all-important radar stations on the island. The only plane they possessed was a single-engine Piper Cub. There were also 150 officers and men of the navy, which consisted of one patrol boat, the *Leventis*, and five torpedo boats, *TB* 1, 2, 3, 4 and 5. (The *TB* 5 was laid up for lack of spare parts.)

(b) The Greek regiment of 1,000 men which was officially stationed in Cyprus under the 1960 agreement. This went under the name of ELDYK, or Elliniki Dynamis Kyprou.

(c) The Turkish regiment of 600 men, stationed there under a similar agreement; known as TOYDRYK.

(d) Makarios's personal army, 'the epikouriki,' or auxiliaries, a force of about 4,000 men heavily armed with Soviet-made AK-47's, Czechoslovakian anti-tank guns and heavy machine guns. (Makarios had consistently refused to modernize the National Guard's arsenal, claiming lack of funds. But he did manage to furnish his 'epikouriki' with the latest light weaponry. After his overthrow a large cache of AK-47s was found in the basement of the Archbishopric. He had also sneaked into Cyprus, in crates marked 'refrigerator trucks,' four British-made tanks to be used by his personal army.)

This, then, was the state of affairs when, on the morning of July 12th, Brigadier General Georgitsis called a meeting of his top officers and announced that on Monday, July 15th, they were to overthrow Makarios. Present at that meeting were Colonel Constantine Kombokis, commander of the Greek special unit of rangers; Commander George Papayannis, head of the Navy; Lieutenant-Colonel Gregory Lambrinos, chief of the tank force; Brigadier Petros Giannakodimos, and a few others. (ELDYK was *officially* not involved.)

These officers, in turn, informed their subordinates and, by Sunday morning, twenty-four hours before 'D-day,' all officers who were to participate in the coup had been briefed and were ready. Some Greek-Cypriot reserve officers of doubtful allegiance, along with men of the National Guard whose allegiance was also dubious, were given a long weekend off or hastily sent on leave.

However, no officers based outside Nicosia—no matter what their loyalties—were informed. This inexplicable omission led to many of them being shot in cold blood by Makarios supporters once the coup was under way.

Zero hour was set for 8:15 a.m. During the summer months, when temperatures hover around 100°F, offices start the day's business as early as 6 a.m. By 8:15 a.m. people are already hard at work and the roads relatively clear of traffic.

The five main targets of the attack were to be the Archbishopric, the presidential palace, the airport, the telecommunications centre, and the building of the Cyprus Broadcasting Corporation (C.B.C.). Secondary targets were the police headquarters, the Kykkou Monastery—where a large segment of Makarios's auxiliaries were housed—and, of course, the various 'epikouriki' strongholds. (The orders were for the occupants to be surrounded, informed of the coup, asked to lay down their arms, if any, and allowed to go free. Despite reports to the contrary, these orders were followed to the letter. The alleged massacres of supporters of Makarios were committed by E.O.K.A.-B specials and were vastly exaggerated by the press.)

By noting the priority given to prominent targets it is easy to see just how important the death of Makarios was if the coup were to be successful. Armed camps were not to be attacked until the Archbishop was overcome and his death announced over the air. This, the plotters believed, would stop all resistance.

Although the coup was timed for 8:15 a.m., a pre-arranged signal was to set it off. That signal was to be the passage of Makarios's car, bringing him back to Nicosia from his weekend retreat in the Troodos Mountains.

At precisely 7:25 a.m. Makarios passed Wayne's Keep, a sprawling base that housed the Greek contingent in Cyprus. He was driven, as usual, by his younger brother, Yacoumis Mouskos, and accompanied by two car-loads of bodyguards.

After the passage of the presidential convoy the two armoured forces which were to lead the attack began to link up. It was reported at the time that the ELDYK force was also involved. This was not so. The Greek contingent—which under the 1960 agreement was restricted to automatic rifles, mortars and light artillery—never officially took part, although certain officers of the Greek troops mingled with the coup-makers. Furthermore, the National Guard possessed all the armour, thirty-eight Russian T-34s.

At 8 a.m. sharp, Major Tsolakis—the Greek officer who, after the Turkish invasion, worked with U.N., British, and Turkish representatives to draw the ceasefire lines—started handing out weapons and ammunition to soldiers of the headquarters company of the National Guard. Simultaneously, the tanks of Lieutenant-Colonel Lambrinos started rolling toward the president's palace. They were supported by a company of infantry, as well as one hundred rangers.

For Commander George Papayannis, the brave, soft-spoken, popular naval officer, zero hour had come with the break of dawn. His orders were many and had to be executed within a short timespan so as not to arouse suspicion. One of these orders was the transfer of all military dependents (wives and children of National Guard officers and of the Greek contingent of ELDYK living outside the capital) into naval bases, or some other safe place, in case the 'epikouriki' took hostile action against them.

Papayannis's first thought that day was to send his wife out of the city. He wrestled with his conscience but, in the end, decided to say nothing. Leaving the house earlier than usual, he told her he couldn't sleep.

At 7:30 a.m., upon receiving the signal that Makarios had arrived in Nicosia, he started firing off orders to his units. First he sent a message to the patrol boat *Leventis* to remain in Paphos—a stronghold of pro-Makarios elements. He then ordered all naval personnel to a state of alert and two torpedo boats to blockade the port of Famagusta. Naval personnel at the Kyrenia base and at Paphos were also ordered to blockade those ports too. By 7:45 a.m. Cyprus was effectively sealed off by sea. Finally, he ordered the immediate transfer of all military families.

At 8:10 a.m. he transmitted a message to all naval units that Makarios had been assassinated and that the National Guard had taken over the running of the country. (A similar message was simultaneously sent out by other officers to their units.)

At 8:15 a.m. Papayannis secured the headquarters of the National Guard by posting ten of his men there, and then drove at top speed to the United Nations headquarters. The building was situated on the 'green line,' which separated the Greek and Turkish sectors of Nicosia.

At U.N. headquarters he asked to see the Indian General Chiant, and was ushered into his office immediately. General Chiant had already heard the news and was highly excited. Papayannis informed him of the coup and told him that Makarios was dead. This was intentional in order to forestall any move by the U.N. Papayannis stressed that it was a purely internal matter concerning the Greek community and that Turkish rights would be guaranteed. He asked General Chiant to reassure the Turkish leaders, and departed. The time was 8:21 a.m.

By 8:22 a.m. Lieutenant-Colonel Lambrinos's tanks had reached the presidential palace and were starting to spread out for the attack. Two tanks were in the lead in a reconnais-

43

sance pattern; the rest of the squadron followed about a quarter of a mile down the road.

Another squadron of armour headed for the airport, securing it without a fight and sealing it off by positioning three tanks on the runway, two on the approach road, and one at the entrance to the terminal.

Meanwhile, the unsuspecting Makarios had been driven to the Archbishopric, his official residence as head of the Orthodox Church in Cyprus. He preferred the more comfortable, if less opulent, surroundings of this mock-Byzantine building to the presidential palace, and used the latter only for his official duties as Head of State. He spent only a quarter of an hour at the Archbishopric and then left for the presidential palace.

On that morning Makarios was scheduled to meet a delegation of Greek children from Cairo. His Minister of Justice, John Vakis, and his Deputy Minister, Patroclos Stavrou, were also waiting for an audience, as he arrived at the domed former colonial residence just ahead of Lambrinos's tanks at 8:20 a.m.

The palace is situated on an incline and surrounded by a wooded park. A winding road leads into the area, which covers approximately thirty acres. On the righthand side of the park, at a distance of about one thousand yards, an 'auxiliaries' camp housed about 500 'epikouriki' in three low, barracks-type buildings. There were also several houses occupied by families of senior police officers, a police station, and a radio station.

Inside the grounds of the palace, to the left of the manor, was a building which housed the presidential guards. The front of the palace, with its large verandas and bay windows, faced north.

Just as Makarios started to greet the visiting children, the first shots rang out. Within seconds firing became heavy. A member of his guard rushed in and informed him that two tanks were crossing the outer perimeter of the palace grounds.

Makarios tried to call the Cyprus radio station, but the lines had already been cut. His two ministers, Vakis and Stavrou, who were waiting in the ante-room, burst in and told him that commandos were about to storm the building. (Both ministers were convinced that these commandos were from the Greek contingent, as the uniforms of both the Greek and the Greek-Cypriot élite forces were more or less identical. But they were mistaken.)

Makarios remained calm, urged the children to lie down for their own protection and, as bullets started to crash through the windows, left the reception room. He went into his private office and disappeared through a small door that led to the back of the building, the southwest side, which had not yet been surrounded.

Upon reaching the back gate, the Archbishop removed his black amulet and robe and, in a plain white shirt, left the palace. He slipped down a small bank towards a dry river bed and carefully climbed up on to the other bank. From there, crouching to avoid any stray bullets, he ran until he reached the main road. Throughout this operation he was accompanied by the head of his guards, Major Nicolaos Potamaris, by his personal bodyguard, Major Thrasyvoulos and by his nephew, Andreas Theofanou.

Once on the road the four men proceeded under cover of the trees and bushes lining the avenue. Suddenly a group of armed men appeared from nowhere and started running towards them. Fortunately for the Archbishop, they turned out to be 'epikouriki,' themselves on the run from their nearby camp which was by now in flames.

A young subaltern, George Tsagarakis, told Makarios that his only chance of escape lay in passing through the lines of the National Guard unrecognized, as all roads leading to and from the palace were cut off.

As Makarios was contemplating his plan of action a car came hurtling around the corner, its driver obviously confused and trembling with fear. He screeched to a stop when the Lieutenant pointed his pistol at him. Upon seeing Makarios, he offered his services, and was immediately accepted; the four men jumped in and told him to drive on. But after one hundred yards the car ground to a halt for lack of petrol. Nevertheless, Makarios's luck still held. No sooner had he left the stalled car than another appeared down the road. Driven by a policeman, this car had a full tank of petrol.

Makarios was now put on the floor of the policeman's car,

under the legs of his bodyguards, and, unchallenged, they headed for the outskirts of the city. As they were nearing the mountains which rise to the north of Nicosia, they heard over the radio, 'Makarios is dead. Long live the National Guard! Hellenism lives in Cyprus!'

By the time Makarios had escaped from the palace—he had, in fact, seen the approaching tanks—resistance by the presidential guard had ceased. However, in the twenty-five minutes it took for Lambrinos's armour to overrun the palace grounds the accompanying infantry unit had suffered heavy casualties. One tank lay immobilized by the entrance, having taken a direct hit from an anti-tank bazooka. Thirty-five to forty national guardsmen were killed while storming the palace, and many more were taken to hospital seriously wounded.

Adding insult to injury was the fact that their objective had not been obtained. In trying to make sure of it, national guardsmen and commandos had scoured the inside of the presidential residence, shooting up empty rooms, and had finally set fire to the building in frustration. But the body they were looking for was not to be found.

Although he had failed miserably, Lambrinos—an experienced tank commander known for his decisiveness—was not entirely to blame. Lack of co-ordination and a failure of intelligence were the real culprits. It must be remembered, too, that the tank column which attacked the presidential residence bore little resemblance to a modern N.A.T.O. armoured unit. The obsolete Russian tanks operated on diesel engines, which were never properly serviced and were not suited to run in such high temperatures. Makarios had bought these 'hearses' from his own arms dealer and, in doing this bit of business on the side, had unwittingly saved his own skin. Of course, the Greeks were to pay dearly for it when, a week later, during the height of the fighting with the Turks, their armour became useless and a change of engine was required for all but two of the tanks.

As Lambrinos's tanks approached the palace they started to spread out so that one column could attack the auxiliaries' camp while the other concentrated on the palace itself. About ten tanks headed for the camp, the other fifteen slowly encircled the palace. Once in position—and here intelligence was sadly lacking—they moved very cautiously, thinking Makarios's defenders were in full strength. When the lead tank was put out of action by bazooka fire, the rest of the armour began to concentrate its fire on the building as the supporting infantry crept up on their bellies.

The commando unit which had moved in to attack from the western side was caught in the fire of the tanks and of National Guard infantry advancing from the front, or northern, side. Many were killed. This fire-fight, plus the fact that some of the tanks' engines failed in the middle of the operation, gave Makarios the time he needed to make good his escape.

The presidential guard, which was normally about 200 strong, had only forty men on duty that day. Eight of these were in the manor, while the rest fought from the adjacent barracks. They managed to stall the attack long enough to justify their presence.

The force that attacked the 'epikouriki' camp also ran into difficulties. Four of the ten tanks stopped due to engine failure: and, although their crews turned them into stationary gun batteries, their effectiveness was reduced to a minimum.

The 'epikouriki' were supposed to be 500 strong, well armed with heavy machine guns, mortars and anti-tank guns. On that day there were only 150 men on duty, but their natural advantage as defenders, plus their better armament, kept Lambrinos's armour and infantry tied up for the better part of three hours. Two National Guard majors were killed leading the attack upon the camp, whose defenders fought valiantly.

The leader of these auxiliaries was Major Pantelis Pantazis, a fanatic supporter of the Archbishop. Being an experienced officer (he was trained in Greece and graduated from the Greek military college), he beseeched his fellow 'epikouriki' to fight on in order to gain time. He knew that, if the camp surrendered, the advancing armour would link up with the force attacking the palace, and Makarios's chances then would be nil. (After eventually surrendering, Pantazis was imprisoned, released to fight the Turks five days later, and is now chief of the 391st battalion of the National Guard.)

Meanwhile, resistance by Makarios's auxiliaries and paramilitary forces continued in other parts of the city. The Archbishopric came under attack and soon fell to the National Guard. The other strongpoint, the Monastery of Kykkou, however, put up a stiff resistance. At one point a National Guard Major asked the defenders for a cease-fire in order to convince the defending 'epikouriki' that their fight was useless. Advancing under a white flag of truce, the Major was shot in cold blood. Artillery was then brought in and used to flush out the holed-up defenders by levelling the stout old stone walls of the monastery.

By 1 p.m. most resistance had ended although isolated pockets within the city fought on. All telecommunications with the outside world had been cut since the start of the coup, while the C.B.C. continued to broadcast military marches and to announce Makarios's death. The radio announcer also stressed that the upheaval was an internal affair concerning only the Greek community.

Immediately following simultaneous attacks against the two pro-Makarios strongholds, the National Guard started rounding up officials of the government. However, the Archbishop's faithful lieutenant, Vassos Lyssarides, one of the leading left-wingers on the island, as soon as he got wind of the coup went into hiding in the Syrian Embassy, because of his close ties with the Arabs. His maquis band took refuge in the Troodos Mountains, and from there continued to harass National Guard movements.

At 2:50 p.m. of that fateful day, Nikos Sampson was sworn in as the new President of Cyprus by Genadios, former Bishop of Paphos and an arch-enemy of Makarios. In retrospect, the choice of President was as great a mistake on the part of the coup-planners as allowing Makarios to escape. Any chance that the coup had of success disappeared when Sampson was made President. 'It was,' someone wrote later, 'the worst choice since Nixon decided to tape his conversations for posterity.'

A thirty-eight-year-old ex-E.O.K.A. fighter, Nikos Sampson has been variously described as a hero, a thug, a blood-thirsty killer, a cold-blooded torturer and as great a Greek as the ancient heroes of mythology. He was loved or thoroughly despised, depending on who was speaking.

Sampson could best be described as the I.R.A. type of fighter. He thought nothing of shooting a man in the back, as he did on occasion when fighting the British during the struggle for independence. He undoubtedly caused havoc in the British ranks when, posing as a journalist, he killed British soldiers and Greeks suspected of collaborating with the British, and then wrote about it, adding that he had been first on the scene.

The significance of these 'exclusives' was finally understood by the British, who captured him and sentenced him to death. His exploits, however, had gained him a large following both in Cyprus and on the mainland. Perhaps for this or other reasons, his death sentence was commuted and, after independence in 1959, he was released from prison.

Financed by friends, Sampson started publishing a newspaper entitled *Machi*, which means 'The Struggle.' Naturally, he turned against his old leader, Makarios, whom he suspected of 'selling out the cause of "Enosis" because he prefers to be the President of a sovereign nation rather than just a Bishop of the Greek Orthodox Church.'

The international reaction to Sampson's elevation to national leader was, as might have been expected, loud and clear. The British, in particular, were horrified that a killer could suddenly become head of a commonwealth nation. Satirical pieces appeared in newspapers and magazines showing him arriving to meet the Queen, dripping with English blood. Yet, as history proves, yesterday's heroes become today's villains, and vice versa. His position was no more farcical, even as far as the British were concerned, than Arafat's appearance in the United Nations a few months later.

Nevertheless, Sampson's appointment was a stupendous blunder because he lacked the qualities necessary for a national leader. At best, he was a very effective fighter, guerrilla and terrorist tactics being his forte. His appointment had come about because of the coup-makers' lack of preparation on the political side. Their first choice, Glafkos Clerides, was Speaker of the House of Representatives, a respected and popular political leader who had, for the last four years, conducted the inter-communal talks between Turks and Greeks.

Clerides, however, declined for obvious reasons. By a fluke of fate the next two choices both happened to be out of the country. With time running out and the situation far from resolved, out of necessity the mantle of power fell on Sampson. His pro-Enosis views and fighting background insured at least some kind of following among the Cypriots, although, as it turned out, even die-hard pro-Enosis elements were shocked when he was named President.

The selection of Sampson, moreover, caused graver damage than the cries of outrage it provoked. As we will see in the next chapter, this act gave Turkey the all-important 'opportunity' she had been seeking for so long to intervene in Cyprus.

Known as an unrelenting Turk-hater, Sampson was not only feared, but detested, by the Turkish community on the island as well as in mainland Turkey. During the inter-communal fighting of the middle Sixties, the new President had personally conducted raids with his followers in reprisal against the Turkish air force bombing and strafing of unarmed Greek-Cypriot civilians. His reputation as a killer—although endearing him to the Greek community—confirmed an undying hatred on the part of the Turks. Upon his appointment, Rauf Denktash, the Turkish-Cypriot leader, remarked that 'it is as unacceptable as Adolf Hitler would be as President of Israel.'

By early afternoon Makarios and his three bodyguards had decided that their only safe refuge would be the village of Paphos. Having stopped at his nephew's house in the Troodos Mountains where they listened to the news on the radio, they proceeded cautiously, arriving at their destination at 4 p.m. There he met a large number of his followers who had managed to arrest the few Greek officers caught outside the naval base.

In addition, auxiliaries, policemen, and citizens loyal to Makarios had demanded the surrender of all officers and personnel of the Paphos naval station. The commanding officer radioed Papayannis and was told to board the torpedo boat *Leventis* and to surrender the station. *Leventis* was ordered to give covering fire while the trapped naval officers and men made their escape. The carrying out of this order was the reason why foreign radio stations reported heavy shelling against civilians in Paphos.

The telecommunications of the naval station were, for some inexplicable reason, not put out of action by the departing men, and it was from there that Makarios broadcast his 'I am alive' message to the Cypriot nation.

Resistance to the coup picked up visibly after his message was flashed by the tiny radio station around the island. Makarios asked the Cypriots to fight against the illegal and murderous coup, repeating again and again that he was alive and remaining with his supporters on the island. He named the station he was speaking from 'The Voice of Free Cyprus,' and his transmission was picked up in Tel Aviv and flashed around the world.

The stiffest resistance outside the capital took place in Limassol, the island's second largest city. But by nightfall of the first day, the National Guard had unquestionably broken all effective opposition. Paphos, on the westernmost side of the island, however, remained under the control of pro-Makarios forces.

In Athens that Monday the meeting of the Prime Minister, Lagakos (the Greek Ambassador to Cyprus), the chiefs of staff and the head of the Cypriot National Guard, General Denisis, took place as scheduled. Nothing had as yet been said on the Government-controlled radio and television stations. Newspapers were not allowed to print the news either.

Nevertheless, the coup was known to almost everyone in Athens by noon. At 'Pinci's' newsmen, foreign diplomats and ex-politicians were saying openly that Ioannides must have gone mad. And for the first time Kissinger's role in the drama began to be discussed. Greeks are notorious for seeing plots and 'dark machinations' by foreign powers behind everything that happens. In this they are not entirely to blame as their politicians have consistently lied to them about the harsh realities of a small nation caught in the middle of a geo-political power struggle between giants. (In fact, the politicians have lied to the people about much more than foreign policy.) The result has been for the average Greek to see plots behind every event concerning Greece, and in case of a national catastrophe to be convinced beyond any reasonable doubt that such plots exist.

It was quite natural, therefore, for the people to believe that

Ioannides and the Athens regime could not have acted alone.

In fact, a well-known economist and editorial writer, Nikos Monferatos, was heard saying that small-time brigadiers (referring to Ioannides) do not make coups involving foreign powers. 'No, sir,' said Monferatos, 'I guarantee that this is Kissinger and the British trying to get their N.A.T.O. installations into Cyprus.'

Late that evening Athens radio announced that the Cypriot National Guard had overthrown Makarios, while the government met for the third time with General Gizikis, President of the Republic, and the Chiefs of Staff.

In an earlier meeting of the government that day, Elias Balopoulos, the Minister of Co-ordination and one of the very few capable men in the Cabinet, had seen a secretary typing a press handout that said the Government was meeting to evaluate the Cyprus situation. The press release was to be issued the next day. Balopoulos told the Council of Ministers that this was pure comedy. 'We had no information before the coup; we have none now,' Balopoulos continued. 'Most of us are bitter and disgusted with what is happening; why don't we all just pack up and go home?'

This was the first time such words had been spoken and they were followed by a more or less embarrassing silence.

The next day, Tuesday, July 16th, mopping up operations continued throughout the island. Press reports said that bloody battles continued on Tuesday, and even on Wednesday, but these reports were highly exaggerated.

At 2 a.m. on Tuesday, three infantry and one armoured battallion left Nicosia for the Troodos Mountains, in order to pacify the countryside. At noon the head of the National Guard asked Commander Papayannis if he could destroy the Paphos radio station from the torpedo boat Leventis, cruising outside the Makarios stronghold. Papayannis reported that with his Bofors 40 mm he could, but that there were bound to be casualties in the houses surrounding the area. The plan was then rejected.

Armoured units and artillery were finally decided upon, and Lieutenant-Colonel Papathanassiou was to lead them. But, as the column approached Paphos, the Lieutenant-Colonel expressed his doubts as to the wisdom of their mission. He became reluctant to shell the city and said so in no uncertain terms. A young Major close to the Athens regime threatened him with drawn pistol. But Papathanassiou, a brave and intelligent officer who personified the good and the pure in the Greek armed forces, did not scare easily. The result was that the Major backed down and, typically, a compromise was reached.

So the task fell to Commander Papayannis's naval unit. He was told to order the *Leventis* to shell the city. The torpedo boat started firing with its 40 mm and 20 mm guns at 3:30 p.m. By 4 p.m. the auxiliaries sent a message that they would surrender without a fight to the approaching columns of Papathanassiou. The Archbishopric and radio station of Paphos were partly destroyed.

Thus ended all resistance in Cyprus, with the exception of the marauding maquis bands holding out in the Troodos Mountains.

Makarios, in the meantime, had put himself under U.N. protection and had flown by helicopter to the Brtish base at Akrotiri, near Paphos. From there he was put on a British Royal Air Force plane and flown to Malta. Throughout his ordeal and final departure he was treated as Head of State.

International reaction to the coup did not mince thoughts or words. The Greek junta was accused of masterminding the overthrow of Makarios. In Ankara, Turkish Premier Bulent Ecevit, declared that Turkey would intervene in Cyprus for the restoration of the Government and the protection of the Turkish-Cypriots unless the Greek officers of the National Guard withdrew.

The Turkish-Cypriot leader, Rauf Denktash, then hastened to withdraw the statement he had made at the start of the coup that 'this does not concern us; it is merely an internal Greek problem.'

In the British Parliament, the Secretary of State for Foreign Affairs, James Callaghan, declared that his government recognized Archbishop Makarios as the only legitimate head of Cyprus, and announced that His Beatitude was on his way to England for talks.

At N.A.T.O. headquarters in Brussels, Secretary-General Joseph Luns and all the representatives of the member nations, with the exception of Greece, condemned the coup and recognized Makarios as the President of Cyprus.

And throughout the world people saw, astonished, a new tragi-comedian acting as the head of a sovereign state. Nicolaos Sampson, the new President, conducted his first press conference on Thursday, July 18th, addressing a sweltering press corps which had arrived in force after the opening of the Nicosia airport on Wednesday evening.

If President Amin has since become the newsmen's darling for his incredible statements, Sampson—a very competitive man indeed—did not fare badly by comparison. He declared that he had accepted the mandate in order to save Makarios's supporters from being lynched by their fellow Cypriots. He also presented proof of Makarios's arbitrary rule by producing various people who showed their scars and told of their tortures at the hands of Makarios's police.

He denied that mass arrests had taken place, giving the number of detainees as one thousand. No matter how doubtful his other statements may have been, there were not many reprisals after the coup. Of course, everything is relative. But in an island like Cyprus, which was an armed camp ready to explode, where passions had reached a peak, and where hate, built up through twenty years of strife, had totally polarized the population, the number of people arrested, or otherwise persecuted, was indeed small.

In fact, most of the reprisals were committed by E.O.K.A.-B specials, in retaliation for all they had suffered from Makarios's auxiliaries. The Greek contingent, whose officers had fought on the side of the National Guard, but which, as a body, had not officially taken part in the operations, was instrumental in stopping any excesses.

Lieutenant-Colonel Bikkos was one of those officers, not having taken part in the coup, who managed to keep E.O.K.A.-B from executing their enemies. He personally saved the Bishop of Morphou, a close friend of Makarios, guarded him and kept him in comfort after his arrest. Commander Papayannis was another who followed this policy, as were the majority of Greek officers in the National Guard and in ELDYK.

The total casualties resulting from the coup did not exceed 150 dead and 500 wounded. These figures have been difficult to verify as the Turkish invasion, coming on the heels of the coup, confused the issue. But it is certain that no more than forty-five national guardsmen, seventy-five 'epikouriki' and twenty civilians were killed.

Aside from the political blunder, the coup was also a failure as a military operation. Although the attack had been skilfully handled, casualties on both sides limited, and immediate objectives attained, the main target had escaped, and with him, Ioannides's pan-Hellenic dreams for Cyprus.

But soon all these matters would be forgotten, and Cypriots who had been fighting each other for a decade would become united, as the Turkish armada appeared on the horizon. It was to turn the happy island of plenty into a blazing inferno, with thousands of dead and hundreds of thousands of refugees, and, because of the 'treachery' of two officers, it brought the doom of Ioannides.

Chapter 5

The Turkish Invasion and The Fall of the Junta

ANY doubt there might have been about who masterminded the coup against Makarios was dispelled early that Monday morning, July 15th. Air force Brigadier General Spyros Alevras saw Ioannides as he was leaving the operations room in the Greek Pentagon with a wide grin on his face. He was being followed by a few officers, all in a high state of excitement and euphoria.

Intrigued, Alevras decided to investigate and was told in hushed tones by a fellow officer that, 'the priest has just got his come-uppance.'

Half an hour later, however, in a hurriedly-called conference of the higher brass, there were no smiles or congratulations. Instead there were grim, accusatory looks and downcast glances. As soon as Makarios's escape became known, Ioannides's worst fears began to come true.

Long suspecting that there was some breach of security within the highest echelons of the Greek armed forces, Ioannides had conducted fine-tooth-comb investigations, but had come up empty-handed. Yet in his conspiratorial mind—and with the sixth sense he had developed because of it—he knew that something was wrong. Now his fears and doubts began to grow.

Ioannides had no way of knowing that Makarios had indeed been caught totally unprepared—a fact which was proved by his miraculously close escape. But there remained certain 'mysteries,' or unexplained events, that did take place. For example: Glafkos Clerides, the Cypriot leader of the House of Representatives, had forewarned Makarios of the coming attempt on his life on Friday, July 12th. A spy within Clerides's inner circle had then sent Ioannides a coded message about this warning the day before the coup. Evangelos Averoff-Tositsa, the ex-Foreign Minister, had sent still another warning to Cyprus telling the Archbishop that a coup was forthcoming. Furthermore, early on the morning of the coup Makarios, protected by only two carloads of bodyguards, had passed within fifty yards of the assembled armour of the National Guard on his way back from the Troodos Mountains. (The National Guard camp was adjacent to the ELDYK encampment, and the road Makarios followed in returning to Nicosia crossed the two units which were both in a state of alert.) Why was the plan to kill him not made simpler by blocking the way and getting rid of him then and there? Why were orders given to attack him, instead, at the supposedly well-guarded presidential palace?

All these questions started to gnaw at Ioannides, but, without concrete evidence and faced with the realities of an explosive international situation, he put them aside and began to draw up contingency plans for a bigger crisis, one that was about to dwarf the coup by comparison.

Throughout the week after Makarios's overthrow, feverish diplomatic activity between the United States, Great Britain, Turkey and Greece dominated the headlines. There were also a few ominous noises from the Soviet Union and from the group of non-aligned countries to which Cyprus belonged.

Great Britain had asked Greek and Turkish representatives to London for talks. Turkish Premier, Bulent Ecevit, had gone to London on the Wednesday after the coup, and had met Prime Minister Harold Wilson, as well as U.S. Under-Secretary of State, Joseph Sisco.

A forty-nine-year-old poet-politician, Ecevit is a rare breed. The son of a professor and himself a cultivated man, a product of Ankara, London and Harvard universities, he loves the arts and is a polished writer. His great love was Ezra Pound, and he has translated Pound's works, and those of T. S. Eliot, into Turkish. Some of Pound's tastes may have affected his own attitude towards life, in his romantic conception of man's aspirations and in his unpopular, but just, stands in political matters.

Nevertheless, Ecevit does not lack resolute efficiency in his work, nor the deviousness which has marked Turkish foreign policy in the past. In geo-political matters, he is a tough—even ruthless—negotiator, knowing full well the advantages to be reaped by 'creating facts' and by gaining the upper hand at the first sign of an opponent's weakness.

Ecevit realized that this was his golden opportunity for a great diplomatic victory—or, better still, a chance of altering the social, geographic and political position of the Turkish minority in Cyprus.

There were internal reasons, too, for Ecevit's aggressive behaviour. Being a minority Premier in Parliament, he was fully aware that the slightest hesitation, or show of weakness, would bring his fragile coalition down with a crash.

Of course, Turkey's case had been greatly bolstered by Greece's total isolation on the diplomatic front. The hostile reaction to the coup and widespread condemnation of the junta had accelerated what was happening in Greece. There was virtually an abdication of government from the moment Ioannides overthrew Papadopoulos in November of 1973. Embassies abroad received no instructions. Civil servants in Athens were left to carry out their functions in a vacuum.

It is a measure of Ecevit's political acumen that he realized—sooner than the Americans—that the destruction of Papadopoulos meant, for all intents and purposes, the end of Greece as a viable, independent nation. He saw Ioannides—the blind, puritanical, naive patriot—as the Trojan Horse which could give the Turks access not only to Aegean oil, but to Cyprus. Plans were made as early as December 1973 for an invasion force to be ready to attack in the south, as well as in the Aegean, in case the junta stumbled. Ecevit's chance came sooner than he expected. (He was not the only person who realized what a golden opportunity the Greek junta was offering the Turks. As soon as he heard of the coup against Makarios, Karamanlis issued a statement from his self-exile in Paris that 'any attempt to exploit the situation by a third country would bring all Greeks, despite their differences, into a united front.' He was to make the same statement many times over after he took power, but without result.)

In London Ecevit insisted again that all the Greek officers stationed in Cyprus had to be recalled. He threatened that Turkey would intervene—a course already decided upon by the Turkish government and armed forces—knowing full well that his threats would be taken as bluff and called by Greece because of two previous occasions when they had gone to the brink of war. He also knew that the Greek junta would not agree to recall the officers, since it had tried to kill Makarios for requesting that same thing.

The Turkish Prime Minister continued his demands throughout his London stay and was supported by Callaghan. (The British Foreign Secretary knew by then that the Turks were committed to invade. Various leaks from his office reached Greek military and diplomatic circles, but were all ignored by the junta as being planted by the British. Callaghan's first reaction to news of the planned invasion was rather indicative of reluctant approval.)

Upon returning to Ankara late on Thursday, July 18th, Ecevit once again accused the Greeks of sending reinforcements to Cyprus and said that, in the circumstances, Turkey had no choice but to mobilize.

In reality, a partial mobilization had already been in effect for months and the actual massing of troops had started well before the coup against Makarios. On July 9th, Michele Bastias, the wife of a Greek publisher, was cruising off the coast of Marmaris (near Rhodes) on the southwestern edge of the Turkish mainland. She was aboard an English yacht that put into the port of Marmaris on the evening of the 9th. There she and her companions saw a Turkish naval force stationed inside the bay which leads into the port. They counted five large troop carriers jammed with soldiers, nine torpedo boats and three destroyers. On the left of the bay there were six submarines. The English captain took down the U-boat numbers: 642, 643, 644, 645, 646 and 647. (They were later plotted during the battle of Kyrenia by *Hermes*, the British helicopter-carrier, as well as by the Sixth Fleet.)

By Friday, July 19th, the air in Washington and London had somewhat cleared. The intensive diplomatic activity had convinced the press in both capitals that Turkey—amenable to

American suggestions—would not move. U.S. Under-Secretary of State, Joseph Sisco, had arrived in Athens along with the American Under-Secretary of Defense, Robert Ellsworth. They had immediately closeted themselves in the presidential palace for talks with the government.

The Greek press, which had not published anything about the international outcry over Greece's action in Cyprus, wrote that the United States was leaning towards acceptance of the Sampson regime. In the aftermath of the Turkish invasion Greek public opinion was to be reminded of these statements by the Greek press, as if Greek newsmen's guesswork about Sampson constituted Washington's official foreign policy. Thus the entire blame for Greece's humiliation was placed on Uncle Sam.

On that same day, Friday, Turkish naval units set out from Mersin, the southern port of Turkey and only sixty miles northeast of Kyrenia, towards an unknown destination. Journalists counted at least thirty craft, among which were landing craft carrying tanks.

That evening in an official communiqué Turkey demanded from Britain the following: (a) the use of British military airfields on Cyprus; (b) the withdrawal of the 650 Greek officers of the National Guard; (c) the restoration of constitutional order; and (d) a Turkish base in Cyprus.

These were the last demands made by Turkey through diplomatic channels. The Greek government heard about them as Foreign Minister Kypreos was about to leave for London to continue negotiations.

At 5:15 a.m. on Saturday, July 20th, Turkish Foreign Minister Gunes summoned the Greek Chargé d'Affaires in Ankara and informed him that Turkey would invade Cyprus in order to safeguard the rights of the Turkish population on the island. Gunes based this action on his country's position as a guarantor nation under the 1960 agreement.

Before the final move was made on Friday evening, Joseph Sisco had gone to Ankara after having talks with the Greek government in Athens. He had conferred with Prime Minister Ecevit in a last desperate attempt to avert war, but had failed to convince the Turkish leader. There are reasons to believe that, in his last conversation with Henry Kissinger, he had informed the American Secretary of State that war was imminent.

Meanwhile, the Greek high command was aware of Turkish military movements. The acting head of the Cypriot National Guard had told Athens that a high-ranking British officer on the island had leaked information about an imminent Turkish invasion. The British officer had even given the name of the invasion plans as Attila I and II.

Brigadier General Sotiriades, head of the Greek mission to N.A.T.O. in Smyrna, Turkey, had also warned about a Turkish attack. In a coded message to Armed Forces Commander, General Gregorios Bonanos, he had spelled out Turkish military movements, adding that other N.A.T.O. officers were frantically signalling their respective countries about these movements.

Finally, Lieutenant-Colonel Perdikis, assistant military attaché in London, had been approached by a Foreign Office official at a cloak-and-dagger meeting in Hyde Park, and plainly told of the Turkish intent to invade. Perdikis's warnings were ignored by Athens.

Instead, the Greek high command chose the days of Thursday and Friday to replace 700 soldiers of the Greek contingent with raw recruits, thus giving the Turks an opportunity to allege that Greece was pouring troops into the island.

The inexplicable behaviour of the Greek high command was due, primarily, to the confusion reigning among the armed forces. The various power struggles which had taken place before and after Papadopoulos's demise had brought about a paralysis in the chain of command. And, as the hierarchy of the armed forces was challenged by junior officers, decision-making and correct evaluation of information and events became more difficult. In addition to this was the fact that the men in high positions were not up to the task of taking drastic steps once the handwriting on the wall was clear. During the last frenzied days of diplomatic negotiations, both the civilian government and the higher echelons of the army were hampered by constant checking and double checking with so-called strongmen before any decision could be made.

At dawn on Saturday morning a heat haze hung over Kyrenia. Despite the coup of the previous week, there were still some 2,000 tourists—mostly British—left on the island. Everyone was asleep as zero hour approached.

In the Turkish quarter of Nicosia, however, Turkish paramilitary forces had taken up defensive positions near the Green line as early as 2 a.m. They had been told of the forthcoming invasion.

Commander Papayannis had also spent a sleepless night. At 9:15 p.m. on Friday evening, he had been informed by the S.T.W. 'A' (the early-warning station on Cape Andreas) that a six-vessel formation was approaching the Kyrenia area from a distance of forty miles. At 9:40 p.m. the same early-warning station's radar had signalled another formation of eight to ten ships heading toward Cyprus from Mersin. By plotting the course of the second formation, he established beyond any reasonable doubt that it was steaming full speed ahead for Kyrenia.

Papayannis immediately called the acting head of the National Guard who, in his presence, reported the sighting of the Turkish fleet to Athens Armed Forces Headquarters.

The answer from Athens had a reassuring sound. 'Probable naval manoeuvres,' it said, adding that 'further plotting is advised.'

Nevertheless, Commander Papayannis ordered his naval stations to be on the alert and directed the patrol boat *Leventis* to proceed to the naval base north of Famagusta. Throughout the long night he received reports from the radar tracking stations of the approaching fleet. With growing apprehension, he continued to inform all National Guard units of theses movements.

When the Turkish armada passed the twelve-mile mark—the limit of Cypriot territorial waters—Papayannis ordered his units to be ready to fire if attacked. The time was 4:30 a.m.

Kyrenia, sixteen miles north of Nicosia, was to be one of the two landing points of the Turkish invasion. It can be reached from the capital by a direct road which passes through a low gorge in the mountains. Its horseshoe-shaped harbour is the most vaunted in Cyprus, and the Byzantine castle of St.

Hilarion towers over the town, whose frontage toward the sea is one of the most beautiful in the world. The Kyrenia mountain range rises abruptly from sea level to a height of over three thousand feet.

The first Turks to land on those northern beaches were frogmen, who swam from landing craft lurking offshore. At 5 a.m. all hell broke loose. In a textbook amphibious assault, using warships and aircraft to soften up all visible strongpoints, the Turkish armada struck the sleeping town with the force of a thunderbolt.

Five warships pounded the town while two large transports disgorged the invading troops from twenty medium-sized and five small landing craft. Paratroopers were dropped on the southern side of the Kyrenia mountain range, and they proceeded to double back toward the harbour in a classic pincer movement which sought to link up with the amphibious troops to the north.

At 'Five-Fingers Crag,' which lies south of Kyrenia, the first bloody encounter took place between the encircling Turkish paratroopers and Greek rangers. Simultaneously, Turkish-Cypriot forces based on the strategically dominant St. Hilarion fortress moved to join the invading units

But the Greek rangers were not to be denied. Led by an experienced officer, Colonel Costas Kobokis, a veteran of the Korean War, the élite rangers butchered the Turkish paratroopers and put the Turkish-Cypriots to flight. This all-important victory by the three companies of rangers in the first hour of the war gave the beleaguered Kyrenia defenders time to organize and fight back. If the paratroop unit had succeeded in its mission, it would have overrun the Greek garrison and two to three thousand Turkish lives would have been saved.

At naval headquarters Commander Papayannis had, by this time, ordered his six vessels to disperse and conceal themselves in sheltered areas. As torpedo boats, TB-1 and TB-3, were receiving these orders, they came under aerial attack. Taking evasive action they sped towards the main part of the Turkish invasion fleet. TB-1, having its commander, first mate, and chief engineer seriously wounded, tried valiantly to reach shore, but sank three miles from land. TB-3, firing torpedos and using its machine guns, attempted a suicide attack on the Turkish destroyers and was blown up by the combined fire of Turkish warships and jet fighters. The captain of TB-3, the young, brave Gouzelis, had spoken to Papayannis over the radio only seconds before his death. He asked permission to attack because, as he put it, 'We haven't got much of a chance of making it back anyway. And I will not be the first Greek officer to put up the white flag of surrender.'

The Turkish objective in the Kyrenia area was to establish a bridgehead on the beaches of Glykiotisa and Pentamili, west of the town. Because of faulty intelligence reports the attempt to land at Glykiotisa was a disaster. The area is full of reefs and rockier than the Turks expected. Faced with the possibility of getting stuck on the reefs, they kept to a westerly course, one thousand yards off the coast, while looking for a suitable site to land. They found it in Pentamili, but not before two National Guard platoons, supported by an artillery unit, zeroed in on them. Turkish casualties were heavy, with only 150 out of the 600 men making it ashore.

Initially, the Turks had three limited strategic objectives: to seize the port of Kyrenia on the northern coast, to take the sixteen-mile corridor from there to the capital of Nicosia, and to secure control of the international airport outside it. Until then, all ports had been controlled by the Greek-Cypriot community, an enormous strategic advantage in any confrontation with the mainland Turks. Although they were to achieve the first two of these objectives, the airport—through the heroic stand of ELDYK units, which suffered almost 100 per cent casualties—did not fall. But this is jumping ahead of the story.

In Nicosia, Saturday morning broke very hot and clear. During the week following the coup an unending stream of reporters, cameramen, photographers, commentators and political correspondents had invaded the Ledra Palace Hotel, which is situated just across the street from the United Nations headquarters and adjacent to the Green line. The hotel is a pale-coloured mock-Byzantine building; it offers comfortable quarters and has impeccable service. It also has great charm, as well as being a perfect location for covering both the Greek and Turkish sides. Because of these attributes, the Ledra has long been the favourite stop-over point for newsmen who, over the years, covered the never-ending Cyprus drama.

On that Saturday there were about 200 newsmen staying in the Ledra Palace. Among them was Joe Fried of the New York *Daily News*, one of the 'firemen' sent to cover the coup. Joe had moved to the Mediterranean beat after eleven years in Vietnam. There he had been considered the dean of the foreign press corps, and his exploits in heckling government spokesmen at the 'five o'clock follies,' as the daily military briefings were called in Saigon, are legendary.

Fried is a small wiry man, described by one of his colleagues as a 'walking ulcer' because of his nervous mannerisms acquired through long years of chasing down stories and meeting dead-lines for his five daily editions.

During his Cyprus sojourn, Fried had to share a room with John Harris of Hearst Newspapers, as the Ledra was packed with tourists as well. He had gone to bed, bone-tired, early on Saturday morning after filing his final copy for the late edition in New York. Fifteen minutes after he had fallen asleep, Harris shook him yelling, 'Look out the window, Joe, look out the window!'

Joe's unprintable remarks were drowned by the whine of a dive-bombing jet, followed by the staccato sound of machine-gun strafing and the swooshing noise of rockets. Both men hit the floor. The time was 5 a.m.

When Joe eventually did look out of his window, he saw hundreds of brown parachutes floating in the clear blue sky towards Nicosia's Turkish quarter. Simultaneously, a heavy aerial bombardment was blitzing the airport, the camps, and the artillery positions of the National Guard and of ELDYK.

American-made Turkish transport planes were dropping paratroopers by the hundreds, coming in successive waves under cover of fighter-bombers. The airport was the target of concentrated attacks by the jet fighter-bombers, while the ELDYK camp was being plastered with deadly napalm.

National guardsmen were running around in confusion trying to set up roadblocks near the Green line as Turkish troops started to move toward the Greek section of the city. Two guardsmen set up a machine gun on the fourth floor of the Ledra Palace, despite the protestations of the trapped newsmen that it would make the hotel a target for attack. But no sooner had the machine gun started firing than it was silenced by a perfectly-placed bazooka shot that tore through the wall killing one guardsman and seriously injuring the other.

A rocket attack from a diving jet had flattened a psychiatric hospital in the Greek section. Thirty of the patients were killed and many others wounded. Running around in a daze, the inmates were one of the most pitiful sights in the memory of battle-hardened newsmen.

Despite the perfectly-coordinated attack from the air, the ELDYK units of the Greek contingent managed to throw 300 men into the defence of the all-important airport. Colonels, Majors, and Captains fought alongside Privates in a desperate attempt to hold the Turkish tide. Undermanned and without air cover, bombed and strafed constantly from the air, they grimly held on against superior forces. Most of them were to die as they held the airfield until well after the ceasefire three days later.

From the beginning the Turkish invasion force behaved as if it were storming the Normandy beaches instead of taking on what was, in reality, a bunch of reservists and irregulars, lacking modern weapons, air cover and proper fortifications. The onslaught began with simultaneous strikes from the sea and from the air at Nicosia, Kyrenia and west of the Kyrenia horseshoe. There were also paratroop drops of men and material into Turkish enclaves lying between Greek-held territory. Twenty helicopters had flown over the mountain range near Kyrenia and landed in the Turkish sector of Nicosia.

By 8 a.m., after three hours of fierce fighting, the invasion's progress was as follows:– Using about seventeen Hercules troop carriers and eighty helicopters in airborne landings, the task force had discharged around 6,000 men and established a bridgehead 500 metres deep inside the port of Kyrenia in the northern part of the island. It had also dropped 1,500 para-troopers in Nicosia's Turkish quarter, and in various other Turkish enclaves. Twenty tanks had come ashore in support of the invading forces. The Turkish contingent on the island, which had a strong unit based on the strategically dominant sector overlooking Kyrenia, was also engaging the Greek forces.

Facing the invading Turkish army were 10,000 men of the Greek-Cypriot National Guard, the 1,000-man Greek contingent, and Makarios's paramilitary forces, which comprised about 4,000 men.

Neither the Greek-Cypriot forces nor ELDYK had any heavy artillery. They were armed with M-1s and vintage World War II Enfield rifles. They had thirty-eight medium Russian-made tanks (T-34s), the previously mentioned patrol boat and five—now three—torpedo boats (Two were lost in the first hour of the invasion.)

The Green Line in Nicosia had not been penetrated by the Turks, nor had the airport been overrun. The Greek rangers were battling Turkish paratroopers dropped behind Kyrenia, while in the harbour itself the Turks had made only slight progress although their troops and material continued to come ashore. The vital road from the capital to the sea was still not in Turkish hands despite fierce armour and infantry efforts to link up with Turkish forces in Nicosia.

Twenty minutes after the invasion began, Lieutenant-Colonel Sgouros drove under fire to the west of the capital where the main jail holding 1,200 of Makarios's auxiliaries was situated. He asked for Major Pantazis—the same Pantazis who held off the tanks attacking his camp near the presidential palace, thus giving Makarios time to escape—and told him that he and his men were free. Major Pantazis, with tears in his eyes, thanked Sgouros, organized his men, and after leading a rousing cheer for the Lieutenant-Colonel, left for the Green Line and his new enemy, the Turks. He was later to reinforce the Kyrenia front and distinguish himself during the three-day battle.

Throughout the island Greek-Cypriot reserve officers and men were rushing to reach their units in the midst of chaos from Turkish aerial bombing. Despite the confusion National Guard units had managed by noon to infiltrate the Turkish quarter in Nicosia and cut the Turkish area of Kionelli in half. Military observers have since concluded that, if the Greek-

Cypriot forces had had the minimum amount of heavy artillery required, as well as some air cover, they might have turned back the Turkish invasion during those first crucial hours and, of course, the Greek navy might have engaged the Turkish fleet as it stood waiting outside Kyrenia.

Other units of the Greek-Cypriot National Guard moved swiftly to neutralize Turkish-Cypriot forces in the pockets of Lefka, Koina and Limnitis. The Turkish-Cypriots fought valiantly and, in doing so, tied down the National Guard units, thus preventing them from going to the aid of the embattled Kyrenia defenders.

A few miles inland between Nicosia and Kyrenia, at Morphou, Lieutenant-Colonel Michael Bikkos was ordered to organize a reserve battalion as soon as the invasion force struck. He was to move his unit, which was not fully mobilized, due to the confusion around Kyrenia, and link up with Lieutenant-Colonel Papathanassiou's 281st Battalion at Aghios Georgios. From there the two battalions were to reinforce the Kyrenia defenders.

When Bikkos arrived in Aghios Georgios with his rag-tag unit, he saw Papathanassiou's column in the distance blacked out—a long charred chain of twisted metal and disfigured bodies. The Turkish air force had caught them in the open and had napalmed them at will.

And so it went with most of the columns rushing to help Lieutenant-Colonel Kouroupis, the chief officer defending the Kyrenia beaches. In response to his repeated demands for reinforcements, units would be dispatched from various areas surrounding Kyrenia, but not one managed to get through intact. In the front line of fire since the invasion began, Kouroupis and his defenders had come under the repeated barrage of the Turkish navy and of dive-bombing jets. He was further pressed by the Turkish-Cypriot units from St. Hilarion.

Having suffered heavy losses, Kouroupis ordered his battalion to retreat to the first 'line of deterrence'; that is, to the foot of the Kyrenia mountain range, the Pentadaktylos. The time was now high noon.

Bikkos tried desperately to reach Kouroupis who was being swamped by heavy artillery fire and napalm in his second line of defence. They had been classmates at the Military Academy in Athens and had remained close friends. However Bikkos never got the chance to help his friend nor to see him again. Kouroupis died defending his position to the last, all the time exhorting his men not to leave, but to fight on to certain death. After he fell, his unit dispersed.

As the news of Kouroupis's death came in to the National Guard Headquarters, the prospect of losing the Kyrenia battle-front became a grim reality. Lieutenant-Colonel Boutos, commander of an armoured column, was summoned and ordered to move in fast to stop the gap. (The Nicosia battlefield now being under the control of Greek forces, Boutos's armour could be spared.)

Boutos was told that he had to hold his ground at all costs. Nearing the Kyrenia area, his column was detected by the Turkish air force. A merciless fight developed between the determined to-the-death Greek officer and the relentless fire-spitting jets. Time and time again in the space of an hour, Boutos kept his column rolling forward while the preying fighters overhead showered it with rockets, machine gun fire and napalm.

The forty-five-year-old Boutos—a quiet, stocky father of three—was commanding his column from the open turret of his tank. He was hit repeatedly, his left arm almost severed, but still he led his troops forward, shouting commands over the radio to his junior officers.

A remnant of his unit finally reached its destination and immediately started a holding operation against the Turkish forces. Boutos himself was brought back after the battle in a comatose state and later flown to Athens. He died in his native land two days after the change of regime. (While in hospital, not a single senior officer visited him. After his death his widow was denied an increase in pension. Like the other brave men who died, he received no recognition of his valour.)

As the afternoon shadows lengthened, Turkish-Cypriot enclaves throughout Cyprus were surrounded by Greek-Cypriot troops, as well as Cypriot irregulars. A Greek vessel, the *Lesvos*, taking ELDYK troops to Athens, had turned back at news of the invasion and, making a wide arc to avoid

69

Turkish aircraft, landed the men in Paphos, on the south-western coast of the island. From there it shelled the fortified Turkish enclave. The encircled Turkish garrison surrendered after a ninety-minute fire-fight, and the men were herded, along with the unarmed population, into a make-shift camp. But, before surrendering, the militia commander had radioed Ankara that Greek warships were shelling the village.

This message, given in good faith by the Turkish commander, was to be the cause of Turkish aricrafts' attacking and sinking one of their own destroyers, and damaging another, on the following day. The inexperienced Turk had failed to report that the vessel which was shelling him had the marking L 172 on her bow—a transport ship sailing without escort and equipped with eight Bofors 40 mm guns and six lighter 20 mm ones. About fifty Turkish sailors lost their lives aboard the Turkish destroyer D 35, which was sunk, and on the damaged un-identified ship that was put out of action for the duration of the war.

By Sunday morning the battle along the Green Line in Nicosia had developed into a static slogging match, with local forces on both sides blazing away at each other with mortars, machine guns and rifles.

The Turks had not sent reinforcements to their paratroopers, preferring instead to consolidate their positions on the northern front around Kyrenia. Into that enclave, after the initial thrust inland, they began pumping thousands of men and hundreds of tons of equipment throughout Saturday and Sunday.

But, in order to establish that bridgehead and the road corridor to Nicosia—which was being fought over inch by inch—making an overall enclave of 150 square miles, the Turks had to leave the Turkish minority groups in other towns at the mercy of the Greeks.

In Limassol, some 1,700 Turkish-Cypriot men had been herded into a football stadium where they remained under armed guard. In Famagusta, the community fled into the walled city and, assisted by Turkish auxiliaries, resisted Greek attempts to overrun them. The Greeks tried desperately to dislodge them, but the valiant Turkish defenders held out. On

Monday at noon, the Turks hoisted a white flag and United Nations troops went in to negotiate the surrender. But after a brief argument among the encircled Turkish leaders, the U.N. officers came out and said that the Turks had changed their minds. Up once again went the Turkish half-moon and star, and it was to stay there until the truce.

By Sunday evening most of the Turkish enclaves were under the control of Greek forces. Paphos was in Greek hands, so was Limassol. So were the Turkish quarters in Morfou, Lefkas and Limnitis.

In Nicosia the static battle continued, while the real fighting raged around Kyrenia at the fortress of St. Hilarion—the Turkish stronghold—and the village of Kionelli, which controlled the all-important artery from Nicosia to Kyrenia.

Greek-Cypriot attempts to prevent the Turks from spreading their bridgehead and widening the corridor from the capital to the sea met with disaster on Sunday. The Turkish air force, facing no opposition, saw to that. After organizing a makeshift battalion, Lieutenant-Colonel Bikos, together with Lieutenant-Colonel Papathanassiou, whose column had been wiped out the day before, and Major Pantazis, had tried a counter-attack. They were once again massacred from the air, although they did manage to harass the Turks and to delay their advance. Bikos was hit by shrapnel and lost consciousness from excessive bleeding. Pantazis and Papathanassiou were both injured, but got back to safety. (Bikos was to survive and eventually return to Greece. He is now posted in K.Y.P.)

The Turkish forces had also suffered heavy losses by Sunday evening. The commander of the Turkish contingent in Cyprus was killed bravely defending the St. Hilarion fort against the Greek rangers. At one moment the Greeks had almost overrun the stronghold, but Colonel Datirgioglou had personally led a counter-attack to repulse them, and died in the effort. His body was flown to Turkey to be awarded full military honours, then given a hero's funeral by a grateful nation.

In the fighting around Kyrenia, fourteen aircraft had been shot down by the Greeks, and the Turks had suffered heavy losses. But by Monday morning 10,000 troops had landed, along with some 200 tanks. With their beachheads now secured, a concentrated effort was begun to take the town. Kyrenia finally fell to the Turks at 1 p.m. on Monday, as 5,000 Greek-Cypriot civilians streamed out toward the Greek lines. The Turkish air force did not inhibit their flight. Inside the town itself, however, the Greek-held fortress, manned by seventeen sailors, refused to surrender. Eventually they managed to escape by breaking out in a grenade-throwing dash toward the mountains on Tuesday, twenty-four hours after the ceasefire had taken effect. Their chief, Ensign Galiatsos, managed to lead them back to Nicosia after a nine-hour march.

The Turks did not take the last Greek position on the Kyrenia range overlooking the port until ten hours after Monday's ceasefire. The Turkish army, despite a military tradition dating back for centuries, did not distinguish itself during the three-day war. However, Turkey's armed forces had not been engaged in a conventional war since Korea. The long period of inactivity seems to have produced some heavy-footed staff work and a reluctance by the field commanders to innovate and depart from the master-plan laid down by General Headquarters.

Nevertheless, the overall objective had been reached, as the corridor from Nicosia's Turkish quarter to the sea was at last secured and the Turkish flag finally fluttered above Kyrenia. The airport near Nicosia remained in Greek hands, although it was to be taken over in the end by United Nations forces.

The battle for the airfield had political repercussions. After the cease-fire, Turkish attempts to overrun it brought Greece and Turkey to the brink once again, and the price that was paid for it involved the fall of the Colonels.

If there was one single thought which sustained the Greek defenders throughout the Turkish blitz, it was: 'Wait until the Greeks come!' During the first hours, when the situation looked grimmest, it was on everyone's mind. Officers handing out weapons to raw recruits and confused reservists repeated the phrase, 'Just hold on for a while, Greece is sending help.'

Even when the battle for Nicosia turned in favour of the Greek-Cypriots, and the Turkish quarter was about to be overrun just before the ceasefire, the same thought persisted:

'With a little bit of help we'll throw the Turks into the sea.' But it was not to be. The Turks, using their fresh troops with impunity, and with total air superiority, finally broke the Greek resistance.

No one can venture to say what the outcome would have been if the mother country had interfered. That is a matter for military experts. However, judging by the lack of co-ordination in the Turkish landing operation and the stubborn Greek-Cypriot resistance, it is safe to assume that, during the first hours of the invasion, the Turkish amphibious forces might well have been beaten back, even destroyed, right there on the Kyrenia beaches.

So what happened? Why wasn't even one shot fired? Was there a betrayal involved, or were the rumours sweeping Athens that the U.S. Sixth Fleet had blockaded Greek naval units true? Had Washington ordered American personnel to sabotage Greek aircraft on the ground and blackmailed the Greek junta not to interfere? For the answers to these questions we must go back to Athens during the early hours of the Turkish invasion, on Saturday, July 20th.

By Friday evening when Under-Secretary of State Joseph Sisco left for Ankara, the Greek Government and the chiefs of the armed forces were convinced that Turkey would compromise. Unfortunately, the inexperienced persons who were running the country had mistaken the feverish diplomatic activity, and American concern over the explosive situation, as a sure sign that a plan of compromise would be found.

In this the Greeks were also misled by the fact that Kissinger did not spell out to them—through Sisco—that a Turkish invasion was a strong possibility. When Sisco warned them that it could happen, the Greeks interpreted this as an American threat. The spirit of the Athens regime was 'Why should America allow two of her staunchest allies to go to war against each other?' As it turned out, the United States did get involved, but not in the way the Greek regime had imagined.

When Sisco arrived in Athens on Friday, July 19th, he met the Government and reached a sort of compromise. The chief point was that, if Turkey remained adamant in her intention to invade, the Greeks—after the passage of a few days, in order to save face—would eventually recall the Greek officers from Cyprus, change the Sampson regime, and install in its place a government of their own choosing.

Under-Secretary of State Sisco departed for Ankara hoping that the Turks might realize that a face-saving device would be good for both parties involved, that Makarios was not exactly a Turk-lover, and that Turkey could use the eventual recall of the officers as a diplomatic victory.

Nevertheless, the Greek high command met immediately following Sisco's departure and formulated contingency plans in case of a Turkish invasion. The plans were the following: (a) To support the Cyprus forces with air cover and naval units. (The limited logistical landing capability of the Turks meant that Greek intervention could easily prohibit an effective invasion and possibly destroy the Turkish armada. (b) At the same time, to initiate heavy artillery bombardment on the Greek-Turkish frontier at the Evros River, which would be a diversionary tactic to pin down Turkish units, and also to convince the Turks of Greece's resolve to enter the war. (The Evros plan included the possibility of a lightning armoured thrust inside Turkey with the intention of capturing real estate as an ace-in-the-hole for future negotiations.)

Given the limited capability of both countries to wage a protracted war, the Greek plan seemed perfect, on paper at least. Turkey could not possibly invade Cyprus without committing the bulk of her navy, air force and élite paratrooper units. At the same time, she would be sorely pressed by the Greek thrust against her northeastern frontier. There the Greeks had their best-equipped, best-trained armoured forces, as well as crack infantry divisions.

By late Friday evening the deployment of the powerful Third Army, under the experienced and reliable General Davos, was complete. Units of the second army had moved into reserve positions in the areas east and west of Salonica, Greece's second largest city. On the Evros River itself, Colonel Byron Velissaroulis had given the last orders to his tank commanders and had coordinated with the engineers for a possible crossing.

Units of artillery and an air force support liaison officer had moved into the headquarters of the field commanders.

The morale of the population in the areas adjoining the Greco-Turkish frontier was high. Also the support of the people could be counted upon, as many living in those parts were refugees from Asia Minor. Throughout the years, the animosity of these Greeks towards the Turks had certainly not diminished.

'On to Constantinople!' was the cry that Friday night, as the people, aware of the army movements, brought fruit and wine to the troops. Thus, everything was 'go' when Saturday morning found the Turkish fleet attacking Kyrenia.

In Athens, Minister of Information Karakostas was told of the invasion, while still in bed, by a journalist who had been listening to the B.B.C. broadcast and wanted to know if he could publish anything about it.

For hours the people of Greece remained unaware of the event. The national broadcasting programme had reported earlier that 'complete stability reigned in Cyprus.' Finally, Christos Mavrogeorgios, Papadopoulos's ex-political adviser, telephoned air force Brigadier General Skoutelis, head of the military propaganda section, and told him in no uncertain terms that the people had to be informed immediately. At 11 a.m. the Government-controlled radio put the news on the air.

This broadcast also announced total mobilization of the armed forces. With military marches blaring away, citizens hurried to close their shops and offices, and somehow find where their mobilization centres were located. Amid a chaotic scene of streets jammed with traffic, housewives started buying and hoarding food. Most grocery stores were sold out within hours.

Again, the decision to mobilize turned out to be a colossal blunder. Every N.A.T.O. country has the ability, during the first phase of military mobilization, to transport and equip about ten to twelve classes, or age groups. But the total call now was for more than twenty, and the ensuing confusion brought the country to the brink of complete chaos.

All means of transport were tied up and mobilization centres were unable to handle the crunch. Many reservists were told to return to their homes, while others were not given arms or specific orders. The blow which this confusion struck at the people's morale quickly became evident.

The decision to mobilize was taken at an early morning emergency meeting of the Greek military leadership, in which President Gizikis and Prime Minister Androutsopoulos participated. But the meeting decided on limited, rather than complete, mobilization. It was only revealed later that the Commander-in-Chief of the Armed Forces, General Gregorios Bonanos, had changed the order. The reason was that Bonanos, fearing internal opposition by dissident elements, wanted to absorb these elements into the reservists and get them out of Athens. Also, in his mind, a total mobilization order would serve to impress international opinion that Greece was about to go to war.

The situation typified the confused attitude of the military heads of the nation. Although the armed forces were ready to strike, their leaders were still hesitant and unsure of themselves. The responsibility for taking such a decision appeared to weigh heavily on their minds, and, for a few hours on Saturday, it seemed as if the nation were adrift and pilotless.

Military observers believe that, if Greece had gone to war, her chances of coming out better than Turkey were about even. The military line-up was as follows:

For Greece: Army—120,000 men, including one commando brigade of 5,000 men. Navy—80 ships, including 7 submarines, 9 destroyers, 13 torpedo boats, and 8 landing craft. Air Force—225 combat aircraft, including 60 transports and 150 jet fighter-bombers.

For Turkey: Army—365,000 men, including 8,000 paratroopers. Navy—120 ships, including 15 submarines, 14 destroyers, 25 torpedo boats, and 20 landing craft. Air Force—290 combat aircraft, including 180 jet fighter-bombers.

Returning to Athens at 7 a.m. on Saturday, U.S. Under-Secretary of State Sisco met Prime Minister Androutsopoulos and the chiefs of staff at army headquarters and tried to persuade them not to go to war. He asked, and got, from the

Greek high command a time limit within which to negotiate a cessation of hostilities with Turkey.

Reports from Cyprus said the Turks were still stalled on the beaches, with the Green Line intact and the Greek-Cypriots more or less in control of the situation. The Greek Government therefore decided it could still avert war without too much loss of face. In fact, it believed that, if Sisco could stop the Turks at that particular moment, this might be considered a victory for the Hellenes.

After communicating with President Nixon and Kissinger, Sisco flew back to Ankara at 11 a.m. The Greek high command, meanwhile, was awaiting the results of his meeting with the Turks, having set a time limit on negotiations of five hours, which was due to expire at 3 p.m.

About this time also former political leaders had issued statements condemning Turkish aggression and asking all Greeks to unite in the face of a common enemy and forget their internal differences.

Throughout Saturday afternoon the Greek people waited anxiously for Sisco's reply. He managed to stall them in two cryptic messages and, with the mobilization order confusing the issue further, a war council meeting was planned for Sunday morning.

Then the drama started to unfold. With the situation in Cyprus still far from resolved, and the Turks continuing to pour men and material into the island, the rulers of Greece met in the old palace.

Present at this meeting were President Gizikis, Prime Minister Androutsopoulos, Commander-in-Chief Bonanos, the three armed forces chiefs—Galatsanos, Arapakis and Papanikolaou—and strongman Ioannides. The President asked for a true evaluation of the situation. Vice-Admiral Arapakis reported that two of his super-modern German submarines were cruising near the beaches of Kyrenia. Each of them, Arapakis said, carried fourteen torpedo rockets. They had in their sights the whole of the Turkish landing fleet and its escorting destroyers. He explained how these submarines could not be detected by the enemy because of their technical capability of moving below the surface at a speed of 21 to 22

77

knots and at a depth of 200 metres. (The sonar equipment of the Turkish destroyers could only detect submarines moving at a speed below 18 knots.)

Arapakis stated: 'I can responsibly guarantee you that we can destroy the enemy without fail.'

Air force chief Papanikolaou reported that some of the newly-arrived Phantoms were ready with bombs and torpedoes and stationed in Crete, the island closest to Cyprus. 'The Turkish fleet cannot escape,' said the General, adding that the Turkish air force did not possess Phantoms, and that the older planes the Turks were flying had already been on continuous duty for twenty-four hours.

Commander-in-Chief of the Army Galatsanos reiterated that the Third Army and crack artillery units were ready to start shelling the Turkish positions across the Evros River as a diversionary action. He also said that a Turkish attack across the Greek border would be almost impossible because of the natural impediments to be overcome by the invading force, the strong defensive positions built up by the Greek side, and the narrowness of the front itself.

The decision was then taken by the war council for Arapakis to order the two submarines to attack the Turkish fleet and sink it. A simultaneous attack by six Phantoms was to be ordered by Papanikolaou, while Galatsanos was to start heavy shelling against Turkish positions on the northeastern frontier. (It should be noted that no crossing was ordered.)

The Government also decided that, after Sunday, Prime Minister Androutsopoulos and Foreign Minister Kypreos would become unavailable to Mr. Sisco, in order to avoid giving the latter any further opportunity to stall for time. (The press reported at the time that Sisco went about shaking his head and saying he had never had to deal with a disappearing Government before. Although a true statement, the inference drawn that the Government had collapsed was false, for the war council had decided that the two men should become unavailable.)

When Sisco returned from Ankara around noon on Sunday, he brought with him Turkish proposals for a cease-fire which, in effect, simply left Turkey in possession of its gains on the island. Prime Minister Androutsopoulos had no choice but to reject them. Sisco, of course, was expecting that. He did not hope to obtain any sort of a ceasefire in Cyprus until the military situation on the island had clarified. He asked for a guarantee that the Greeks would not go to war until Monday noon. By then he hoped that either the Turks would have consolidated their positions and the Greeks would agree to a ceasefire or that the invading force would be amenable to one.

Androutsopoulos demurred, saying that he did not think that he could hold back the armed forces any longer. Then Sisco asked for a compromise, saying 'Will you at least stall them until 7 a.m. tomorrow when we shall meet?'

The Greek Premier answered that he did not know where he would be on Monday morning. Foreign Minister Kypreos, whom Sisco contacted afterwards, made the same reply.

Meanwhile, Ioannides had personally ordered 200 men of the élite commando unit of L.O.K. to be flown to Cyprus. Civilian and military transport planes braved the withering fire and landed most of the men. One plane, however, was hit in the darkness by the Greek-Cypriot National Guard and blew up, killing everyone on board, as it was about to land.

These élite 200 were the turning point in holding the airport. Although sustaining very heavy losses, they held their objective. This was the only help given by the mother country to the embattled defenders on the island. It was done by Ioannides without the permission of the high command, and not through required channels.

When the Turkish government was informed of Greek troops landing on the island, it told Under-Secretary Sisco in Athens that the ceasefire offer was off.

From that moment on, the plot visibly thickened. An American Embassy official asked to see Lieutenant-General Stathopoulos, head of the Greek Central Intelligence Agency (K.Y.P.), and told him in confidence that Bulgarian army units were massing on the Greek-Bulgarian border. The official strongly hinted that the Bulgarians—traditional enemies of the Greeks—were about to invade the country. He also said that the excuse used by the Bulgarians would be an obscure clause in the 1922 Treaty of Lausanne which prohibited the Greek army from crossing the Evros River.

This was an obvious ploy, but the K.Y.P. chief had to check it out. Lieutenant-General Stathopoulos informed the Chiefs of Staff about the confidential information that had just been obtained, and was ordered by them to investigate it.

The heads of the armed forces then decided to wait and see if the information could be verified. In a way, they were relieved that a little time had been gained before their fateful orders must be given. The enormity of the decision to go to war had suddenly found the generals hesitant, unsure of themselves and clutching at straws.

The fact that this dilemma existed did not escape the experienced and highly intelligent Sisco. Moreover, he was determined that a disappearing Government was not going to deter him from stopping the two N.A.T.O. powers from going to war against each other.

An unidentified person arranged a meeting between Sisco and Commander-in-Chief Bonanos. Sisco told the General that, if Greece did not go to war, he would guarantee a Turkish withdrawal immediately following a ceasefire. The vacillating Bonanos agreed, but asked the American Under-Secretary to confer with the other chiefs of staff.

This Sisco did, selecting Vice-Admiral Arapakis as the one most likely to go along with him. He told the ambitious Admiral that this was his chance to become a national hero. He reminded him of the dangers involved in going to war and that, if the result were a Greek defeat, the people responsible would surely be shot. Sisco also said that America was against the Ioannides regime, that all of the West was looking for a change in the Greek Government, and, furthermore, that ex-Premier Karamanlis was waiting in the wings.

'You could bring all this about by cooperating with us,' Sisco told Arapakis, 'and the future regime will be aware of your actions.'

The American envoy, moreover, guaranteed that a Turkish withdrawal would take place if Greece did not engage in hostilities and agreed to a ceasefire.

He did not have to go any further. Arapakis agreed with

alacrity and told Sisco that the ceasefire terms being offered by the Turks seemed reasonable. Sisco then asked the Admiral if Ioannides could be handled. Arapakis said that he could.

Thus Sisco got the deal that he sought. In the early hours of Monday the Turkish Prime Minister also agreed to the package. Reports from Cyprus said that the Greeks were about to overrun the Turkish sectors of Nicosia, so that, although the Kyrenia front was being enlarged, the expedition had hardly turned out as the Turks had forecast—which had been control of the island within twenty-four hours.

On Monday morning Brigadier Ioannides went to the operations room of the Greek Pentagon on the outskirts of Athens. Throughout Sunday afternoon and evening he had waited in vain for the order to attack. By morning he realized that Cyprus was about to fall through lack of ammunition for the defenders and the complete exhaustion of the garrison.

In a third floor room he met his adjutants and staff officers of the three armed forces. He informed the twenty-five officers present of the armed forces chiefs' refusal to implement the war council's decision, and asked for their advice. In a calm manner Ioannides told the assembled men: 'We have two choices. Either we arrest these men, try them for high treason, and proceed with yesterday's plans—accepting all the dangers involved in trying to wage a war while purging the high command—or we look for another solution, one that will not include my person.'

The officers unanimously demanded the arrest of the armed forces chiefs and the implementation of the decision to attack the Turkish fleet. (Most of the officers throughout the Cyprus ordeal had openly expressed the agony they felt over their fellow officers' fighting and dying without being given assistance.)

Some of them wanted to arrest the air force chief, Papanikolaou, immediately.

They were restrained by Ioannides, who had agreed to the suggestion of one of Bonanos's deputies that they meet President Gizikis before taking any final decision. (Once again, final decision-making was to be postponed.) Ioannides then left for the presidential palace.

During this time the Chiefs of Staff had not been idle. They ensured that no hostile action against the Turks would be possible by recalling the two submarines from the Kyrenia area—Arapakis gave the order personally—and made sure that the Phantoms in Crete would stay on the ground.

When Papanikolaou gave the order concerning the aircraft, two of the pilots who were in the air patrolling called him, 'a yellow bastard' and a 'cowardly son-of-a-bitch'. The officers who received these orders from Papanikolaou in person began to argue with him. But he refused to take any blame, saying that a massive Bulgarian force was about to attack in the north, and that Greece would lose part of her mainland if she intervened in Cyprus. Although he knew by then that this was false, it seemed a good excuse to use. (This incident made the deputy head of K.Y.P., Stoforos, recall Papanikolaou's visit to America earlier that year, and the suspicions he had felt about Papanikolaou upon his return.)

Army Chief-of-Staff Galatsanos likewise ordered the Greek artillery units to desist from firing.

When Ioannides reached the palace he was immediately ushered in to see the President. The two men were soon joined by Ioannides's first assistant and close friend, Lieutenant-Colonel Michael Pylihos, and by Major Palainis.

Pylihos complained about the leadership's inertia during those critical hours and suggested a change of regime. He had been in contact with the Chiefs of Staff, had been told about the American assurances of a Turkish withdrawal and the promised smooth transition of power from the army to the politicians.

Pylihos looked at his old friend, Ioannides, smiled, and said: 'What the hell, Mimi,' (Ioannides's nickname) 'you don't really want to go to war the way things are now. Maybe those chickens have the right idea. The game is up.'

Ioannides nodded his head understandingly, and said that he had already agreed to step aside.

General Bonanos was then summoned to the President's office. Informed of the decision to turn the government over to a political person, Bonanos readily told his adjutant, Major Matasis, to produce the list of people already drawn up by the

Chiefs of Staff in anticipation of such a change. The list included all the usual political personalities of the past, with the exception of Constantine Karamanlis.

Ioannides refused to take part in a decision that would bring back to power the very people who, in his mind, were the epitome of corruption. He wanted an apolitical person, like the ex-Governor of the Bank of Greece, Xenophon Zolotas, or an experienced diplomat, like Xanthopoulos-Palamas. Nevertheless he told the gathering that he would go along with them if they felt it was best for the country. He then left the meeting and headed back towards the Pentagon.

There Ioannides told the assembled officers of the decision to turn the nation's destiny over to civilians. Despite some grumbling he asked them to follow the President's wish for a smooth transition of power, and, after an emotional farewell, left for his home in Galatsi, a working-class district of Athens.

Rumours, in the meantime, were sweeping the city. A foreign broadcasting station had said, in its Greek language programme, that 250 officers of the Third Army had signed a statement asking President Gizikis to invite the former politicians to take over. The broadcast also said that the commanding general of the Third Army, General Davos, was threatening to march to Athens with his tanks unless such a course of action were taken.

Although unaware of the drama being played out in Athens behind the scenes, the broadcast was, by pure luck, right in many respects. There was never any petition, however, nor did General Davos threaten to march on Athens. In fact, the contrary was closer to the truth. Davos and the Third Army officers, perceiving their fellow Greeks' agony in Cyprus, were itching to go to war.

Nevertheless, Athens once again became a madhouse of activity as housewives swamped grocery stores for canned food, and people closed their shops and offices and headed for home. More foreign stations picked up the news and by Monday night Athenians were convinced that a change was imminent.

Fortunately for the Greeks, the Turks were unaware of the drama unfolding in Athens, or of the decision by the Greek armed forces chiefs not to go to war. As the time of the ceasefire approached, an all-out Turkish effort to overrun the airport and improve their positions began. The National Guard, by now totally exhausted as well as demoralized by Greece's lack of assistance, was at the end of its tether. It barely hung on in a succession of grim holding actions.

The airport was under increasingly fierce attack from the air and from Turkish armour, but miraculously the Greek contingent held on. After the ceasefire went into effect the Turks increased their pressure. Finally, nine hours after the ceasefire, the British contingent of the United Nations took the airport under its control and threatened the Turks with aerial intervention. (The British forces in Cyprus included 5,000 men of the air force, 3,000 army and 17,000 dependents. Also included were two squadrons of Vulcan jet bombers, one squadron of Lightning interceptors, and Bloodhound interceptor missiles.)

The Turks, moreover, continued to advance to the west of Kyrenia and to the east of Nicosia, taking the villages of Trakonas and the Nicosia suburbs of Kaimakli and Neapolis. To the west of Kyrenia, and well after the ceasefire, they overran the prosperous townships of Lapithos and Karavas. They also reached the village of Larnaka and, to the east, they took over the vitally important 'white nose' mountain, thus bringing the towns of Dicomo, Vouno and Sihari under their guns.

Tens of thousands of refugees were by then streaming toward Nicosia and Limassol in the south, some of them still hoping for a Greek intervention, none of them aware that before long another 200,000 of their fellow Cypriots would be in the same straits.

In Athens, Tuesday morning brought a flurry of closed-door discussions and meetings. The continuous Turkish advance in Cyprus made some junior officers—aware of the deal between Sisco and the chiefs of the armed forces—shake their heads. U.S. Ambassador Henry Tasca met some of the senior officers and first mentioned the name of Karamanlis as a possible candidate. The Ioannides group of officers—Pylihos, Palainis, Loukoutos—was trying for a compromise between a few of the former politicians and some of the young technocrats who had emerged during the seven-year Papadopoulos regime.

A compromise was in the offing and a transitional government by an apolitical person seemed at the time a likely solution. But because of the worsening situation in Cyprus, and the threatening noises from Turkey, President Gizikis preferred to call in the old politicians to take a decision.

The Government had met in the morning and, after a stormy session, had decided to hand in its resignation. Ministers, having been kept in the dark about what was happening, complained bitterly to the Prime Minister that they were being treated as puppets. Some of them, like Co-ordination Minister Elias Balopoulos and Minister to the Prime Minister, Constantine Rallis, laughed at their colleagues' naiveté, telling them that puppets is what they had been all along.

After the resignation of the Government en masse, they went home. The Prime Minister was later accused by the press— among other more serious charges—of absenting himself during Tuesday's important meeting on Cyprus in the President's office. However, he had by then become redundant and Gizikis had told him to go home.

At noon on Tuesday, Colonel Bravakos, the President's aide, asked Commander Kouvaris of the President's office to find the telephone numbers of the various ex-politicians. This the handsome navy officer was unable to do. After all, seven years had elapsed since anyone had needed to call them. So he, in turn, had to call K.Y.P. for their numbers.

Over the phone, Lieutenant-Colonel Stoforos, the second in command at K.Y.P., gave him the numbers. Stoforos then called Bravakos, momentarily suspecting that Kouvaris could be up to something. Bravakos told Stoforos of the decision to invite the former politicians to take over, and Stoforos winced. A quiet, honest, and in many ways brilliant officer he had done a commendable job in counter-espionage. But he was leary of the former politicians and their—in his mind—corrupt ways. Nevertheless, he went about his job, though telling one of his aides that their days in K.Y.P. were numbered. (He was right. As soon as the new regime took over, he was fired.)

Around 2 p.m. the old politicians started gathering at the palace. There was Panayiotis Kanellopoulos, the philosopher and successor to Karamanlis after the latter's resignation from

85

his party's leadership. Kanellopoulos was a septuagenarian and the last Prime Minister to be appointed by the King before the 1967 coup. There were Georgos Athanassiades-Novas and Stephanos Stephanopoulos, both nearing their eighties, who had been Centre Union leaders under the Papandreou government; George Mavros, another Centre Union politician, who had inherited the mantle of leadership after Papandreou's death; Spyros Markezinis, the former leader of a small political party and the civilian Premier whom the Ioannides coup of 1973 had deposed; Xenophon Zolotas, a former Governor of the Bank of Greece; Evangelos Averoff-Tositsas, the ex-Foreign Minister under Karamanlis and a writer and intellectual of note; and Petros Garoufalias, an ex-Defence Minister under Papandreou, who had done more than any other service minister to bolster the Greek garrison in Cyprus—he kept 8,000 men under arms there—and had been the cause of a split between Papandreou and the King, which caused the King to fire the Prime Minister. (Incredibly, after the new regime came in, Garoufalias was to run in the elections which took place and his opponents were to brand him a 'man of the junta'. They seemed to forget that Garoufalias had instigated the navy coup against Papadopoulos and had been imprisoned as a result.)

These, then, were the man President Gizikis called in to take over. Present at the meeting also were the four Chiefs of Staff, as well as Gizikis himself.

The only politician who seems to have been tipped off about the conclave was Averoff-Tositsas. He had always maintained close contacts with the military, and certain officers—anxious to see Karamanlis return if there was to be a change of regime—had talked to him. It is unconfirmed, but seems true, that General Agamemnon Gratsios, the Athens and Central Greece commander, asked Averoff to insist on choosing Karamanlis as head of a new government. This was hardly necessary since Averoff was of the same mind.

When the meeting got under way, President Gizikis quickly brought the politicians up to date with the situation and asked them to form a government of national unity. A long discussion followed without any result. Although united against the junta, the politicians had not completely forgotten their differences. Nevertheless, after about three hours, Panayiotis Kanello-poulos and George Mavros had agreed to form a government. All the people present were to be included and assurances given by the military heads that absolutely no one from the armed forces would interfere.

The politicians had resisted attempts by the four military chiefs to retain the Ministries of Defence and of Public Order. Markezinis had insisted that the diplomat Palamas be appointed, with an eye to the coming United Nations discussions, but was also voted down. Finally, at 5 p.m., the meeting broke up while Mavros and Kanellopoulos went to confer with their inner circles.

Averoff, however, stayed behind. He went inside, into the President's private office and, in the presence of Pylihos and Bravakos, asked the President to consider Karamanlis. His name had already come up during the discussion, but Gizikis had said that there was no time to find him in Paris and explain everything that had happened.

Averoff now revealed to President Gizikis that he had already spoken to Karamanlis and that the latter was standing by in the Greek Embassy in Paris. A hurried call went through but Karamanlis, after having waited all day, had gone home and would return in half an hour.

After a brief interlude, the President called again and this time got Karamanlis on the line. After listening to what he had to say, Karamanlis promptly accepted. (The newspapers at the time reported that Karamanlis had said, upon hearing Gizikis's voice, 'What took you so long?' He meant why was the call so late in coming that day, not why did they wait seven years to call him, as the papers implied.)

When the politicians returned about 6 p.m.—amidst the growing crowds gathering around the palace—Gizikis stunned them by announcing that the armed forces had decided Karamanlis was the best man to take charge in such critical times, thanked them for their support, and asked them to remain in the palace until a government could be sworn in.

Despite a few disappointed people, his decision was unanimously accepted and the long vigil began. It was to be nearly a nine-hour wait before Karamanlis finally arrived. After the usual warm greetings and wishes for success, everyone got ready for the swearing-in ceremony.

Everyone, that is, except Karamanlis. The sixty-seven-year-old leader wanted to find out exactly what he was getting into before taking the oath. He said he needed assurances that the army really intended to give him a free hand, as well as needing to learn what was happening in Cyprus. And he wanted to know what deals, if any, had been made, and with whom.

At this point Petros Garoufalias and the military chiefs stepped in. They reminded Karamanlis that the army's morale was almost at breaking point, that it had been on alert for days, was now leaderless, and expected immediate decisions. 'It is now or never,' they told him, and he acquiesced.

An hour after his arrival at the old palace Karamanlis was sworn in.

The rapidity of events was probably the main reason why a very important detail was omitted by the military leaders; that, and the sheer physical exhaustion of men who had lived through the drama of the last fortnight. With junior officers threatening to open fire on the Turks in the north, with the ceasefire being violated in Cyprus, and occupied by the business of turning the government over to the politicians, men like Pylihos, Bravakos and the Chiefs of Staff forgot to ask for any kind of guarantee for themselves.

As things turned out, they were to regret that omission for the rest of their lives.

The Cyprus disaster was somehow mitigated by the return of democracy to Greece. Apart from the Cypriots who lost their lives, their homes, and their lands, the biggest reverses were suffered by America—in prestige, that is. The great majority of the Greek people were convinced that the United States had pushed Ioannides into the Cyprus adventure, although the facts point in the opposite direction.

For months Ambassador Tasca had been warning the State Department that the situation in Cyprus was coming to a head. Once the Turkish fleet had set sail for Kyrenia he had even suggested that the Sixth Fleet intercept it. Secretary Kissinger turned the suggestion down because a direct American intervention would have been unacceptable to the American public. In addition, such an act would have brought the Soviet Union into the picture with its massive fleet lurking nearby in the Mediterranean.

Newspaper reports in Greece distorted the initial American response to the Sampson takeover. The wait-and-see reaction was reported as an approving one; a distortion fanned by Communist propaganda. These distortions by the Greek press were, thereafter, to make the United States—three months after the Cyprus invasion—the most-hated nation in Greek eyes, even more than Turkey.

The human price that was paid in Cyprus was about 2,000 casualties for the Greeks, and roughly the same number for the Turks. But the civilian casualty list was also important. Rumours of large-scale killing of civilians spread fast after the first hours of fighting. Although it became difficult to substantiate them—one side would accuse the other, while denying any accusation directed at itself—a definite, and extremely ugly, pattern emerged of Greek attacks on Turkish villages, and vice versa.

The Turkish invasion force finally totalled 15,000 men, equipped with TOW missiles, armoured personnel carriers and tanks, and backed by naval forces and planes which dominated the sky. Ranged against them and somewhat worn out from two days of internecine fighting, were 10,000 national guardsmen, 4,000 paramilitary police, 600 of Makarios's personal reserve, and the 1,000 men of ELDYK. They had no modern weapons to speak of, and sometimes fought in jeans and old British helmets, with ancient, bolt-action Lee-Enfield rifles.

Both sides fought valiantly, but the biggest Turkish losses were incurred at their own hands. Turkish aircraft sank one of their own destroyers, rendered two others useless, and brought down one of their own planes. The Turks admitted losing five aircraft, while the Greeks claimed to have shot down fourteen.

Ironically, Cyprus was to undergo her greatest agony and defeat after Greece had acquired a democratic government. By acting in this way, Turkey showed that her plans to invade had nothing to do with the overthrow of Makarios, as she had claimed at the outset.

Brigadier Ioannides continued to deny having been influenced by the American C.I.A. to overthrow Makarios. In his present position (sentenced to life imprisonment) he would have certainly revealed any secret deals if they existed. He had been offered, unofficially, a probable lighter sentence if he had talked. But Ioannides clearly had nothing to say which would have been damaging to the United States.

He resolved to overthrow Makarios when it became obvious —through K.Y.P. information—that Turkey had plans to invade Cyprus or the Aegean, as the oil war began to heat up. When Makarios refused his requests to bolster the Greek contingent, Ioannides decided to get rid of him.

Makarios was encouraged to send the fateful letter. The Soviets may have urged him to do it—or some other power. But, shrewd as he is, he would never have acted alone. A close associate of his alleges that the decision to send the letter was made after his Moscow visit.

Sisco, for his part, bargained for an end to hostilities and brought down the junta in the process. Greeks, however, will never accept this. They like to believe that the will of the people did it; which is poppycock. The Colonels fell by themselves, by overestimating their own strength and that of their ally, the United States, and by underestimating the Turkish resolve to fight. In the end the Colonels resigned for the good of the country, not because they were pushed out.

In the ensuing daily anti-American riots a journalist remarked that if the United States could not bring President Thieu to accept the Vietnam truce, and had to bomb Hanoi flat while the 'little man' was thinking it over in Saigon, if it could not get Golda Meir to sit down and talk with Sadat, while she was totally dependent on America for Israel's existence, how were the poor Americans supposed to get Ioannides to kill Makarios, the Turks to attack Cyprus, the Greeks not to counter the invasion, and the Turks to advance in Cyprus?

His question made a lot of sense, but few people were listening. Greece was entering a new and crucial period. The euphoria felt on the night of July 23–24 would not last for long.

PART II

Chapter 6

The Historical Background

THE return of democracy to its birthplace, and the Cyprus disaster which was the direct cause of its return, cannot be accurately explained without a brief look at the history of Greece and at the events leading to the breakdown of the democratic process.

Unlike those who believe that the reasons for today's developments can be found only in the whims of the C.I.A. or in the machinations of 'dark foreign forces,' serious observers of the Greek scene believe that the history of modern Greece is the natural evolution of affairs caused by age-old characteristics and idiosyncracies of the Greek mind and of the Greek people in general. In order for non-Greeks to comprehend both the post-World War II situation and the current political developments a basic understanding of the past is essential. Although this could be said of any nation, no modern state—with the exception perhaps of China—believes so strongly in the continuity of its national existence from the dawn of prehistory to the present.

For the Greeks, their history flows in an uninterrupted stream beginning with the Neolithic peoples who inhabited this area in the thirtieth century B.C. During these fifty centuries, triumph and tragedy, illustrious creative achievements, periods of stagnation, conquests abroad and foreign occupations at home have created a rich historical and cultural heritage, which has indelibly stamped its imprint on their way of thinking. They have come to see Greece throughout the ages as the personification of the ideal tragic hero described by

Aristotle—achieving renown, but through some flaw or frailty bringing *nemesis*, or retribution, upon himself.

After the glorious centuries of antiquity—from the Mycenean Age and the Classical era to Alexander the Great and the Hellenistic period—the Greeks became an integral part of the Eastern Roman Empire with its opulent capital, Constantinople, founded in 330 A.D. by the Emperor Constantine.

Later known as Byzantium, the Eastern Empire incorporated within its ill-defined and fluctuating boundaries parts of Egypt, Syria, Palestine and Asia Minor, as well as lands in Italy, North Africa and most of the Balkan peninsula. In this huge area Greeks soon became the dominant element, establishing their language and cultural heritage alongside Christian beliefs and Roman political traditions, until they finally 'Hellenized' the Empire.

Byzantium lasted until 1453 when Sultan Mohammed II and his Ottoman Turks captured and sacked Constantinople. Four hundred years of Turkish domination followed and with it came most of the ills which, in retrospect, have plagued modern Greece in its recent history: civil disobedience, distrust of authority, and a lack of political maturity. It is not without reason that Tuesday, the day of the fall of Constantinople, became an unlucky day for Greeks who, superstitious even now, will not start a new business or a long trip on a Tuesday.

During the long period of Turkish rule much administrative authority was delegated to the Greek Orthodox Church. Because the Ecumenical Patriarch in Constantinople was accepted by the Turks as the national leader of all Christians, it was natural that the bishop should become the most influential local official in each Christian province. Thus the administrative structure helped to maintain the language and culture of the Greeks, whose churchmen were for a period the only educated persons throughout the Ottoman Empire.

While the Turkish administration left the Greeks mostly on their own, many who came into conflict with the Turks took refuge in the craggy mountains which cover almost sixty per cent of the country. These 'klepths,' or brigands, led a guerrilla existence for centuries, and their exploits caught the imagination of the people. The fiercely independent Greek spirit thus managed to survive, along with the inherent belief that taking the law into one's own hands is not a crime, especially when the regime is an unpopular one.

In 1821, revolution broke out in the Peloponnese, terminating successfully in 1829 with the assistance of England, France and Russia. The new sovereign Greek state encompassed all of the Peloponnese, the southern part of 'continental' Greece and several islands.

A long and continuous struggle for the incorporation of other Greek lands was then set in motion and was to dominate Greek politics, as well as foreign policy, for the next 150 years up to the recent Cyprus drama. The reason for this struggle was that, during the long period of occupation, many parts of the Greek-speaking world within the Byzantine Empire had alternated between Turkish and Venetian masters, causing boundaries to become uncertain. In the circumstances it was natural that the lands with predominant Greek-speaking populations and traditions should be considered Greek, although this was often disputed by others.

As the Great Powers of Europe had played an all-important role in the birth of an independent Greek state, they were not going to allow the infant nation to escape their influence. Those were the days when the balance of power between the leading European states was sensitive to the slightest shift in spheres of influence over territory. Greece's geographical position as a crossroads between three continents was—and still is—of the utmost strategic importance.

This influence was exerted by appointing a monarch acceptable to the Big Three. Young Prince Otto of Bavaria was chosen as the first king of Greece. He arrived in 1833 aboard a British warship. With three Bavarian regents, some 3,500 Bavarian troops, and a three million pound loan, he was to ascend the Greek throne and endeavour to create a modern European state.

This turned out to be more difficult than he at first imagined. The Greek people were just emerging from five centuries of darkness, and their backwardness—still prevalent to this day—was extreme, accompanied by a deeply-ingrained distrust of authority. Civil disobedience, which had been considered right and good for more than 400 years, was suddenly regarded as a crime. Few Greeks understood this. The result was that the democratic and liberal ideas incorporated into the first constitution had to be scrapped as the newly-found freedom of the people turned into lawlessness.

The vicious circle of freedom-anarchy-repression has marked modern Greek life up to the present day. No sooner did some liberalization take place than excesses forced a crackdown.

Otto's autocratic rule managed to bring some semblance of law and order to the country, but with the obvious result: the Greeks began to resent the King almost as much as they had resented the Turkish Pasha (Sultan) a few years before. The social problems confronting Greece were not the only reason for the malaise. The infant nation had not had the opportunity to 'emerge' from the Dark Ages like its European counterparts, nor had it experienced the 'enlightenment' which followed. Thus it was inevitable for the people of this infant nation to confuse democracy with anarchy, laws with tyranny, and normal political evolution with the resolution of differences through violent means.

It was also inevitable, as well as natural, for the newborn nation to seek a sense of identity. This it found in its glorious past. The dream of the 'Great Idea'—meaning the bringing of all Greek-populated areas under the new state—was to plague its politics for the next hundred years. Preposterous as it may sound today, this dream of 'national fulfilment' was a natural consequence of the desire of those Greeks living in predominantly and traditionally Greek areas to seek 'enosis,' or union with the motherland. Supported by inherent delusions of grandeur the 'Great Idea' stimulated the vision of a new Greek empire centred, as of old, in Constantinople. Needless to say, this vision was mercilessly exploited by politicians; it became an obstacle to any realistic foreign policy.

In 1843, an infantry battalion led by Colonel Demetrios Kallergis, forced the King to grant a constitution and parliamentary institutions. In bringing about modern Greece's first coup d'état, Kallergis became a hero overnight and established, from that time on, a tradition of military meddling in politics. Major coups took place in 1862, 1909, 1923, 1925, 1926, 1933,

1935, 1967 and 1973. There were also three major Communist-inspired mutinies, which shook the Greek armed forces in the Middle East during the Second World War.

In 1862, a revolt caused the abdication of King Otto. Although the King had found learning the Greek language difficult, and was never quite accepted by the Greeks as one of their own, his reign, nevertheless, was good for the country. During thirty years at the helm he saw the population of Greece doubled and foreign trade quadrupled. Athens had acquired new public buildings, a university, and a library. A legal code had been established, while commerce and the mercantile fleet had been greatly expanded.

After Otto's deposition the Greeks typically looked for a replica of the person or institution that they felt had been the root of their troubles to begin with. And once again the Great Powers obliged by choosing a new king for the Greek throne. A seventeen-year-old Danish prince became George I, 'King of the Hellenes,' or of all the Greeks. His title was significant as it personified the 'Great Idea'. Imbued with this concept, the royal family believed—like the rest of the nation—that the titular head of Greece embraced all Greeks irrespective of national boundaries.

George I arrived in Greece in 1863, bearing an unprecedented gift from the British: the cession of the wealthy Ionian islands, an acquisition which greatly enhanced national prestige.

A new constitution was adopted in 1864, providing for universal male suffrage even before the idea was accepted in most other European countries. In the years immediately following, the people began once again to struggle with a new and unfamiliar parliamentary system. During George I's entire reign the country remained beset by difficulties—foreign aggression, deep internal divisions fostered by opportunistic and squabbling politicians, corruption and inefficiency in the civil service, and, not least, impudence and abstention in Parliament, which made the passage of essential bills impossible.

In 1884, Greece recovered the province of Thessaly, with its fertile plains, and southern Epirus. In 1897, however, war was declared against Turkey over territorial demands by both

95

countries. The ill-prepared Greek armies, led by Crown Prince Constantine, suffered a humiliating defeat. A shocked nation saw its glorious illusions replaced by harsh reality and the war turned into a national disaster.

Political and administrative anarchy then set in, and the people became even more disillusioned with the politicians and the royal family. This disenchantment grew more acute when a military coup, led by Kemal Ataturk, overthrew the ageing Sultan of Turkey, and, riding the crest of a wave of popularity and Turkish nationalism, Ataturk forced the Greeks of Crete, Macedonia and Epirus to repudiate their claims of union with Greece.

By 1909 the military revolution in Turkey had infected the armed forces of Greece. A newly-formed Military League, under Colonel Nickolaos Zorbas with 3,000 officers and men, seized power from its camp in Goudhi on the outskirts of Athens. It was from this same camp that, on the night of April 21st, 1967, Brigadier Pattakos was to order his tanks to roll into the heart of the city.

The difference between the two coups was that the officers of the Military League did not form a dictatorship. Nor did they dissolve the National Assembly. Their sole purpose was reform. They then summoned the young Cretan politician, Eleftherios Venizelos, to take over the government and to hold elections within one year.

It is ironic for those well acquainted with Greek history to hear the outraged cries of protestation by foreigners about the Greek military's meddling in politics. Especially is this true of the British and American press, which treated this meddling as though Her Britannic Majesty's Government or the American Congress were being dictated to at gunpoint by some obscure Colonel. Foreign public opinion does not realize that the equivalent of an amalgamation of Britain's Young Pitt, Disraeli and Winston Churchill, and America's George Washington, Abraham Lincoln and Franklin Roosevelt— which is what Greeks consider Venizelos to be—first came to power by force of arms. And, furthermore, that he tried a few coups of his own when he found the electorate going against him. The romantic concept built around the birthplace of democracy has always coloured international public opinion, so that it will accept a military takeover in other countries—especially in the Third World—as a necessity, but never in Greece. Nor will it accept that, despite a geographical position which makes Greece barely a part of Europe, the country's volatile politics, the people's restless nature and climatic conditions, all combine to make Greece more of a Middle Eastern country than a modern European one. This illusion will persist as long as ancient Greek history is confused with modern times.

Venizelos turned out to be a towering figure in the modern history of his country. No Greek politician has approached him since, in international prestige or political stature. After winning the 1910 election he revised the constitution (there have been as many revisions as coups) and set about reorganizing the armed forces and bringing new faces into politics.

In revising the constitution he strengthened the rights of citizens, introduced liberal ideas, and applied democratic principles by protecting private property, personal liberty and freedom of the press. The few large estates were broken up and given to landless peasants. Greece has never known the phenomenon of large estates owned by absentee landlords. The huge fortunes one hears of today have all been accumulated outside the country by poor emigrants. Greek industrial empires are minute in comparison with their European or Western counterparts, while the main utilities and heavy industries have, since the early 1900s, been in the hands of the State.

The great inequality in wealth which was apparent until very recently—a middle class did not really exist in Greece until the late fifties—did not result from a lack of equal education or of opportunity. Nor have there ever been distinctions between people because of birthright or feudal traditions. The modern nation had no indigenous aristocracy nor families of great means. The richest people were merchants trading outside Greece, or captains who owned their ships and slowly built up fleets.

Thus the wealth of the few was more a phenomenon of

creative success than the result of an inequitable system. State-imposed egalitarian measures have always been prevalent, but have been resisted by a populace which fundamentally distrusts central authority. This was—and is—largely due to the 'spoils system' practiced by succeeding governments up to, and including, the present one.

Possessed by the 'Great Idea,' Venizelos believed that the recovery of the northern provinces would fulfil the nation's sense of identity and remove the frustrations which seemed to plague its people. Unlike his predecessors, however, he waited for the right opportunity. By superb diplomacy he formed the Balkan Alliance with Serbia, Montenegro and Greece's archenemy, Bulgaria.

The alliance was victorious in the First Balkan War against Turkey, through which Greece obtained southern and western Macedonia, Crete and another part of Epirus. Disputes over the partition of Macedonia, however, occurred among the allies. True to type, they split up and fought each other. This time it was Greece, Serbia and Turkey against Bulgaria. As a result Greece secured most of Macedonia, and in early 1914 the Great Powers recognized Greek sovereignty over most of the Aegean islands.

In five short years Venizelos had doubled the nation's territory and made Greece a coveted ally for the super-powers. Meanwhile, a mad assassin's bullet had killed King George I just a few months before his fiftieth jubilee. He was succeeded by his son, Constantine, who was married to the sister of Kaiser Wilhelm II.

The buoyant and promising conditions of 1914 were soon to be shattered by the outbreak of World War I and the 'National Schism' which effectively divided the nation for a long time to come. The schism developed over which side Greece would join in World War I. Venizelos favoured the Allies, who dangled as bait territories in Asia Minor, Constantinople and even Cyprus. Constantine—emotionally involved with Germany, being the Kaiser's brother-in-law—believed in the final victory of the Central Powers, who had promised him parts of Serbia and Albania in return for Greek support.

Going against the popular mood, the King consequently

resisted efforts by Venizelos to join the Allies. Venizelos was finally dismissed and fled to Salonica, where he established a provisional government and declared war on Germany and Bulgaria.

The nation, from then on, was divided between royalists and Venizelists. Excesses were carried out by both sides, and the scars of the wounds inflicted then were still visible in the political upheavals of the sixties.

In 1917, King Constantine was forced to resign in favour of his second son, Alexander. Venizelos became Prime Minister of a re-united government on the winning Allied side.

However, the final unification of the Greek people, after nearly a century of struggle, was not to be realized at the Paris Peace Conference which followed. Promises made in wartime adversity were easily forgotten in the flush of victory. The Treaty of Sèvres proved more fragile than its porcelain. Though favourable to the Greek cause, the Treaty was never fully applied.

Following the death of King Alexander in 1920, national elections were held. Volatile, fickle and unpredictable, the Greeks voted this time against Venizelos. A plebiscite brought King Constantine back by an overwhelming majority.

Greece now faced the displeasure of the Allies over Constantine's return, while France and Italy were supporting the revitalized Turks under their great leader, Kemal Ataturk. The Greek forces occupying Smyrna and its hinterland on the coast of Asia Minor—they had been there since 1919 under a treaty with the Allies—were soon to come under Turkish fire. A classical military blunder followed. Led by Constantine, the Greeks decided to march on Ankara. A long string of victories was cut short because they had over-extended their supply lines.

The Turks then counter-attacked, and what followed was the greatest military debacle in Greek history. The Turks broke through the Greek lines, entered Smyrna, burned the city and literally drove 1,300,000 refugees into the sea. The panic and subsequent retreat of the army saw thousands of Greeks butchered by the Turks. After 3,000 years the Greek presence in Asia Minor had come to an abrupt end.

Back in Greece the news of that momentous defeat brought the obvious result. A coup d'etat took place under Colonél Nickolaos Plastiras which forced the King to abdicate in favour of still another son, George II. The new regime also court-martialled the King's military and political advisers and executed six of them, including his Prime Minister.

The 'Great Idea' had finally come to a tragic end. Greece had to begin anew, facing the huge problems which the influx of refugees created.

The 1,300,000 destitute and dissatisfied refugees, representing almost one-quarter of the Greek mainland population of that time, quickly became a breeding ground for unrest. Living in squalid conditions, their demands exploited by opportunistic politicians, they were to create profound political instability. National humiliation helped to spread discontent among a people already divided into pro- and anti-Venizelist factions, for and against the King. This post-World War I period is usually pointed to as an example of Greek ineptitude and incapacity to cope with modern liberal ideas and parliamentary institutions. These accusations are not totally fair, however.

Greek intellectuals and historians have generally blamed the 400-year Turkish occupation for the nation's ills. And it is a fact that, where humiliation persists through several genera-tions, the oppressed begin—in defence of their own dignity— to imitate their oppressors. The cruelty, vindictiveness and harshness shown by warring political factions testify to this theory.

But this is not sufficient explanation. The volatility of the Greek character, probably the only remaining link with the glorious past of antiquity, is another. The highly individualistic Greek is too self-seeking to submit easily to the dictates of others. His unruliness has helped him survive throughout the centuries of oppression, as well as to rise above adversity, economic or otherwise. But it has also made him unaware of the advantages of a communal spirit and true democratic attitudes. He will go to any lengths to attain his goals, not hesitating to lie and cheat in order to achieve them. This has—brutal though it may sound—created a climate where cheating is a way of life, and where the highest and lowest of citizens do not hesitate to use dishonesty, especially where politics are concerned.

A direct result of this way of life has been the 'spoils system'. Although not a Greek invention, nowhere has it been practiced more assiduously than in Greece. Succeeding Governments have shamelessly brought in their favourites, returning favours and expecting new ones in the future, and changing laws to suit their purposes; thus encouraging resentment, divisiveness and a 'wait-until-my-turn-comes' way of thinking. No Greek government has ever come to power which truly tried to reconcile the people. There has always been too much vindictiveness among political leaders for such a course of action. Even Karamanlis, after returning to rescue the country from the Cyprus débâcle—at the invitation of the military—proceeded to hound the very people who brought him back.

The failure to attain national goals has probably also served to increase the political instability of the country. There seems to be a definite inability by the people to conceive of a common good or to achieve a community spirit. The fault lies, at least partly, in the Greek character. Whether or not it was influenced by the Turkish occupation, this self-seeking, opportunistic streak must bear the blame. All parts of the political spectrum and all sectors of society are guilty of it.

Poor economic conditions following the disaster in Asia Minor—unemployment, inflation and an almost non-existent balance of payments—were fueled by the profound political instability caused by the schism between Venizelists and royalists. It was only to be expected that these chaotic economic conditions should have severe repercussions on the political situation. From 1922 to 1936, there were nineteen changes of governments, three changes of regime, seven military coups and innumerable minor acts of sedition.

A multitude of political forces competed with inept politicians, irresponsible governments and intervening military dictators for the complete bankruptcy of proper government. To existing royalist and republican factions were now added communist and fascist ideas, which completed the political spectrum.

Communism did not catch on easily in Greece. It had to

wait for World War II and the opportunities which that conflict offered to armed insurrectionists. The true electoral strength of the Communists has never passed 15 per cent, and has been as low as 8 per cent. This relatively poor showing can be attributed both to the Greek character and to certain basic errors made by the K.K.E., the Greek Communist Party.

Greek individualism cannot easily adapt itself to the rigidity of Communism. Also, the fierce nationalism, not to say chauvinism, of the Greek does not readily take to communist internationalism. Finally, the Greek's belief in private property is almost sacrosanct, making him unlikely material for communist indoctrination.

The K.K.E.'s advocacy of an autonomous Macedonia and Thrace was a serious tactical error, as it repelled many Greeks who were otherwise sympathetic to communist propaganda. In propagating its ideas, however, the K.K.E. had no peer. It found the perfect place for such activity in the refugee camps, and willing politicians to spread its gospel. The instability of the country obviously helped.

Meanwhile the King, George II, had been exiled in 1923, only to return in 1935, after seven coup d'états, nineteen changes of government, and two dictatorships. The plebiscite which brought him back indicated that 97 per cent of the electorate—voting is compulsory in Greece—favoured his return. As almost half the population have always been fervent republicans, especially while Venizelos was alive, it is not difficult to guess how the electorate experienced such a change of mind: ballot-tampering has always been the rule, rather than the exception, in Greek elections.

The results of the 1936 election created a political impasse as the Monarchists won 143 seats in Parliament, the Liberals 142 and the Communists 15, thus giving them the balance of power. Under the circumstances General Metaxas—a man who was to play a decisive and heroic role in Greek history— was assigned by Parliament to rule by decree for six months. (During that period Venizelos died of natural causes after having survived numerous attempts on his life, as well as having tried two coups during his last years.)

In the ensuing political vacuum, the small K.K.E. achieved

an importance disproportionate to its size. Under the leadership of Nikos Zachariadis, a Russian-trained Asia Minor Greek, there were 344 strikes and disorders during the first six months of 1936 alone, reaching a climax in the Salonica Communist demonstration in which twelve people were killed. An army unit joined the Communist demonstrators, then took over the city, while Zachariadis openly called for revolt and invited the army to join the people.

National discontent resulting from the internecine political bickering and the cynical manipulation of the people's misery by the Communists, stirred too by the 'gathering storm' over Europe and the Spanish civil war, soon led General Metaxas to convince the King that he should dissolve Parliament and declare martial law. On August 4th, 1936, on the eve of a Communist-declared general strike, which was to be the decisive *tour de force* by the K.K.E., a dictatorship was established. Even the most faithful believers in parliamentary democracy heaved a sigh of relief.

The Metaxas dictatorship (1936–1941) is usually relegated to that inhuman species of political monsters which were unhappily emerging throughout Europe at the time. But this is much too broad and convenient a generalization by Western liberals. Although John Metaxas's contempt for parliamentary rule was a well-known fact, it should not be assumed—as it has been by the majority of historians—that his opponents took an opposite view. Neither the Populists, who had been in power for the two preceding years, nor the Republicans, had shown much respect for democratic principles. While holding almost 90 per cent of the popular vote, they had placed petty differences above their responsibilities, leaving the country without leadership or a working government.

It must also be said that the Metaxas dictatorship was one of the mildest of the species, certainly when compared to those in Germany, Italy, Spain and the U.S.S.R. No political executions were carried out, which itself was a sharp contrast to the Republic which preceded it and to the parliamentary governments of the forties and fifties. Sensing that war was inevitable, Metaxas built up the armed forces. In addition, he attempted many social reforms, passed badly-needed labour laws to protect the worker, cancelled farmers' debts, and disciplined the civil service. He cracked down hard on dissident Communists, while largely turning a blind eye toward the Fascists.

Metaxas was later to become somewhat of a model for George Papadopoulos, who tried to emulate Metaxas's ideas concerning a 'national regeneration,' which involved a utopian view of 'Hellenic-Christian civilization' and the indoctrination of the people about their glorious past. But censorship of the press, and sometimes even of classical Greek texts, made neither man popular with thinking Greeks—something each in his turn had desperately desired.

The inevitable establishment of a no-matter-how-mild police state, the arbitrary arrests of dissenting elements and the creation of police files, contradicting the peoples' strong sense of liberty, never permitted Metaxas to become popular. His greatest moment came when he uttered his historic 'No' to the Italian demand that Greece allow Fascist troops free access to its territory.

His firm stand against the Italian ultimatum in October 1940, and the subsequent success of the Greek forces on the Albanian front brought him a certain national glory. He died in January 1941, while the Greek troops were still victorious. Even his opponents admitted that his untimely death was a blow to the Greek cause.

Greek military successes drew Germany into the war, and, on April 27th, 1941, Nazi troops entered Athens. King George II and his Government, some remnants of the Greek army and the British Expeditionary Force, fled to Egypt after making a brave, but bloody, last stand on the island of Crete.

The Axis occupation forces did not concern themselves with the greater part of Greece; their interest centred on the major cities and other strategic areas. Mountainous, and with poor communications, most of the countryside was left to starvation and to the whims of the roaming guerrilla bands which started to appear.

The Greek Communist Party clearly understood the vast opportunity which was now presented. Recognizing that most Greeks were distrustful of Communism and would not readily join a solely Communist movement, it formed the National Liberation Front (E.A.M.) as a national resistance movement, thus hiding its real objective for the moment. The K.K.E.'s immediate aim was to monopolize the Greek resistance movement. E.A.M. was led by a central committee of hardcore Communists, whose names remained secret and who were well accustomed to working underground. The movement spread rapidly throughout the country, became powerful and—most important—offered the enslaved nation the political leadership which was so desperately needed.

In April 1942 E.A.M. established its military arm, E.L.A.S., under the leadership of Thanassis Klaras, who took the pseudonym of Aris Velouchiotis. It was this military organization that was to wreak havoc eventually on other resistance groups and, finally, on Greece itself; on all those who did not believe in communism.

Although it is undeniable that E.A.M./E.L.A.S. together constituted the main force behind the resistance, their motives and subsequent actions cast doubt on the genuineness of their contribution to the Allied cause. Their most spectacular effort was an operation which destroyed the vital Gorgopotamos viaduct in December 1942. The guerrillas, including E.D.E.S., which was a nationalist group under Napoleon Zervas, wiped out the Italian garrison defending the bridge and blew it up, thus disrupting German transportation to North Africa for several weeks.

When looked at from the vantage point of history, the real contribution of the resistance was that it offered the Greeks a chance to defend their honour and dignity against the Fascist invaders. This the Communists understood better than the other resistance groups which slowly emerged. Once the war was over they used this nationalist sentiment to advance their real aim of taking over the country.

How did the leadership of what had been, before the war, a most insignificant party suddenly gain widespread popular support? The answer lies in the fact—and this is where historians have managed to rewrite history to suit their own purpose—that most of the people who joined E.A.M. were not Communists. A political vacuum had been created by the death of

Metaxas and the King's departure for Egypt along with his Government; this situation left the nationalist element leaderless and discouraged.

The only alternative was to join the well-organized Communist-led E.A.M./E.L.A.S., which had conveniently located cells, both civilian and military, throughout the country. The young were quickly proselytized to Communist dogma, while the nationalists were slowly weeded out, or fed with false information about the nature of the war being fought. For these reasons the Communist organization became much the most important element of the resistance movement in a country where 90 per cent of the electorate was either royalist or liberal.

E.A.M./E.L.A.S., however, did more than just fight the powerful Axis occupiers. They also betrayed many nationalists to the Germans, and, after a time, began the drive toward their 'ultimate objective'—the seizure of power after the war—by carrying out repeated attacks on all guerrilla bands which refused to be incorporated within the Communist fold. They managed to wipe out most of these groups with the exception of E.D.E.S., which barely survived though limited to a small area in Epirus.

Communist infiltration of the armed forces in Egypt led to two anti-royalist mutinies in the springs of 1943 and 1944, lessening the role the Greek army could play during the liberation. The King—determined to maintain his prerogative—refused either to yield or to compromise when confronted with the realities of the situation at home.

In March 1944, E.A.M./E.L.A.S. announced the formation of its own Government as a challenge to the Greek Government in Cairo. George Papandreou—a liberal political leader who was to play a fateful role in his country's fortunes later on—became Prime Minister of the Cairo Government-in-exile after a short tenure by Sophocles Venizelos, the son of the great Cretan politician.

As liberation approached, the time seemed ripe for a *rapprochement* between 'the Government of the mountains' and the one in Cairo. A conference was held in Lebanon, which created a Government of National Unity under the premiership of George Papandreou. Representatives of seventeen political parties and resistance groups participated. After some hesitation by the Communists, and perhaps through the influence of Colonel Gregori Popov—the head of the Sovet mission in Greece—six E.A.M. members were sworn in as Ministers.

Another agreement was signed in Caserta, Italy, between the guerrillas of E.A.M./E.L.A.S. and the nationalists, along with Papandreou and representatives of the British government. This pact placed all guerrilla bands in Greece under the Greek Government. The King agreed to return to Greece only after the holding of a plebiscite. On October 12th, 1944, the last German troops left Athens.

Liberation had finally come, but at a very high price. Over 1,000,000 Greeks had died in battle, from starvation or in internecine fighting: and the killing and the misery was not to end yet.

The national euphoria sparked by the liberation did not last long. The bloodiest civil war in Greek history broke out two months after liberation. The Communists could not trust a Government whose purpose was to render E.A.M./E.L.A.S. powerless and to bring back the King. Although the Cold War had not yet begun, it was obvious that the British-backed Government of George Papandreou could not co-exist ideologically with the Soviet-inclined E.A.M. group. The Communists were also convinced that all their efforts during the war would have been vain if Greece were to return to the pre-war situation.

On the nationalist side, the Greek Right had ample reason to mistrust E.A.M./E.L.A.S. The cynical way in which the Communists had wiped out resistance groups which did not accept their ideology was proof enough. It was obvious that the K.K.E. and E.A.M. were seeking nothing less than the communization of Greece without allowing the people to decide in a manner remotely resembling democracy.

After a Communist-called demonstration resulting in fifteen deaths (some say a policeman started firing; others that it was an *agent provocateur*), the battle of Athens was on. E.L.A.S., which controlled nine-tenths of the country, had 50,000 superbly-trained and well-armed men. Facing them were

7,000 nationalist guerrillas under Colonel Napoleon Zervas, the Greek army's 'mountain brigade,' and a token British force which had arrived as the Germans departed.

Within a fortnight E.L.A.S. took over most of Athens, as well as most of the rest of the country. The E.D.E.S. forces were driven into the sea, and took refuge in the island of Corfu. Only a small section of the capital remained in nationalist hands. Non-Communists throughout the country were killed in an orgy of blood and hate. Priests, civil servants, teachers, policemen, the well-to-do, anyone who was not at least a communist sympathizer, was executed. Mass graves filled the gardens of Athens, and for years afterwards more and more bodies were discovered—all victims of the 'Red Terror'.

Soon, however, superior British forces arrived by sea from Egypt and managed to turn the tide. This was the first open confrontation between East and West in the Cold War. Only Churchill's decision to send in troops saved Greece from disappearing behind the Iron Curtain. He defended his action by recalling the understanding he had reached with Stalin in Moscow in October 1944, which expressly left Greece out of the Soviet Union's sphere of influence.

The Varkiza agreement, by which the Communists consented to surrender their arms, was signed in January 1945. Although a large amount was in fact handed over, just as much was cached away for future use.

By the end of the war the majority of the people were ready for a liberal government; so they turned to the British and to the Right as the only guarantors of peace and order. The battle of Athens and the Red Terror had seen to that. Unfortunately, the Right was unwilling to let bygones be bygones. A relatively mild White Terror then took place, dividing the country even further.

The first elections in ten years found the Populist party—the royalists—winning a clear majority. Six months later a plebiscite, in which 69 per cent of the population voted for the King's return, re-established the monarchy. The Communists abstained both from the elections and from the plebiscite, charging that fraud and terrorism had shaped the outcome.

One month after the plebiscite the Greek Communist Party

(K.K.E.) declared war on the Government and proceeded to form a Democratic Army (D.S.E.). At first, the D.S.E.—openly supported by Greece's northern neighbours—was quite successful. However, one basic thing was lacking: popular support. After the recent wholesale massacres the support which the Communists enjoyed during the German occupation had evaporated.

With the announcement of the Truman Doctrine in 1947, the United States replaced Britain as Greece's major ally. And when Marshal Tito closed the Yugoslav frontier to Communist guerrillas, the fate of what the Communists called the 'Second Round' was sealed. A mass retreat took place in 1949; the Communist forces withdrew into Albania, abducting 28,000 children in the process. The civil war had cost 150,000 casualties, some 100,000 Greeks had fled behind the Iron Curtain, and 700,000 refugees had flocked into the cities. The Communist insurrection had failed, but the scars of the conflict—piled upon so many previous ones—left the nation in a state of economic and moral collapse.

Once internal peace was secured Greece entered a period of reconstruction under an American 'protective' umbrella. In the early stages of that period the old parties—the Populists and the Liberals—as well as some newly-formed parties failed to establish strong governments or even working governments. This happened because an electoral system of proportional representation fragmented the vote.

In May 1951 Field Marshal Alexander; Papagos formed a new rightist party, the Greek Rally, and instituted a new electoral system which favoured the party of the majority. Political stability was finally at hand. In the November 1952 elections Papagos received 50 per cent of the vote and 240 out of 300 seats in Parliament.

The Papagos administration was to govern for three years, until the Premier's death in 1955, and to inaugurate ten continuous years of stable right-wing rule. During this time economic confidence was restored by the drastic monetary measures of the Minister of Co-ordination, the young Spyros Markezinis. The death of Papagos also brought forth the most important political figure of the post-war period, Constantine

Karamanlis. King Paul, who had succeeded his brother, George I, after the latter's death in 1947, bypassed Papagos's logical successors and named Karamanlis to head a Provisional Government until elections were held. It was to be one of the Crown's wisest decisions.

The forty-eight-year-old son of a Macedonian school teacher, Karamanlis at the time of his appointment was the Minister of Public Works in Papagos's cabinet and relatively unknown. He became the youngest Premier in Greek history, but he had already launched a programme of road-building and public works that were to be the first steps in a nationwide reconstruction effort.

With his heavy northern accent and lower middle-class background, Karamanlis was at first looked upon by élitist political observers as a temporary and rather comical solution. But, again, the political observers were to be proved wrong. Efficient, immensely hard-working, the new Premier soon displayed a dynamism and forcefulness that had rarely been seen in Greek domestic affairs. Having initiated his public works projects, he became the architect of Greece's industrialization programme.

Politically right-of-centre, Karamanlis laid the basis for an economic resurgence which pulled his country out of its perennial economic slump. Domestically, he became known as 'Mr. Law and Order', for his emphasis on due process and open elections. Internationally, he believed strongly in the Western Alliance and led the country into the European Economic Community.

A man with a rigorously logical mind, Karamanlis is exceptionally taciturn for a Greek. He uses adjectives sparingly in a land where hyperbole has become an art form. This disconcerting habit of developing his thoughts in a few sentences and then refusing to say a word more earned him the reputation among his associates and parliamentary opponents of being an obtuse authoritarian.

Nevertheless the premier's simple tastes—he had been very poor as a boy, and struggled hard to support the family after his father's death—and unpretentious style of living endeared him to the people, who had been used to crooked politicians living high on the hog. After winning the election in 1956, he began the political processes that were to give Greece its greatest stability for 150 years.

In 1958 Karamanlis called for elections once again and won them comfortably. A disturbing sign, however, was the surfacing of the Communists as the official opposition. Under the euphemistic name of United Democratic Left (E.D.A.), the Communists managed to secure 25 per cent of the popular vote. This was a direct result of the bickering between George Papandreou and Sophocles Venizelos, the two leaders of the Liberals, who fought for the leadership of their party, causing its near disintegration.

As the sixties approached, Karamanlis had without doubt turned Greece into the 'economic miracle of Europe'. Never had an undisciplined, under-developed nation come so far in such a brief period of time. Never had Greece enjoyed a stable government for so long, except under a dictatorship. Never had the standard of living been so high. And all this was due to the remarkable Mr. Karamanlis and his firm-but-fair government.

But it was not enough. True to their past, the Greeks emulated their ancestors by biting the hand that fed them. Inside three short years Karamanlis was to flee his country, clandestinely, using a false name and under charges of fraud and corruption. Riots, political murders and coups were to follow. And it all began with an old man calling for an 'unyielding struggle.'

PART III

Chapter 7

Preamble to a Dictatorship: The Fall of Karamanlis

I N September 1961 Karamanlis resigned and called for elections to be held within forty days. A caretaker Government was appointed by King Paul and headed by General Dovas, the chief of the Crown's military retinue. Karamanlis was then at the peak of his power.

Greece was no longer, as it had been immediately after the war, a ravaged, bankrupt and divided country, but an emerging, confident nation, about to join the European Economic Community.

The economic accomplishments of Karamanlis's government were undeniable and proof that the Greek people could, under smooth parliamentary conditions, act in unison toward the common goal of a better standard of living.

Karamanlis's hopes for the election were not merely to gain a majority. An overwhelming victory at the polls—an impressive national mandate—seemed to him imperative, so that he could push through constitutional changes. These changes were badly needed. An impatient, autarchic man, the Premier was particularly exasperated by a procedure under which essential bills might be passed by Parliament but still require another two years to become law.

Along with the proposed constitutional revisions Karamanlis also hoped to 're-define' the position of the throne, as he had found its privileges, and the interference by the royal family, to be causes of embarrassment to his government.

Party cadres were instructed to apply maximum pressure in the civil service, the military, and other state institutions so that this overwhelming majority would be achieved. In retrospect, Karamanlis must have felt as foolish as Nixon eleven years later, because his lieutenants, like Nixon's men, risked the position of their chief by trying with excessive zeal for a mandate which was already in the bag.

This, then, was the state of affairs as Karamanlis and his E.R.E. ruling party conducted their campaign in the autumn of 1961. Opposing them was the newly created Centre Union (E.K.) and the Communist Front (E.D.A.).

The creation of the Centre Union in 1961 was an important turning point in Greek politics. Karamanlis himself was relieved by its appearance as the main opposition party. Since the centre liberals were always busy quarrelling among themselves, effective opposition in Parliament had been limited to the Communists of E.D.A., who were concerned purely with sabotaging legislation even if it was vital for the nation's needs.

The Centre Union, which was led by George Papandreou and Sophocles Venizelos, was a coalition of the centre's political personnel, containing such middle-of-the-roaders as the two leaders, Petros Garoufalias from right of centre, and Elias Tsirimokos belonging to the extreme left of the party. (It is interesting to note that many of the old politically-established families of Greece were represented in the Centre Union, and continue to be now. The right—although also containing some 'old boys'—was mostly made up of young, up-and-coming technocrats of modest background, typified by their Macedonian leader.)

The results of the hard-fought campaign showed that the Greek electorate did not want a change. E.R.E. received 50 per cent of the vote and 176 out of 300 parliamentary seats. The Centre Union obtained one-third of the vote and 100 seats, while the Communists suffered a severe set-back from their previous high point by gaining only twenty-four seats, a loss of fifty-five.

Two days later, however, George Papandreou made a public statement claiming that the results were a fraud and the product of violence. He declared an 'unyielding struggle' against the 'illegitimate majority and the illegal government.'

This statement marked the first step in the deterioration of the democratic process in Greece and its subsequent abolition.

Ballot-rigging was not a new phenomenon in Greek political life. In fact, it was more the rule than the exception. It has been said that 'democracy in Greece is no virgin.' It has always been common for the electoral system to be manipulated in favour of the ruling party.

The characteristics of village life in rural Greece—50 per cent of the active population work and live in the country—make it easy to cheat at ballot-time. There the local gendarme, priest, teacher, and prefect reign supreme. Let us take the case of a typical village of 3,000 people near Sparta in the Peloponnese:

The town is in need of a doctor, modern medical equipment for its antiquated hospital (if there is one) and an asphalt road making it accessible to Sparta's merchants. A promise to provide all three, or at least two, of the demands is extracted from the Central Government by the area's parliamentary representative. In turn, the authorities demand assurances that the village will vote for the Government candidate at election time. If the Member of Parliament happens to be from the opposition party, the prefect or community leader of the village will bypass him and deal directly with Athens.

At election time the local gendarme will warn 'suspicious' elements that they had better not risk the promised benefits by voting against the ruling party. He might even go so far as to examine ballots cast, so as to make sure that the village will outshine all others in its support of the Government, thus gaining attention and the fulfilment of promises.

In small villages and hamlets where everyone knows everyone else and needs are more or less the same, these practices do not outrage the inhabitants' democratic principles; which is why they have been tolerated throughout the years, exacerbated by the lack of communication between the political parties.

The old maxim of 'to the victor belong the spoils' is the best way to describe the transition of power from one party to another in Greece.

With the exception of the extreme Communist Left, the parties have traditionally lacked any hard-and-fast ideological base. They tend, instead, to revolve around the personalities of their respective leaders and, as such, are liable to the leaders' volatility. Party structure and discipline are more or less alien to Greek politics, in contrast to the Western world where political parties tend to be highly organized, semi-permanent groups with elected heads.

Fraud, or rather an intensification of irregularities, in the 1961 election was never proved by the opposition. That this took place, however, was undeniable. An objective guess would be that it did not exceed the degree of such activity in past elections and referendums. If anything, manipulation was less extreme than in some of the plebiscites which showed the Greek people voting, with Stalin-like percentages of approval, to bring back the King.

That these irregularities took place at all was due to the fear by Karamanlis's para-governmental mechanism that the 1958 electoral successes of the Left—25 per cent of the vote—would be repeated. However, with the presence of the Centre Union this was unlikely. The Communist atrocities during the civil war were still fresh in the minds of the people in key positions—police officers, town prefects and municipal leaders, even priests. It was those very people who had been butchered by the Communists in December 1944, and who feared them most.

Greece's 500-mile frontier with Communist Albania, Bulgaria and Yugoslavia, as well as with her arch-enemy Turkey, has maintained fear of a Communist menace in the minds of the people. But the Government's desire for a large majority, and the orders to party cadres, assured that the election would be fraudulent.

As compared to the past, the important difference in the fraud claimed in this election was not the extent of it (at most 2–3 per cent) but the reaction it caused. The repetition of methods used in the past by all parties was suddenly no longer tolerated by the electorate. This crucial point dawned on George Papandreou who had, in the past, after his numerous electoral defeats, always charged fraud on the part of his opponents, only to let the issue drop soon afterwards.

The 'unyielding struggle' which was to topple Karamanlis within two years caught the imagination of the urban masses. Athens, in particular, was to become paralyzed as crowds rampaged the streets and fought pitched battles with the police. And George Papandreou, the seventy-year-old has-been, was the prime mover behind this struggle.

An old Venizelist Liberal, the head of the Centre Union was the man who had returned to Greece some seventeen years before as Prime Minister of the wartime Government-in-exile, only to be forced into early retirement by the Communist uprising. By 1961 he was past seventy, but was still recognized as the most formidable of the old Liberal politicians, although never having held office again.

A tall, imperious figure with a gift for public speaking, Papandreou had been actively involved in politics for the better part of fifty years. He had served Eleftherios Venizelos as Education Minister and the Plastiras revolutionary Government as Home Secretary. Metaxas had exiled him to the Aegean island of Andros, and the Italian occupation forces had imprisoned him. After his release he escaped to the Middle East in time to head the Government-in-exile. Although a man of great natural ability, he was notoriously volatile, quickly carried away by the sound of his own voice, and plainly addicted to wishful thinking. His oratorical style was his greatest asset, and his theatrical manner and histrionics were made to order for the passionate Greek public.

Papandreou was, nevertheless, fiercely anti-Communist and committed to a pro-Western Greece within the N.A.T.O. alliance, although having some reservations about the latter.

The enormity of Karamanlis's mistake in giving the opposition such a plum of an argument against his victory was explained by David Holden in his penetrating book, *Greece Without Columns*.

'Obsessed with anti-Communism, they reacted to the mildest liberal criticism as if it were the voice of Lenin himself, and in the chain of patronage which descended from Athens down to the lowest level of rural affairs, they did not hesitate to insert their own men and exclude all others, so that local police stations or village councils were sometimes dominated by people who were little better than bully-boys, out for what they could get, or men who were still paying off old scores from the Civil War. Instead of trying to close the desperate fissures that ripped apart Greek society in those tragic years, such men actually kept them open; and whether they did so out of greed, fear or simple misunderstanding, they produced an equivalent reaction from the other side as inevitable as it was depressing.'

In his last sentence David Holden gives us an inkling of the vicious circle caused by the Greek electoral system. Later on, when Papandreou's hour struck, the same excesses were to take place. And even worse, terrorist tactics were to be used on unsuspecting citizens simply for reading conservative newspapers.

Needless to say, the dictatorship that came in 1967 refined such tactics. But even after the restoration of democracy this Greek cancer was not to disappear. The spoils system, patronage, retribution, even kangaroo courts were to continue.

Widespread dissatisfaction throughout the country became evident as Papandreou heated up his campaign for an 'unyielding struggle'. Strikes and demonstrations jolted major cities in general and Athens in particular. The Greek Left, of course, was not going to let the chance of a lifetime pass by, and so threw its excellent organization behind Papandreou's supporters in the streets.

One must surely wonder why, if Karamanlis's past tenure had been so successful and productive, the crowds supported the minority's call for street demonstrations and civil disobedience? After all, election irregularities had taken place before without causing even embarrassment to the winners.

The reasons are manifold and complicated. As previously mentioned, the electorate had matured and started to resent the hanky-panky which always took place at polling time. There was also the famous Greek propensity for disgracing its idols. And Karamanlis had become an idol after the longest period in office in modern Greek history. (From Themistocles to Socrates, Kapodistria to Kolokotronis to Venizelos, the Hellenes have always repaid their greatest leaders by disgracing, or even killing or imprisoning, them. Or exiling them. Aristides, the Athenian wise man, was exiled when the people decided that there must be something wrong with a man who was always called 'the Just'.)

Along with Karamanlis's drive for economic recovery and development profound social transformations had taken place.

Although Greece still remained essentially an agricultural country, urbanization had proceeded rapidly. The influx into the cities had begun in the Civil War period when hundreds of thousands of peasants fled to the safety of the towns. With the subsequent industrialization, more and more people left their villages and the meagre living they could eke out in the harsh countryside for newly-created jobs around the cities.

This influx caused Athens to double in size by 1961, as compared to its pre-war population. Comprising more than 2,000,000 people, the capital now represented almost a quarter of the total population of the entire country. Thus, inevitably, profound social contradictions appeared. A severe housing shortage was one example. The unfamiliar urban surroundings, the cramped and dingy quarters, the noisy, bustling streets, pollution, and the competitive pace of a modern city—all these alienated the migrants.

Accustomed to the clean air and pleasant peaceful surroundings of the countryside, the Greek villager found himself frustrated and unwilling to cope with the sudden deterioration in the quality of his life. He became a perfect and willing target for the demagogue. His lack of education was another important and influential factor.

Education had suffered adversely from Greece's turbulent history. Oppression, revolution and war did little to foster creative intellect. Rural primary education often consisted of local priests doubling as teachers for the children of their parishes. Although attendance at primary schools was compulsory for all children reaching six years of age, the secondary education that followed was neither compulsory nor free. In fact, primary and secondary education for all remained a goal rather than a reality. Progress was hindered by the poverty of the country. School buildings were inadequate, teachers too few, and their salaries a pittance.

With the sudden influx of the peasantry to the cities, the education problem became very acute. No government could have solved it overnight. Nor could any democratic government have prevented the poorly educated, frustrated urban masses from being further alienated and divided by the press.

The Fourth Estate in Greece has been called divisive and,

at times, counter-productive; unfortunately both charges have some foundation. The press has—unwittingly or not—contributed to the country's problems by arousing passions, serving individual interests, and, in general, failing to unite the people toward a national goal.

That is not to say that the role of the press has been solely negative. Far from it. But the press has failed in its primary role, which is to report the facts accurately and objectively. This is especially unfortunate because, if any people can be said to be addicted to newspapers, it is the Greeks.

As radio and television are state-controlled, the press plays a very crucial role in influencing the ordinary person in Greece. The Athenian public alone supports more than twelve dailies with a combined circulation of 600,000. Being of a naturally inquisitive nature, the average Greek desires above all to be 'in the know', considers himself a political animal, and delights in talking, preferably about politics. The numerous papers fulfil these desires and are, in turn, taken seriously by their public.

Yet the journalistic level has remained low. Although yellow journalism is not a Greek invention, it might well have been. Editorialising while reporting a story is allowed, even encouraged. Tendentiousness, false rumours and character assassination are not considered improper newspaper techniques.

The importance of objective journalism has never been understood in Greece, and there is neither a school of journalism nor any effort made to teach objectivity to aspiring newsmen. Newspapers are privately owned and naturally reflect the political opinions of their owners. They support the candidates of the owner's choice, and most politicians have found it impossible to rise and stay at the top of the political ladder without the support of at least one of the major publishers.

Since the early Fifties the most powerful newspaper concerns have been the Lambrakis, Vlachos and Botsis groups. The largest circulation has been enjoyed by publications of the Lambrakis group, which has traditionally backed liberal and left-of-centre candidates. The other two publishers have been conservative in political ideology, backing Karamanlis and the palace. The rest of the newspapers have varied between the extremes of the political spectrum, dividing 60 to 40 per cent in favour of the centre.

It was common knowledge that no major decision was taken by the heads of political parties without first consulting certain newspaper owners. Christos Lambrakis, the son of the founder of *Vima* and *Nea*—morning and afternoon papers respectively—played a pivotal role in deciding the Centre Union's course of action. Lambrakis's presence behind the scenes has been a formidable one throughout, making and breaking careers according to his whims, which are many and said to be rather strange.

Helen Vlachos also inherited her position as an influential conservative publisher—owning the morning *Kathimerini* and the evening *Mesimvrini*—and enjoyed no less political power. Like Lambrakis, she too was a kingmaker and changed favourites according to her whims.

Nassos Botsis, the publisher of Greece's oldest daily, *Acropolis*, was more a follower than a kingmaker, preferring the good life of girl-chasing and gambling to political infighting.

As Papandreou's charges of fraud and calls for an 'unyielding struggle' mushroomed, newspapers aggravated the tense situation by what can only be described as extremely irresponsible journalism. The Communist press, in particular, overstepped all bounds of propriety and decency. It accused Karamanlis of every conceivable crime and—libel laws being what they are in Greece—pretty well got away with it. Others followed suit.

It was small wonder, therefore, that factions were at each other's throats. Rapid urbanization, the lack of education of the masses, a yellow and divisive press, irresponsible conduct by politicians of both Right and, Left, and finally, undeniable excesses by certain military and security organizations—all combined to make the people forget the good things Karamanlis's tenure had brought. Instead they spilled out on the streets in protest.

The one institution which could have had a calming influence on the bitter political feuding, the Crown, then came under attack. The Centre Union proclaimed that palace involvement in politics should be curbed, indirectly pointed an accusatory finger at the King's meddling and pressed him to disclaim the election results.

The Greek monarchy had never become an apolitical institution like its surviving European counterparts. The basic problem between the Crown and the politicians lay in the Crown's interpretation of its position, which can only be described as extra-constitutional. In simpler terms, the royal family adhered to the feudal concept of king and state, fervently believing that they were the guarantors and personification of that state.

This attitude was tolerated and actually encouraged by servile politicians in return for royal favours and patronage. Needless to say, whenever a strong political personality of independent views appeared, a collision course between him and the Crown was inevitable. In post-war Greece the Crown collided with Papagos, Karamanlis and, subsequently, Papandreou. All three men attempted to re-define the role of the King and that of the politician in a modern political system.

Despite continuing to think in traditional terms while reigning over a modern state, King Paul was a popular monarch. His naval background—he had served in the merchant marine and in a British factory as an engineer during his youth in exile—simple tastes and unassuming manner, as well as his love for rugged, outdoor activities, endeared him to the people. His straightforwardness also charmed the politicians, most of whom grovelled in his presence. In a land where charm counts more than talent and ability, the monarch made the most of this attribute.

His wife, however, was a different story. The strong-willed grand-daughter of Kaiser Wilhelm II, a great grand-daughter of Queen Victoria, she managed to arouse as much controversy over her person—and, through her, the throne—as her husband aroused sympathy and respect.

Much has been written about Queen Frederika's excesses during her reign. Communist and other left-wing papers have presented her as a monster and an outright thief. This, of course, was nonsense. Just as the mob spread vicious stories about Marie Antoinette and her personal life, the Greek Left saw a golden opportunity to discredit the Right through its association with 'the German woman'.

The facts about the Queen and the reasons for the controversy surrounding her seem to be these:

Her political meddling and general behaviour can be explained by three main factors,

(a) Her family and national background. She was born into an authoritarian family within an authoritarian system, in a state where the concept of 'absolute monarch' had been glorified by her grandfather, Kaiser Wilhelm II. From an early age her life was filled with constant reminders that it was up to her and her family to guarantee the welfare of the country and its people. She believed in the divine right of rulers and, in that medieval spirit, saw herself as a lioness protecting and dominating her young. (When she and her husband ascended to the throne in 1947, in the midst of the Civil War, she showed great courage and compassion for people involved in the conflict. Touring the battlefields she not only gave needed moral support, but also managed to gain great popularity for the throne.)

(b) Her own personality formed by ambition and supported by a lively and clever mind. Among royalty, an institution which has been called, among other things, 'a biological blunder' and 'a race unique in the world for the depth of their stupidity', she was a rare example of intelligence and courage. These qualities were bound to cause a reaction from progressive people, who found in her a difficult and recalcitrant opponent.

(c) She found in Greece a political leadership in which everyone had his price. By the Sixties Frederika was like the proverbial leopard, unable to change her spots. She had become used to political meddling—which she thought normal in the first place—and, being unaware of the winds of change, continued to indulge in it. And the politicians, in return for royal patronage, continued to accept her meddling.

Given the fact that in Greece authoritarian leadership has more or less been tolerated for the good of the country, Frederika's and the monarchy's eventual failure can be explained by a series of mistakes. First was the throne's blunt intervention in politics and total disregard of basic constitutional norms. There was also the failure to create a popular image, which inevitably undermined the position of King Paul, eventually resulting in an acute deterioration of the early popularity enjoyed by the King and Queen. Another contributory factor was the royal family's immediate entourage, the supposed 'aristocracy' of Greece.

The literal translation of the word aristocracy is rule by the best and the ablest. It also means a hereditary nobility. In Greece's case, there was none of the latter, and, among those around the Throne, definitely none of the former. Instead, the royal family surrounded itself with a bunch of nit-witted, dishonest, uneducated sycophants. Frederika and Crown Prince Constantine, in particular, drew *nouveau riche* shipowners as a flame draws moths. Having achieved financial rewards without social distinction, such people threw themselves at the royal family's feet while making available their considerable accoutrements—yachts, private planes, gifts and large donations for the Queen's Fund. (One elderly and rather undistinguished shipowner became so enamoured of his Sovereigns that he built a very expensive and speedy yacht just to receive them on board and take them for a quick spin, this wish having been once casually expressed by the Queen, who scarcely realized the shipowner's willingness to go to any lengths to please her.)

This sort of thing was manna from heaven for the opposition. The extreme Left, as well as the Centre Union, exploited these mistakes by the Crown and blew them up out of proportion.

Karamanlis was aware of the ammunition which was being handed by the Crown to the opposition. And, in trying to curb it, he came into direct conflict with the King himself. Two incidents broke the already crumbling relations between the Prime Minister and the Crown.

The first one involved the Queen's Fund, a charity personally supervised by the Queen, and one she had created at the time of the Civil War to help destitute people. Unpleasant insinuations by the opposition about the allocation of its funds compelled Karamanlis to defend her honesty in Parliament. Approaching her in person, the Prime Minister hinted that although she would be free to operate the fund as she saw fit, she must give him an account so that he would be able to defend her against the false charges of the Left. Frederika—who as far as anyone knows never touched a penny from the fund for her personal use—became very angry, and told Karamanlis that her honesty was above reproach. 'I don't need to prove to people who are known to have taken bribes that I am honest.' Both the Prime Minister and the Queen considered each other's interference a threat to their position, thus drawing further apart.

The situation was aggravated by the marriage of Princess Sophia, the king's eldest daughter, to Prince Juan Carlos, heir to the Spanish throne. The Crown asked, and was given, a $300,000 dowry from the tax-payers. Although the nation's economy would hardly suffer from the expenditure of such a sum, the moment was scarcely opportune to ask for it. When the Queen requested a similar amount for her younger daughter, Princess Irene, a fierce row broke out. In view of the controversy over the first dowry, as well as the outcry over the handling of the Queen's Fund, Karamanlis flatly refused.

But the immediate occasion of the break between the Palace and the Prime Minister was the famous state visit to London. In early 1963, King Paul and Queen Frederika accepted an invitation from the British Queen to visit London in July of that year. It was the first time in fifty-seven years that the Greek royal house had received an official invitation from the British monarchy, and the ambitious Greek Queen—knowing that her husband was a very sick man, a fact of which even her children were not aware—decided they would go at all costs. She thought of it as a glamorous farewell trip.

Unfortunately, the Prime Minister did not see it that way. Nuclear disarmament groups, co-operating with dissident Greeks, had organized protests against the visit, claiming that political prisoners from the Civil War were still being held in Greek prisons. Although this was true—about 1,000 men were, in fact, in prison—they had all been found guilty of criminal acts and could not properly be considered political prisoners. Or so the Government claimed.

Nevertheless, the Prime Minister was adamant in his refusal to allow the King and Queen to accept the invitation, claiming, and rightly so, that their trip would re-open old controversies and receive unwanted publicity. The question of political prisoners had already become an issue in the European and American press, as left-wing groups took up the rallying cry.

In April, the intrepid Queen went on a short private visit to London to attend the marriage of Princess Alexandra, again contrary to Karamanlis's advice. Coming out of Claridge's with her younger daughter, Irene, she was physically attacked by a mob led by Betty Ambatielos, the British wife of a Greek Communist trade union leader in prison for crimes committed during the Civil War.

Frederika and Irene after being severely jostled, had to run about a quarter of a mile and finally took refuge in Deanery Mews, in a house owned by an American socialite-singer called Rise Stevens.

Betty Ambatielos, an activist in her own right, claimed that she was trying to hand the Queen a petition demanding the release of her husband. The next day, amid widespread demonstrations in London, Mrs. Ambatielos's petition was received by Queen Elizabeth. The British Foreign Secretary officially apologized in the House of Commons to the Greek Queen amidst protest and criticism by Labour M.Ps.

On May 22nd, meanwhile, a shocking crime—and as it turned out, a colossal blunder by right-wing bully boys—shook still further the now dubious foundations of Karamanlis's conservative government.

A left-wing rally had been called in Salonika, Greece's second largest city, in the northern part of the country. The guest speaker was Gregory Lambrakis—no relation to the publisher—an Assistant Professor of Medicine, a former athletics champion and a Member of Parliament belonging to E.D.A., the Communist front party.

Lambrakis had only recently returned from London where he took part in the anti-Frederika demonstrations, for which he had received much publicity—mostly favourable—in the Greek press. The organizers of the gathering had found it difficult to secure a satisfactory hall large enough to accommodate the expected crowd. Pressure had been applied by the police to owners of large premises not to accept offers by the organizers.

Finally a hall was found, and Lambrakis was lodged in a hotel across the street from it.

Soon after 8 p.m. Lambrakis crossed the street on his way to the hall and was met by a large group of right-wing hecklers. Two or three hecklers approached him and, yelling insults, punched him in the face. Lambrakis got away from them, with no help from the police who were standing around.

Once inside the hall Lambrakis publicly blamed the authorities for the actions of the mob outside and asked for police protection. Just as he was speaking, another Communist Deputy, by the name of Tsarouhas, arrived and was similarly attacked.

Finally, a little after 10 p.m., as Lambrakis emerged from the hall, having been given assurances by the police, a motor bicycle carrying two men ran him down, injuring him fatally.

Needless to say, his death made him a martyr overnight, and was later romanticized in the film Z. The portrayal by Yves Montand of the murdered Lambrakis—indeed the whole film— was more a figment of the author's imagination, based on true happenings, than a reconstruction of what actually took place that night, which is what the film gave the impression of being.

In Z, almost the entire army, gendarmerie and government, including the judiciary, were involved. Nothing could have been further from the truth. The two bully-boys who ran over Lambrakis were, in reality, only trying to scare him, injure him and warn him to get out of town. These are typical tactics used by extremists all over the world.

Thirteen years later the case is still being written about and discussed. But it is safe to say that the two hooligans really were only trying to injure him, at most. Their orders had come —if they received any orders—from people still unknown. Public Prosecutor Stylianos Boutis and the Investigative Judge, Christos Sartzetakis, accused the General of the Gendarmerie, Constantine Mitsou, and the Chief of the Salonika police, Colonel Efthymios Camoutsis, of involvement in the murder. This has never been proved, but bystanders testified that Lambrakis's life could have been saved if the police had really been trying to protect him.

The uproar that followed nailed the lid on Karamanlis's coffin. The fanatical core of his military and security forces had suddenly damaged him, and he was caught totally unprepared. Being a shrewd politician he realized that his time was up. The crowds were out in the streets screaming fraud and now murder; Papandreou had become the man to save Greece from the Fascist monster. Knowing the Greek character and its love for dramatic exits, he looked for reasons to step down gracefully.

The royal trip to London gave him the excuse he wanted. By resigning over his disagreement with the Throne he killed two birds with one stone. He put himself against the unpopular monarchy and dissociated himself from the extreme right of the party.

Karamanlis's resignation was accepted and a caretaker Government sworn in under P. Pipinelis, a firm royalist, to approve the trip to London and carry out elections. The Centre Union, however, objected to the Pipinelis appointment, fearing a repetition of the 1961 electoral fraud. They pressed the King until he finally yielded.

Stylianos Mavromichalis, a highly respected judge, headed the new caretaker government which was sworn in on September 27th, 1963. Elections were proclaimed for November 3rd.

In the meantime, the Crown started its invisible machinery rolling, to ensure that Karamanlis would not win the coming elections. Having had a taste of Karamanlis's independence of mind, the royal family revised its opinion about Papandreou. Perhaps the septugenarian would be easier to handle.

Their calculations were encouraged by the presence of Sophocles Venizelos as co-leader of the party. Unlike his illustrious father, he was known for his royalist views.

A suave, sophisticated gentleman, Venizelos was a great lover of women and a world-class bridge player. Enormously wealthy through his marriage to the Zervoudaki family, he had been thrust into politics more because of his name than through personal ambition.

The royal family saw a great ally in Venizelos. They calculated that, if Papandreou were to die in office, the Centre Union's leadership would not revert to the extreme Left while

Venizelos was at the helm. (The exact opposite was to happen. Venizelos died a short while after, in the time-honoured tradition of a well-known French President and other lovers of the good life.)

During the campaign there was a notable lack of energy shown by Helen Vlachos's newspapers in support of Karamanlis. Undoubtedly, this was a result of his break with the Palace. On November 3rd the Centre Union received 42 per cent of the national vote and 138 seats in Parliament. E.R.E. came a close second with 39 per cent and 132 seats.

Papandreou had finally achieved his lifelong ambition of returning as Prime Minister, but he had failed to gain a majority, lacking thirteen votes to ensure the passage of bills. King Paul gave Papandreou the mandate, although he would have to face Parliament on December 16th with the distinct possibility of needing to call new elections unless he accepted the support of E.D.A.

Karamanlis, the great administrator, proved not to be a great fighter. After eight years in power he did not possess the fortitude required to stay on as opposition leader. He resigned as head of E.RE., and Panayiotis Kanellopoulos, a noted historian, was elected head of the party.

Then, inexplicably, Karamanlis decided on self-imposed exile. He left Greece under an assumed name and was not to return for eleven years. People have often speculated that, if he had stuck it out and remained, the country might not have been plunged into the chaos that was to follow his fall from power. One thing anyway is sure. He abandoned his ship just as it began to flounder; and his capriciousness, one might almost call it cowardice, was to have an adverse effect on all Greeks.

Chapter 8

The Papandreou Government and the "Royal Coup"

ITH the November election of 1963 George Papandreou regained the premiership—his lifelong ambition—after a lapse of nineteen years. Although E.R.E. had pretty much cut its own throat by the excesses of its lunatic fringe, his vigorous campaign had administered the *coup de grâce.*

Everywhere Papandreou went, throughout the country, he had promised more welfare, more pensions, more schools, and a better life for all Greeks. He had also vowed to redress the evils of the Karamanlis regime which were—according to him—corruption in high places, a financial oligarchy, and the para-governmental organization of the Right.

Although the Centre Union did win a majority of the popular vote, it was not able to muster an absolute majority in Parliament. In order to pass essential bills it would have to rely on E.D.A. votes, thus enabling the Communists to hold the balance of power. This Papandreou found unacceptable.

The 'Old Fox,' as his colleagues called him, knew that he was riding the crest of a wave of popularity which the election had not truly shown. Many people had voted for E.R.E. purely because of Karamanlis's undeniably great record, despite the party's recent disintegration. With him out of the way, the Centre Union and its leader were sure of an absolute majority in new elections.

Therefore, without hesitation, Papandreou called for yet another national vote to be held on February 16th, 1964. But, first, he wanted to ensure victory. So he cancelled farmers' debts and introduced higher farm subsidies, offered free education for all, expanded the social services, announced tougher terms for foreign investments, and raised the salaries of members of Parliament. (He also gave Members of Parliament the right of free transportation and telecommunications. This resulted in first class seats being unavailable on Olympic flights in and out of the country as M.Ps. took advantage of their new-found privilege.)

Without a commensurate attack on other forms of government spending, Papandreou then proceeded to further strengthen his position by appointing his political supporters to vital civil service posts around the country. Although this was considered normal for the ruling party, it did contradict many of the slogans about clean government which the 'Old Fox' had brandished during his 'unyielding struggle' campaign.

The February 1964 elections proved to be George Papandreou's greatest moment of glory. He and his party received 53 per cent of the national vote and 171 seats in Parliament out of a total of 300. He was assured of an uninterrupted four-year rule.

In addition, the death of Sophocles Venizelos ten days before the election strengthened his position as party leader. This loss, however, was the first of a series of events which were to undermine Papandreou's reputation as a responsible leader. The royal family had felt secure in backing Papandreou against Karamanlis—however underhandedly—confident that, if the seventy-six-year-old Papandreou strayed too far toward radical policies, his intra-party support would crumble, because Venizelos would have none of it. As things turned out, the 'Old Fox' was left unchecked to pursue policies which were certain not only to divide the country, but to bring the army once again into active political involvement.

Three weeks after the election, King Paul died of cancer. His son became King Constantine II. Twenty-three years old, handsome, tall and athletic, Constantine had won an Olympic gold medal in the dragon class of the sailing competition during the 1960 Rome Olympiad. Undoubtedly immensely popular, his zest for living endeared him to the hot-blooded Greeks. Although he was more inclined to fast cars and sporting activities than to serious contemplation, this fact was looked upon favourably by the politicians. Palace involvement in politics was becoming a serious issue, and the fun-loving young King, it was thought, would be less liable to interfere in the running of the country.

The installation of the new King soon after Papandreou's overwhelming victory seemed a further guarantee that the nation's mood would revert to the constructive ways of the late Fifties.

Although irreparable damage had been inflicted on the country's institutions by Papandreou's charges against Karamanlis and the 'establishment'—charges which he continued to use against his political opponents—most people were ready to forgive and forget. A new and fruitful atmosphere of collaboration was emanating from the palace as the young monarch called the septuagenarian Prime Minister a 'second father'. In the hundreds of cafés flanking the sidewalks of Athens the word was out that the political shrewdness of the 'Old Fox' would blend perfectly with the young athlete's desire to reign, but not rule.

And when Constantine married the beautiful young Danish princess, Anne-Marie, the sight of the seventy-six-year-old Premier walking arm in arm with the radiant couple occasioned genuine rejoicing.

Thus, amidst the widespread belief that this was to be the dawn of a new liberal democratic era for Greece, George Papandreou set out to turn his loosely-connected Centre Union coalition into a disciplined political party.

Readers of ancient Greek history will not miss the resemblance between the tragic heroes of classical times and the leading figures of the Papandreou period. As the story unfolds one cannot help but notice the flaws in individual characters that eventually lead to destruction. But, unlike the classical pattern, the downfall of these modern heroes was to be almost immediate. Could anyone have guessed that Papandreou, after such an auspicious beginning, could be arrested before his tenure was up? That a total split within his party would occur after only eighteen months? That the young King would be discredited and exiled in less than three years?

The essence of this book is to examine just this point in Greek history. Was the death of the democratic process to be blamed on fascist forces resisting Papandreou's reforms? Was the King acting on his own when he dismissed the people's choice with a whimsical ukase? Who was really to blame for the ensuing chaos that brought the nation to its knees?

Some answers to these questions have already been given by several of the participants. But, as is often the case, those who have chosen to write about the events of the period have coloured them either to suit their own views or to justify their behaviour at the time. This book, then, will try to give objective answers to these questions by examining the Papandreou era and showing that the military dictatorship which followed was almost inevitable.

Although the downfall of Karamanlis through the machinations of the Palace, combined with the bad faith of the opposition and of the press, had started the nation's slide toward chaos, the situation was by no means irretrievable. The volatile Greek character welcomes change and finds it salubrious, especially where politics are concerned. Therefore Papandreou's election was a good thing. A fresh start was needed after all the slanders and accusations that had marred the end of Karamanlis's period in office.

What was not needed at all was the pursuit of short-term expediency with which Papandreou lived up to his campaign promises. By acceding to his supporters' demands, he eventually swamped the Centre Union and risked the nation's fiscal stability which had been carefully nurtured under Karamanlis.

Despite Papandreou's rise to power the old political divisions and quarrels were still very much present. So were the social problems which he had exploited in attacking Karamanlis. Now the masses who had flocked to the cities in search of a better life, and who had been promised an immediate improvement in their standard of living, were impatiently demanding both.

The consumer society which had been revealed to the people through Karamanlis's economic miracle, made possible by a period of generous American aid, also posed problems. The rising demands of the workers, the precarious balance of payments, the small luxuries and large possibilities open to the consumer, were all necessary 'evils' of a growing society.

Papandreou, however, had promised everything to everyone and, worst of all, was determined to juggle things in an effort to keep everyone happy. In order to accomplish this, the State's reserves, so painfully husbanded by Karamanlis, were to be spent. He instructed the commercial banks to lend money freely, both to industry and to private individuals. The Defence Ministry's budget was cut as the least unpopular measure of economy, while a huge increase of imports was permitted. In addition, he reduced income taxes by 10 per cent while prices shot up alarmingly and inflation set in.

When imports rose by 27 per cent and exports by only 7 per cent, Papandreou reverted to the 'spoils' system to bolster his waning popularity. Having already filled most civil service posts throughout the country with his supporters, he proceeded to create new jobs for his followers, totally disregarding the expense.

In a country where a middle class was only just beginning to emerge, and where taxation had always been a half-hearted affair, this indiscriminate spending was to alarm the financial community and some of the ministers. Nevertheless, Papandreou was not to be restrained in his spending, for he associated it with his popularity at the polls. An honest, if foolish, man he was not about to renege on his promises of a better life for all Greeks. In his heart he was sure that government spending, no matter how indiscriminate, would somehow lead to utopia.

Besides his campaign promises which had prompted this loosening of the purse strings, Papandreou was also bound by his fragile coalition. Centre Union ministers ranged from royalist conservatives, like Stavros Costopoulos and Petros Garoufalias, to the confirmed leftists congregating around George Papandreou's son, Andreas. The only element holding these unlikely partners together seems to have been a common desire to leave the opposition benches. Once in power, the ideological differences of the Union were to prove insurmountable. And Papandreou's son was the proverbial straw which broke the coalition.

No matter where one's feelings toward Andreas Papandreou lie, it is an undeniable fact that, during his short public life, he became one of the most divisive factors in Greece since the great schism. His father was to be mercilessly attacked by the Right over Andreas's alleged subversive activities. The elder Papandreou was also to be betrayed by some of his Centre Union Deputies, outraged over Andreas's meteoric rise within the coalition. And the 'Old Fox' was finally to be dismissed from office by the King, who feared Andreas's socialist designs and radical re-organization of the army.

From the start the past of the younger Papandreou was not one to endear him to most Greeks. An avowed Trotskyite in his youth, he had fled to America when his activities were investigated by the police during the Metaxas era. When war with Italy broke out and his age group was called up, he refused to return to Greece despite assurances by the government that his past activities would be forgotten. He remained in the United States and became an American citizen after he was drafted during the war. He did not, however, take part in combat, but became a male nurse in a naval hospital. He subsequently married his second wife, an American of Bulgarian descent, Margaret Chant. After the war he taught economics at various universities, including the University of California at Berkeley.

The refusal of Andreas to return to Greece during the Italian invasion, his subsequent Medical Corps record away from the front, even his marriage to a foreigner—especially a foreigner of Bulgarian descent—have all been used by his opponents to discredit him. As most Greeks had fought and suffered greatly during the Axis invasion and occupation, Andreas's enemies could use his past to undermine him. The traditional peasant distrust of intellectuals and foreigners, coupled with the aggressive *machismo* of the Greek male, found a ready-made target in the man who wanted to lead them and their army but who had spent the war years rolling bandages.

These prejudices, of course, were ridiculous and childish. As it turned out, the irony of the matter was that Papandreou junior showed more courage and spirit than the pusillanimous politicians of the right who were attacking him. In fact, it was his brazen and outspoken frontal attacks on the system that brought about his downfall.

After a twenty-year absence the younger Papandreou owed his return to Greece to Karamanlis's munificence. In 1959 the elder Papandreou asked the Prime Minister to persuade his prodigal son to return, by making Andreas some offer which he could not possibly refuse. Karamanlis obliged, offering him the newly-created post of Director of Economic Planning at the then very generous salary of $2,000 per month. (The salary, furthermore, was tax free, since the gravel-voiced, heavy drinking, fun-loving Papandreou Junior still retained his American citizenship.)

Once in Greece Andreas was hardly the type to resist the lure of politics with its traditional pattern of patronage and nepotism. He himself, after all, had been elevated to his present position because of his father. After making sure of his prospects, he gave up his American citizenship and took the plunge into the murky water of Greek politics. He was elected Member of Parliament for Patras, his father's traditional seat, in the February 1964 elections, and was quickly appointed Minister to the Prime Minister, a powerful key position closely resembling that of Lord Privy Seal in Britain.

Andreas Papandreou's strength lay in his ability to gauge the spirit of the times. He sensed that if the established order—both in E.R.E. and in the Centre Union—was to be displaced, a coalition of youth, including underground Communists, the non-Communist radical fringe and anti-royalists, would need to be brought beneath a single banner. All these elements were to be found in urban centres; which is where Andreas concentrated his attacks.

He had brought with him from America a vision of a 'new' Greece, as well as modern ideas which entailed making the government an instrument of radical reform. He had correctly assessed the situation in his native country; which was that, as a result of long delays in post-war social and economic reforms, Greece was losing the development race.

Andreas attacked the traditional methods of the Greek farmer, whose limited knowledge of land use put him perennially in financial difficulty; and the industrial worker's lack of skill and of the rudimentary disciplines which the methods of modern industry require; and the Greek entrepreneur's ignorance of modern organizational techniques, research and marketing studies. He found equally unsatisfactory the structure of the public sector and the behaviour of the civil servants. The highly centralized, rigid, bureaucratic system was thoroughly inadequate, its administrative personnel being unable to assume responsibility or to initiate activity. He quickly realized the unfairness of the public sector where the law was bent and even broken to accommodate the wishes of influential persons.

These criticisms were justified. Andreas's progressive ideas should have been a godsend for the country at large and for the Centre Union in particular. Instead, the effect was just the opposite.

Soon after assuming his ministry, Andreas found himself pilloried by the Right. More significantly, he was also vociferously attacked by the Centre Union, with only the Communists and his own supporters rallying around him.

Andreas had rocked the boat. But that was not the preponderant reason for the attacks against him. The real reason was that he himself contradicted the very ideas he was fulminating against. Nepotism he attacked, yet he was a product of that system. He used patronage as much as any other politician, playing his own favourites unashamedly. He brandished divisive and intemperate slogans, and showed himself as recklessly partisan as any extremist. Finally, he too came under the shadow of financial scandal.

He used the past misfortunes of his country unscrupulously in attacks on his political opponents. Accusing the Right of being responsible for the lack of development, he conveniently forgot that E.R.E. and Karamanlis could take credit for whatever development there was. He absolved the extreme Left of any responsibility for keeping the country in turmoil after the war; which was the undeniable reason for Greece's backwardness.

By not subscribing to the progressive spirit he ostensibly advocated but continually harping on the past excesses of the Right, he became just another rabble-rousing party politician. (The greatest harm of the 'unyielding struggle' was that it brought forth unsubstantiated charges that E.R.E. and Karamanlis represented a fascist regime. This Andreas and the Communists exploited to the utmost, the latter in order to undermine the nation's institutions, the former by pretending that the Right enjoyed absolutely no popular support. Thus, with the help of leftist newspapers, the Communists and Andreas succeeded in convincing even some members of the European community that Greece was being ruled through the C.I.A. and a monstrous K.G.B. type of police.)

The negative, divisive and expedient side of Andreas Papandreou's character was, in a real sense, tragic. Greece was in dire need of an intelligent and charismatic leader with a sound grasp of geopolitical and economic matters. Andreas could have filled that role if it had not been for his flawed sense of values and contradictory policies.

He had a panacea for the country's ills. He accused the Americans and the multinational companies operating in Greece of being the root of all trouble. 'Throw out the Americans, drastically curtail all foreign investment, and our troubles will be over,' he preached. And among the poorly educated masses such slogans found a receptive audience. 'Greek riches for the Greeks,' Andreas said, and the people agreed.

Those who were more sophisticated and responsible, however, could not accept such demagogy, and demanded action against him. He faced a concentrated right-wing press attack.

Totally ignoring the positive side of his programme, a segment of the press presented him as a cross between Jack the Ripper and Lavrenti Beria. Helen Vlachos's newspaper *Kathimerini* was the most virulent in its personal attacks, saying that, 'whenever you touch Andreas and Margaret Papandreou you touch something sick, something steeped in scandal despite the showy smiles.' Needless to say, a commensurate attack from the pro-Andreas press assailed the Right, aggravating the situation even further.

At first Andreas's politics were simply more liberal than his father's, but with the passage of time his views were revealed as extreme New Left, or breakaway Communist of the Tito type.

But it was Cyprus—that Damoclean sword hanging over a long line of Greek Governments—which brought things to a head, just as happened again ten years later.

The Republic of Cyprus had been malfunctioning since its

birth in 1960. The main reason for this was the indiscriminate use by the Turkish minority of the veto power accorded to it in the Zurich agreement. In effect, the Turkish Vice-President had managed to paralyze all attempts at efficient administration. The Greeks, for their part, were also guilty of infringing upon Turkish rights and of treating the Turkish-Cypriot minority as second-class citizens.

The proposal advanced by President Makarios in December 1963 to revise the Constitution—in other words, to govern according to the will of the majority—may have been justifiable but was, nevertheless, illegal.

Accusations by the Greeks that the Turkish minority was committed to disrupting the government, and the Turkish fear of losing minority rights, resulted in deplorable acts of violence by both sides and a show of strength by the Turkish fleet.

Turkey was insisting on a separate administration for the two communities. Greece found the Turkish demands unacceptable, since they would mean a *de facto* partition of the Republic. As always in this part of the world, the Superpowers were quickly involved. In an attempt to keep two N.A.T.O. allies from each other's throats, the Americans produced the Acheson plan. This offered 'enosis' to the Greeks in exchange for a solid military base in Cyprus for the Turks, thus guaranteeing the safety of the Turkish-Cypriot minority.

The Greek Government in Athens saw this as 'double enosis'—the union of the Greek-Cypriot side with Greece and the Turkish-Cypriot side with Turkey—which, in effect, it was. So Greece rejected the proposal outright. While Turkey made threatening gestures with her fleet, George Papandreou decided to re-enforce the Greek-Cypriot national guard. He appointed Defence Minister Petros Garoufalias to direct the operation. Garoufalias managed to pull off a magnificent coup. Under cover of darkness, using only small yachts and fishing boats, 9,000 men and 950 officers, fully equipped and heavily armed, landed in Cyprus. Once this operation was known the Turkish fleet manoeuvres became noticeably less aggressive, although the Greek position on the diplomatic front was marred.

It was to be ten long years—and required a monumental Greek blunder—before the Turks had another opportunity to attack the island. Yet Papandreou's decision to reinforce the Cypriot Republic, and Garoufalias's superb planning, came to nothing. The opportunist and master schemer, Makarios, was not about to allow 'enosis' to take place, nor to permit the Greeks to maintain a strong military posture on the troubled island.

Although Makarios had gone along with George Papandreou's plan for uniting Cyprus with Greece, he had never intended to let such a thing happen. (He had persuaded the Greek Premier not to accept the Acheson plan, telling him that union was possible without granting a base to the Turks. The romantic septuagenarian saw this as an extra feather in his cap and therefore followed Makarios's advice.) The Archbishop's real ambition all along was to remain undisputed head of an independent Cyprus. Although he used flowery rhetoric and convincing arguments in favour of an eventual union, his acts— both overt and covert—were all diverted to the opposite end. He expelled Greek officers from the island, claiming that they had plotted against him: but he also instructed the national guard to prevent Turkish arms from being smuggled on to the island. This eventually led to their taking over Turkish-Cypriot positions in the northwest of Cyprus. A battle royal followed as the Turkish air force strafed the Greeks from the air.

This was exactly what Makarios had expected. He then publicly called for Soviet assistance, which was guaranteed immediately in case of a Turkish invasion. Already alarmed at the sight of a massive Russian armada in the Aegean, the Americans could only make a feeble attempt to cool their two N.A.T.O. allies down and to warn the Turks that no help would be forthcoming if they invaded Cyprus.

Andreas Papandreou had been watching the Makarios machinations with unconcealed glee, for the Cyprus imbroglio seemed to be pushing public opinion into his hands. Andreas had been advocating that Greece should not belong to N.A.T.O. or be within the American sphere of influence. Counting on the Greek propensity for blaming others for their own mistakes, he correctly guessed that the people's sentiments would turn against the Americans and the British.

That is exactly what happened. Because they had not taken

the Greek side unequivocally against Turkey, the Anglo-Americans were pilloried without mercy. The fact that Turkey was also a N.A.T.O. ally and that both America and Britain had 'shaded' their positions toward the Greek side did not matter a scrap. Fuelled by an hysterical press campaign against the 'imperialists,' the people's frustration found a ready 'I-told-you-so' sympathizer in Andreas.

Made even bolder by success, Andreas next called for a Greek-Soviet rapprochement. Thus Makarios and the younger Papandreou's positions synchronized along parallel lines. Their procedures, although not co-ordinated in advance, were interlocking. Both, in the end, undermined American influence over Greek foreign policy, while simultaneously sapping the control exercised by the nationalists in the army.

More important, events in Cyprus, as well as Andreas's public fulminations, were propelling George Papandreou toward a leftist line and a direct collision course with the army, whose leaders watched with alarm as Makarios's pro-Soviet stand was ardently backed by a very strong and influential Cypriot Communist Party. And the entire anti-Communist camp, with equal apprehension, watched Andreas's supporters, who were made up chiefly of left-wing deputies in the Centre Union and their E.D.A. colleagues.

It was Andreas Papandreou's belief then—and is to this day—that the United States wants to establish a base in Cyprus. In order to have this base, according to him, America would like to see Cyprus as part of N.A.T.O. This could be realized either through 'enosis' or by letting the Turks overrun the island. In rumour-filled Athens this Machiavellian way of reasoning found thousands of adherents.

As the year 1964 was ending, a definite pro-Soviet spirit reigned in the streets of the Greek capital. Extreme left-wing agitators found perfect ammunition for their anti-American campaign.

Then something unforeseen happened. The Soviets—always unpredictable—switched horses in midstream. From being whole-hearted backers of Makarios and the pro-independent Cyprus movement, the Russians decided that the Turks, too, had a point. They supported Ankara's proposal for a federal independent republic. This placed George Papandreou in a quandary, as he had openly advocated an independent Cyprus. (His commitment to 'enosis,' proved by his effort to bolster the Cyprus garrison, was never openly declared.)

Needless to say, E.R.E. was delighted by the Prime Minister's embarrassment at having advocated a common policy with the Turks. Pro-'enosis' elements—the army, E.R.E., even the Palace—joined the chorus condemning him. Poor George Papandreou was certainly not to blame. He had done everything in his power to favour 'enosis,' except saying so publicly. But such are Greek politics. The opportunists from all parties jumped on him.

His one clear mistake was to have trusted the Soviet Union, and, beyond that, to have allowed his son to veer towards such a leftist course. Although gaining popularity by the hour, Andreas's charisma with the people was based more on his father's popularity than on his own. When the people veered to the left with Andreas, they did so thinking that George wanted it that way. But the 'Old Fox' was not going to let a thing like the Cyprus embarrassment stop him. Something had to be found to divert the people's attention. So the 'monster' Karamanlis and the old excesses of the Right became the sacrificial lambs.

A Karamanlis witch-hunt was first proposed by E.D.A. and its Communist supporters. The Centre Union, trying desperately to regain the momentum it had enjoyed before inflation and the Cyprus troubles had eroded its popularity, supported the parliamentary demand for a formal investigation of Karamanlis's past activities.

However, the trumped-up charges opened a Pandora's box of surprises for the Centre Union. *Eleftheria*, a liberal afternoon daily, revealed that the Centre for Economic Research—run by the Ministry of Co-ordination, of which Andreas was deputy chief—had granted a contract for the planning of the city of Patras to a personal friend of Andreas. The article also intimated that this friend, Skiadaresis, had been paid twice the amount asked by other town planners who had submitted tenders.

The newspaper openly implied that Andreas had taken a cut

from Skiadaresis's exorbitant fee. Andreas did not sue the paper, although he vehemently denied the allegations. He probably was innocent of the charge. He pushed the Ministry to grant the contract to his friend, but not for personal profit.

It was significant that the allegations came from a paper which normally followed a Centre Union line. And newspapers in Greece tended then, as now, mainly to report scandals involving their political opponents. The revelations of *Eleftheria* were proof of the deep and irreconcilable cleavages that Andreas had caused within his father's party.

On November 16th, 1964, Andreas resigned under fire. He was locked in open warfare with some of his father's ministers, who accused him of meddling in their ministerial affairs. Although offering a perfunctory excuse to Parliament for resigning—he kept his seat as an M.P.—in public he accused the Americans of having put pressure on his father to fire him. (There was friction between father and son. One report claimed that Andreas and Margaret, as a result of his father's action, refused to let him see his grandchildren. The old man was said to have been broken-hearted over this, and his visiting rights were restored only when Andreas became a Minister again a few months later. The veracity of this report was never confirmed.)

The first thing Andreas did after his resignation was to accept an invitation from his friend, the Archbishop, to visit Cyprus. There he made 'useful' contacts with some Greek officers serving on the island, a fact which was to have dire repercussions later in the year. Upon his return a right-wing newspaper, as well as *Eleftheria*, accused both Makarios and him of having prevented 'enosis,' as anticipated in the Acheson plan.

Both Makarios and Andreas had always maintained that the Cyprus problem should be resolved through the United Nations. (Makarios, of course, was telling George Papandreou a different story.) Despite pressure by the Americans, who favoured bilateral talks between Greece and Turkey, Andreas insisted that the U.N. would eventually solve the problem. He attacked American imperialism for favouring direct Greco-Turkish talks, conveniently forgetting that the Soviets also were insisting on this. As he continued to make statements concerning foreign policy, he managed to alienate still further the Ministers of Foreign Affairs and of the Army.

The younger Papandreou would not desist from his public fulminations. He set out to establish a popular base for himself by touring the country, and decided to devote most of his time and energy to the organization and mobilization of the widespread political forces of the extreme left. Placing his emphasis on youth movements, trade unions and agricultural cooperatives, he turned to E.D.I.N.—the Centre Union's youth party—and transformed it into an extra-party militant group. This organization worked closely with the 'Lambrakides'—the E.D.A. youth movement—which was a Communist force, 40,000 strong.

It would be a distortion of history to say that Andreas did not strike a responsive cord with the people during his travels around the country. One case in particular stands out. In Larissa, the district capital of Thessaly, he was mobbed by people who were anxious for a change and were looking to him as the man who could bring it about. Taking courage from such spontaneous public shows of approval—needless to say, both Communist and Centre Union youth movements took part in the demonstration—Andreas then proceeded to Athens, and virtually compelled his father to make him a Minister once again.

While Andreas was busy covering the countryside and setting up his shock troops, matters were deteriorating for the Centre Union. The first manifestation of the Centre's political bankruptcy was the call by Panayiotis Canellopoulos—the E.R.E. leader—for Centre Union Deputies to overthrow George Papandreou and join E.R.E. in forming a new government.

This action by the opposition's leader came as a result of galloping inflation which had all but overwhelmed the business sector, as well as of deepening divisions within the Centre Union which made the passage of essential bills almost impossible. Although a historian of some note, Canellopoulos was a vain and ambitious man. Having succeeded Karamanlis as head of E.R.E., he was in constant fear of being accused of less-than-vigorous leadership. Privately, he was also aware that if the Centre Union remained in power, E.R.E. and the nationalist camp would demand the return of Karamanlis from his self-imposed exile. This Canellopoulos was determined should not happen.

Although his call for defection was unsuccessful, a violent battle between the two major parties began. Slanderous attacks flew back and forth. Parliamentary business ground to a halt, while the Communists sat back and enjoyed the spectacle.

George Papandreou had by now realized that he was in deep trouble. No flowery rhetoric or rousing demogagic speech would get him off the hook this time. The nation was tottering on the brink. So he reached into his bag of tricks, and produced what he hoped would be a fatal blow to the opposition.

On March 3rd, 1965, in a hushed assembly of parliamentarians, he revealed the Pericles Plan. This was a scheme which had allegedly been used to rig the 1961 elections. Its importance lay in the fact that certain documents had been found in the offices of the Army General Staff, implicating not only top army officers, but also the current Chief of Staff, General Gennimatas.

A five-officer investigating committee, which included Colonel Papaterpos—deputy director of K.Y.P., the Greek C.I.A.—had discovered this plan. Papaterpos was a Papandreou appointee to his key position in K.Y.P., as was General Loukakis, the chairman of the investigative committee.

It was further revealed that Karamanlis himself had ordered the Pericles Plan to take effect. Included among those who were implicated was one George Papadopoulos, whose fame was yet to come.

After Papandreou's disclosures all hell broke loose. King Constantine demanded the immediate dismissal of the investigating officers for violation of the army's code of conduct. The army itself went into convulsions.

The reason behind George Papandreou's disclosure of the Pericles Plan was fairly obvious. He needed time and a diversionary action to take the Greek people's mind off the country's troubled condition. There was a deeper reason too. Realizing that time was not on his side, George Papandreou wanted to

Scenes from Parliamentary life before the Colonels' coup. These photographs were used later in a propaganda booklet to show the chaos and political irresponsibility from which the new regime claimed to have received Greece.

Above. *Papadopoulos being sworn in as President. His piety and dedication to the welfare of Greece were sincere, but his opponents regarded the new constitution as merely a cloak for continued one-man rule.*

Above right. *The King, looking glum, has just sworn in the Colonels' Government—an act which rendered their authority just as legal, they believed, as that of the politicians they had ousted.* Right. *The triumvirate— Pattakos, Papadopoulos, Makarezos.*

iii

Right. *Andreas Papandreou in characteristic action, whipping up emotion, urging revolt.* Far right. *The Colonels have gone, but in May 1976 left-wing students and workers were rioting again, now against what they called the 'dictatorship' of Karamanlis.* Below. *'The Old Fox'—George Papandreou.* Below right. *Mrs. Helen Vlachos, newspaper proprietor, one of the Colonels' most relentless enemies, and, together with Melina Mercouri, probably the most highly publicised of the Greeks in exile during their regime.* Below, far right. *Riots broke out when the King dismissed the Prime Minister, George Papandreou in 1965.*

Above. *The siege of the Polytechnic. The authorities held off as long as possible, but finally a tank broke down the gates.*

Below. *The morning after. Twenty-five people had been killed, mostly bystanders. Despite rumours of a massacre, no students died. Hundreds were arrested, but they were all subsequently released.*

Above. *A mass grave in Cyprus.*
Some 2,000 fighting men were killed on
either side during the Turkish invasion.
Nobody knows how many civilians died
as Greeks and Turks attacked each
others' villages.

Below. *The Colonels in captivity after*
the return of Karamanlis. They had
surrendered power without making any
attempt to escape or to negotiate an
amnesty for themselves.

Old politicians back in the saddle—Constantine Karamanlis, the Prime Minister; Evangelos Averoff, the Minister of Defence; and the President of the Republic, Constantine Tsatsos.

reorganize the army by advancing officers sympathetic to the Centre Union. For thirty years, since the time of Metaxas, the Greek army had been royalist and right wing. Papandreou felt that liberal-minded officers should now be promoted to key positions, thus keeping the army in tune with the government.

The mentality of the military in Greece will be examined in detail in the next part of the book. For the moment it suffices to say that the officer corps was deeply anti-Communist and royalist. Americans and Europeans can perhaps hardly imagine now a military which genuinely belongs, not to the elected government, but to the Throne: one that makes its own laws. Yet this was roughly the situation of the Greek army, and it can be justified only if seen in the context of Greece's recent history.

Because of revolts in the army and the navy during the 1943 period in the Middle East, and seeing how the politicians behaved in order to pursue their ends, the military had concluded that its allegiance must be solely to the Crown. And as the post-war period proved so volatile, the military establishment identified itself with the King, who constitutionally was its supreme commander, rather than with elected governments. The Civil War had further convinced most officers of the Communist danger, and they naturally attached themselves to the one sworn enemy of the Communists—the King.

Politicians might come and go, but the Crown and the army were stable institutions which the nation seemed unlikely to change. As Karamanlis, a man of the Right, respected the army's tradition, a collision was improbable. The picture changed, however, when the Centre Union came to power.

George Papandreou's disclosures and his subsequent efforts to promote his own men in the army caused a furore among the Right, the King, and the senior officers. Once again accusations flew thick and fast. Papandreou was accused of turning the nation over to the Communists by undermining the armed forces and, as was normal in Greek politics, there were counter-accusations and investigations.

In the meantime, Andreas Papandreou had been re-installed in the Ministry of Co-ordination. He had applauded the disclosures of the Pericles Plan, which had confirmed his charges of a 'military-royalist plot to overthrow my father.' With his return the Centre Union was once again thrown into turmoil; his economic policies were blamed for the rampaging inflation, and his leftward foreign policies for the Cyprus humiliation.

So, when the Aspida plot exploded in the headlines, many Centre Union deputies decided that both father and son must go, the former in order to get rid of the latter for good.

The Aspida affair has been called a trumped-up charge of the Right, designed to overthrow the Government of George Papandreou despite its large popular mandate. This view was partly substantiated by the military, which took over on April 21st, 1967. George Papadopoulos, the strongman of that regime, quietly amnestied the officers who had been imprisoned.

The Right claimed, and still continues to claim, that there was indeed a plot of left-leaning officers to subvert the army and eventually take over with Andreas at the head. The truth—as always—lies somewhere in between, although the former version is probably closer.

The first secret reports of the alleged plot came from General Grivas in Cyprus. The legendary leader of the Cypriot underground uprising against the British, Grivas was a Cypriot by birth; he was sent back to Cyprus by George Papandreou to prevent Makarios's leftist policies and neutralist manoeuvres from impeding 'enosis'.

An 'enosis' diehard, Grivas reported to George Papandreou that a left-wing conspiracy of Greek officers was under way, headed by his son, Andreas, who had already visited the island and had been in contact with the military there. George Papandreou decided to keep this information quiet. Whether this was to protect his son, or whether he doubted the objectivity of the report, will never be known.

But the rumours got out and soon all of Athens was openly discussing them. The Grivas report had also been sent to the Minister of Defence, Petros Garoufalias, who decided to investigate further and was able to confirm that a secret society by the name of Aspida (Shield) definitely existed.

Secret societies were not new to Greek military circles. I.D.E.A. was the one most officers belonged to. The Sacred Union of Greek Officers had been formed in the late Forties and was mainly a reaction to the Communist threat of the postwar period.

Aspida, at best, was a secret society made up of liberal officers with the purpose of advancing their careers, since I.D.E.A. officers had been getting the plum assignments. At worst, it was an organization conspiring to overthrow the monarchy.

That Andreas was involved is definite. He had openly admitted that he wanted to retire officers who criticized himself and his father, and to replace them with officers more congenial to him. He found a sympathetic audience among the members of Aspida, and, therefore, tried to further their careers.

However, the predominantly conservative army commanders, knowing the vulnerability of the nation's long frontiers and the Communist threat to internal order, were not going to allow Andreas's tampering. Their fears were increased by the Lambrakides Youth, who were becoming more violent by the minute, and by Andreas's irresponsible attacks on the Crown. The Aspida affair thus became a *cause celèbre*—a confrontation between George Papandreou and the King, nationalist officers against liberal ones, the army of the King against the army of Andreas.

Inexplicably, George Papandreou decided to attack instead of allowing the furore to die down. He was advised to do so by Andreas, who believed that the time had come to take over the roots of power. Standing in his way, however, was Defence Minister Garoufalias, who would never permit massive purges of the armed forces.

While the Aspida plot was being investigated, Premier Papandreou decided to sack his Defence Minister and take over the running of the army himself. His son had already been accused of high treason for Aspida, but was protected by his parliamentary immunity. Whether the old man was merely trying to protect Andreas, or if he really intended to rid the army of conservative elements, again we shall never know.

Garoufalias refused to resign, claiming that he had sworn allegiance to the Crown. The Crown agreed; Garoufalias had to stay. The old premier then travelled to Corfu and discussed the situation with the young King, who was spending the summer there with his bride. Papandreou went to see King Constantine again in the Athens Palace on the 15th of July.

'Your Majesty,' said the Premier, 'if you continue to insist that the Defence Minister stay on in his present duties, I shall have no other course but to resign.'

The King thought it over and then firmly repeated his wish that Garoufalias should stay. He suggested a compromise candidate, but reiterated his desire that George Papandreou refrain from taking over the Ministry.

'Then it is my unfortunate duty to submit my resignation to you in writing,' said Papandreou.

'That will not be necessary,' replied the King, 'I accept it verbally as of this moment.'

Thus came to an end the political career of George Papandreou. But the reverberations of that brief encounter were to be felt for years to come and were to cause the eventual abolition of the monarchy and of the democratic process.

Chapter 9
Political Turmoil

THE King's action in firing the elected head of government—however constitutionally correct—raised an uproar among Greeks. Public opinion ranged from mild disapproval by conservative elements within the Centre Union, who called it over-reacting, to outright denunciation by the hard core of Papandreou's followers and by left-wingers who called the King's move arbitrary, undemocratic, even criminal.

What had happened was that the Palace, having for generations regarded the armed forces as its private domain, felt betrayed by a Government which it perceived was trying to replace established army leaders whom it trusted with younger men sympathetic to the Centre Union.

The army felt threatened as cells of dissidents, belonging to the Aspida organization, were found within its officer corps. The financial establishment had become alarmed over the Papandreou Government's inflationary policies. The middle classes and the nationalist camp—anti-communists, peasants living in areas bordering Communist nations, and white-collar workers—felt that the progressive ideas of Andreas Papandreou were entirely irresponsible and would eventually lead to a leftist or Communist takeover. The Centre Union itself was split between conservative and radical factions.

The effect of this state of affairs was to polarize the population. Although a compromise was still possible after Papandreou's dismissal—as it certainly had been before—such a solution was rendered very difficult by the attitude of the press. Never was an institution as irresponsible as the Greek press during the crisis of July 1965. Instead of calling for a semblance of sanity, for an intelligent and responsible government, for an awareness of the national community of interest, the press did exactly the opposite. In large, black, screaming headlines it accentuated the differences and distorted the ills that plagued the nation.

Nor did the politicians do anything to improve the situation. They, too, squabbled, haggled, attacked, and refused to budge an inch except when they had made a deal with a newspaper publisher, the Palace, or some powerful financier.

Although the issue was a constitutional one—whether the king reigned or ruled, and whether or not the monarch had the right to interfere with the Prime Minister's choice of appointees—the real problem was army loyalty. George Papandreou's attempt to replace the army leadership and become his own Minister of Defence was a clear indication to King Constantine that, if this occurred, the monarchy would be rendered powerless, a mere pawn in Papandreou's hand.

For his part, Papandreou felt that the King had no business involving himself in politics and, more specifically, interfering with his choice of ministers. So the question became: Should a Premier also choose the leadership of the army? Was the army an institution whose heads should be replaced every time there was a change in government? If not, how could the army be kept out of politics? How was it that armies in other countries of the free world belonged to no party, but appertained instead to the nation, whose king or head of State symbolized national unity?

Here we come to the crux of the Greek problem in general, and of the July 1965 crisis in particular. The question confronting the nation was: Is the Greek army apolitical? The answer to that was an obvious and unqualified 'no.' It was not then, nor had it ever been. Since 1843, when army officers had forced King Otto to grant a constitution, the Greek army had meddled continuously in politics. For most of the three decades between the 1909 coup and the Metaxas dictatorship, Greek political life was dominated by a succession of coups, most of them pro-republican, a few pro-royalist. All of them were instigated and carried out by the army.

In the aftermath of World War II and the fraternal strife

which saw the Communist minority try to take over the nation by force, the army was once again brought into politics in a very definite, if indirect, way.

Both Papandreous wanted to change all that. But behind the flowery rhetoric about an apolitical army of the people and for the people lay the sneaking possibility that, like everyone else before them, the two Papandreous simply wished to use the army for their own purposes. The automatic installation of their own men to such key positions as the heads of K.Y.P. and of the gendarmerie, as well as Andreas's proselytizing campaign within the armed forces, convinced their opponents of their ultimate intention.

That George and Andreas Papandreou planned an eventual neutralization of the Crown's influence over the army, even the abolition of the monarchy if it resisted, was beyond question. Neither of the contesting parties spoke frankly about the crucial point, but this was the real issue: Who would control the army?

King Constantine, feeling that the armed forces were his personal fief as well as his responsibility, saw meddling by the Government as treason. He had told his intimates, it is reported, that he could not sit by and watch the army being subverted away from royal influence, since this would make it just another pawn in the hands of the politicians. It would, he said, then go the way of the Civil Service, subject to the whims of various influential men, part of the spoils system.

Constantine truly believed that, as a guarantor of the nation's well-being, he had to maintain absolute control over the only institution which guaranteed that well-being, the army. He also believed that he embodied the nation, and saw anyone who preached against him as attacking Greece itself. (His mother's feudal concept is obvious here, a concept completely outdated in most European countries, but, at times of crisis, still badly needed in Greece.)

Despite these beliefs Constantine had tried hard not to steer a collision course with Papandreou. After Papandreou's dismissal much was written concerning a 'royal plot' and how it had been conceived as a contingency plan years before. These accusations continue to be heard in Greece today, as newspapers try to discredit the monarchy and all it stood for. But nothing could be further from the truth. King Constantine was a most reluctant executioner.

Taken within the Greek context—and without trying to find excuses for the King—the young monarch's action that July 15th could not have been averted. If Constantine had not dismissed Papandreou that day, *the armed forces would have led a coup against the Prime Minister and his son.*

This fact has never been divulged by the King. Neither before nor afterwards was he willing to put the responsibility on the army. But the army had watched with increasing apprehension Papandreou's espousal of radical causes, his flirtation with Communist elements, his calls for a rapprochement with the Soviet Union, and his virulent anti-N.A.T.O. and anti-U.S. stand.

Why was this so alarming? Have not other European political leaders pilloried the Americans and denounced N.A.T.O., flirted with the Communists, and proclaimed radical ideas without being dismissed by the head of State?

Obviously yes. But recent Greek history goes some way to justify the fears both of the King and of the army. And if Greece's volatile past is taken into account as well, its geo-political position surrounded by Communist neighbours, the Greek Communist party's calls for intervention by those neighbours, the bloody civil war with its terrible atrocities, and, finally, the proven irresponsibility of politicians in the past, then the army's apprehension over Papandreou's behaviour can surely be understood and even excused.

So, when Army Chief of Staff, General Gennimatas, warned the King that the armed forces would not sit idly by if Papandreou attempted to assume control of the army by firing Garoufalias and taking over the post of Defence Minister himself, the King decided on confrontation. In a naive way he thought that he would be safeguarding democracy.

In this decision Constantine was greatly encouraged by the political leadership of E.R.E. which, after all, represented 40 per cent of the people. Although the then leader of E.R.E. has since munched his words about his position concerning the dismissal, it was pressure from him as much as from the army which convinced the King he was doing the right thing. Only a few months earlier Canellopoulos had tried to wean Papandreou's parliamentary majority away. His Pontius Pilate-like stance since then seems indicative of bad faith and a sanctimonious attitude.

The publisher of *Kathimerini* and *Messimbrini*, Helen Vlachos, was also influential in pushing the King towards confrontation. Although she has denied it since, her articles and editorials testify to the role she played. The worst offender by far, however, was Christos Lambrakis, the publisher of *Vima* and *Nea*. In secret negotiations with the Palace he had assured the King of his support. After Papandreou's resignation-dismissal, Lambrakis's papers lauded the King's move. But when mobs tried to burn down his office building, and did not allow his newspapers to be distributed, he switched horses and became the most vituperative and aggressive accuser of the King. The methods of this publisher have been, and continue to be, indicative of what is wrong with the Greek press. It is a pity that such unadulterated hunger for political influence colours the editorial pages of his newspapers, because they are the only ones in Greece which even slightly resemble what a well written, informative paper should be like.

Another possible catalyst in Constantine's decision—in addition to the army—was Costas Mitsotakis. A Centre Union Deputy from Crete and a man with an impressive war record against the Germans, Mitsotakis, who was George Papandreou's Minister of Co-ordination, hated Andreas, who, he said, had not only tried to take over his Ministry, but had sabotaged it. Mitsotakis held liberal political views, but was conservative in economic matters. Backed by the newspaper *Eleftheria*, he sounded out those of his Centre Union colleagues who felt the country was drifting toward disaster as a result of Andreas's meddling. Many of them resented Andreas's meteoric rise, as well as his extreme radical position, which they felt did not represent the true ideology of the party. By July they were ready to bolt, not the party, but its leader—and told Mitsotakis of their intention.

With the assurance of full backing from E.R.E. and the Mitsotakis group, Constantine felt that he had sufficient popular support to make his move. Under pressure from the army he waited, nevertheless, until Papandreou decided to take over the Defense Ministry.

In getting rid of the Centre Union leader Constantine left himself and the Throne open to attack. It came first and foremost from genuine liberals who resented the interference of a hereditary monarch. From the extreme Left, it was more scurrilous. That the young King suffered the brunt of this offensive was perhaps proof of his courage, if not of his political acumen. Like Marshal Ney, who was accused by Napoleon of fighting like a soldier instead of a General at Waterloo—by courageously and repeatedly attacking the British guns and wiping out the French cavalry, Constantine could have fought from the rear and let someone else take the risks. The army was willing to step in unconstitutionally and then, the job having been done, allow itself to be sent back to barracks by the King. But Constantine would not hear of it. He felt that he alone should bear the responsibility as head of the nation and of the armed forces. Rumour has it that he even castigated his mother for suggesting that some General could do the dirty work for him.

In retrospect, it was perhaps this conspicuous courage—and the lack of rewards it brought—which made Constantine, the Olympic champion, the tough karate practitioner, such a paper tiger when the 21st of April 1967 coup came twenty-one months later. But those events still lay in the future.

Despite the outraged cries of Papandreou and his followers over the King's 'coup,' the 'Old Fox' could hardly conceal a sigh of relief. When thinking over the King's predicament, he must have chuckled with secret laughter; for, by being dismissed, he had regained in one brief royal encounter what he had lost during his eighteen months in office.

Beyond any question, his popularity had been slipping away by the hour, and in the last weeks even his leadership of the Centre Union was under attack. Now, however, with mobs rampaging the streets shouting anti-royalist slogans, he knew how the Deputies of his party would react. And he was absolutely correct in feeling renewed confidence.

More than twenty Centre Union deputies followed George

Novas, who had been sworn in as Premier immediately after the Papandreou resignation. Novas at seventy-two was a respected leader of the Centre Union and the Speaker of Parliament, as well as being a man of impeccable credentials who had spent most of his life in parliament. Stavros Costopoulos, Papandreou's Foreign Minister, was sworn in as Defence Minister, while another Papandreou Minister, Ioannis Toumbas, was named Minister of Public Order.

The King was hoping to keep a semblance of the *status quo* in the composition of the new government. He had not transgressed the Constitution, nor had he exceeded his authority in his handling of the Papandreou matter.

By selecting the Speaker to head the new Government, Constantine hoped to avert an open clash between Centre Union partisans and himself. Novas had asked all the members of the old Government to carry on under him. Although a few accepted, the others went to Papandreou's residence, where they signed a protocol denouncing Novas as a traitor for accepting the premiership.

Until that moment, and despite the accusations by Papandreou that a coup d'état had taken place, Constantine was well within his rights as head of State. But with the fall of the Papandreou government, and the ascension of Novas, Constantine's troubles really began.

The Greek Constitution provided for the kind of crisis that had just arisen. It said that, if a Government resigned, the King could either give the mandate to a caretaker Government, which would dissolve Parliament and hold elections within forty-five days, or he could give the mandate to anyone he believed had a chance of achieving a parliamentary majority.

Constantine opted for the second choice. If he had decided to go for new elections, he would have come up against the man whose resignation he had just accepted. Reviewing the political situation, the King saw that the Centre Union had 171 Deputies, E.R.E. 107, and the Communist front E.D.A. 22. If he managed to lure at least 44 Centre Union Deputies away from Papandreou, he would, with the support of E.R.E.'s 107 members, have a working majority.

Once again the definition of the king's functions was in

question. Because of the political manoeuvring required to wean Deputies away from Papandreou, constitutional experts declared that his activities were contrary to the popular will, and hence unconstitutional. Royalists countered by saying that the monarch was well within his rights in seeking a political government, which would ask for a vote of confidence within the required time limit. They further insisted that it was George Papandreou who had not followed his party's programmes and ideals, and that Deputies had been chosen by the people, not as individuals, but to represent what the party stood for. They were free to bolt Papandreou, but not the party and its principles.

The problem was, to say the least, very complex, with both sides presenting valid arguments. In the meantime, George Papandreou appealed to the masses for popular support. And the masses obliged. Some 30,000 demonstrators shouted their approval of the 'Old Fox' and cursed the royal family in the main streets of Athens. The demonstrators were a mixture of Papandreou followers, Andreas die-hards and militant Communists who were ordered by the Party to go into the streets. The mob burned cars, broke windows, fought pitched battles with the police, and then surrounded the palace chanting, 'take your mother and go,' or 'out with the German woman,' and, of course, 'Yankees, out!'

George Papandreou accused the Palace of behaving like Circe, the sorceress of Greek legend, who cast a spell on the companions of Ulysses, turning them into swine. By now he was deperately trying to isolate the defectors, hide the deep fissures within his party, and pretend that the apostates were a bunch of political prostitutes who had been paid to defect. 'I feel unbounded bitterness,' he said, 'and will leave all traitors to endure the people's wrath.'

This was a warning to other Deputies of the Centre Union. The threat did wonders for any Member of Parliament who happened to be grappling with his conscience at that moment as to whether or not he should stick by Papandreou. Perhaps the apostates had overestimated their following, or perhaps Papandreou's influence within the party was stronger than its conservative wing had supposed. Certainly in the end very few bolted. (It is worth mentioning that the defecting Deputies made up most of the Centre Union's collective leadership. They included such long-time liberal leaders as S. Stephano-poulos and S. Costopoulos, E. Tsirimokos on the extreme left of the party, C. Mitsotakis and others.)

In order to achieve a working majority, as well as a vote of confidence, the Novas government needed 151 votes. In other words, twenty-six defections were still needed. The Novas group finally appeared before Parliament seeking the vote of confidence on August 3rd. A lot of haggling, backroom bargaining, out-and-out bribery, promises of ministerial posts and newspaper support had gone on during the preceding two weeks.

In the pandemonium which ensued, including booing by the Centre Union and the Left, fist fights among Deputies, and a general breakdown of parliamentary procedure, the Novas government was voted down by 166 votes to 131. The magic number was short by twenty votes.

Much has been written since about that 'long, hot summer' of 1965, and most of the opinions offered have expressed a revulsion from the flagrant violations of democratic principle which took place. But very few, if any, Greek commentators have actually touched the root of the problem. Most have simply put the blame on the various participants, each allo-cating it according to his own political ideology. Some have blamed the Constitution and its lack of provision for the kind of crisis which arose in 1965. (Karamanlis is among those who blamed the Greek Constitution, although he singled out one man, Papandreou, as the basic cause of the trouble.)

But all these opinions skirt the real issue. There is no paper or document in the world that can predict or pre-empt all contingencies. A working constitution is simply one which is supported by the country's leaders. It is a guideline whose spirit must be obeyed. Unfortunately the Greek approach tends to be just the opposite. Anything which the Constitution does not specifically forbid is considered all right. Thus extra-ordinary powers are assumed and an inordinate amount of harm can be done by the misuse of constitutional liberties.

In 1965, when democracy really died in Greece, the political leaders were not following the spirit of the Constitution. They were trying to find ways around it. Who was responsible? The only true answer is—everyone, from the monarch and the Papandreous to the army leadership and P. Canellopoulos. (The Communists are a separate case, since their primary aim has always been the collapse of the democratic system.)

It was ironic to hear the outraged cries of the politicians when the eventual military takeover put them out of business; especially the complaints Canellopoulos, who had agreed to play a parliamentary game which trampled on democratic principles and flagrantly abused constitutional norms.

The King was well within his rights in forcing the issue with the Premier, but his plan of action afterwards did exceed his authority in principle. There was no way of knowing at the time that he acted in this way to stop the army from intervening. In other words, he was trying everything to keep Papandreou from the seat of power, because he knew what would happen if the old man ever got back on it again.

On August 18th, the King made his second attempt at forming a new government. More promises had been made, more bribes offered and more bargaining conducted in back rooms. The going price for a Deputy to switch from Papandreou to the apostates had risen from 8,000 to 15,000 dollars. (This writer assisted at one such transaction.)

The mandate was given to the socialist, Tsirimokos. Ten days later Tsirimokos was voted down by 159 to 135 votes. The magic number was now sixteen and Papandreou was obviously losing ground.

On September 16th, the King made his third try, giving the mandate to S. Stephanopoulos. In their efforts to bring Deputies into their camp, the apostates and E.R.E. had managed to wreck whatever semblance of honesty was left in Parliament. People in the streets hooted at Deputies, yelling 'How much, how much today?'

This time the Stephanopoulos Government succeeded where the last two attempts had failed; 152 Deputies voted with the Government. Rightist Deputies watched with glee as the Centre Union tore itself apart: the Communists were delighted to see others doing their disruptive work for them; and what was once called the democratic system in Greece was forever discredited.

The new Government was to rule ineptly—it was to its credit that it managed to rule at all—for over a year. It fell when E.R.E. and P. Canellopoulos decided to withdraw their support in December 1966. The reasons for E.R.E.'s withdrawal were multifold. By early 1967, elections would have to be held, since the four-year term of office for Deputies would have expired. Canellopoulos had reached a secret agreement with George Papandreou and the King which has never been admitted by any one of the three. The deal was that, if Papandreou won the election, the army would be held back by the King, provided Andreas was not included in the Cabinet or was only given a post not close to national security or to key financial matters. Canellopoulos in turn was guaranteed the second place if Papandreou failed to gain an absolute majority and was forced into a coalition.

Canellopoulos was eager for such a solution because he knew that an electoral stalemate would either bring the army in or Karamanlis would be brought back by popular acclaim. This would mean the end of Canellopoulos's E.R.E. leadership. Some people close to him at the time thought he would prefer to lose the election to Papandreou—arguing that the old man would eventually stumble again—rather than lose the leadership of E.R.E. if Karamanlis returned.

A transitional Government, under banker John Paraskevopoulos, was created. That, too, was to fall and the mandate to conduct the coming elections was given to Canellopoulos by the King on March 30th, 1967. The fall of the transitional Government came over an amendment to the new electoral law. The amendment had been proposed by the Centre Union and concerned the extension of parliamentary immunity through the period of elections. The Papandreou supporters insisted on the amendment because, as everyone understood, the moment Parliament was dissolved Andreas would be arrested in connection with his Aspida involvement. The transitional Premier, Paraskevopoulos, understood that, if this were to happen, the streets would erupt. Canellopoulos insisted on voting against the amendment, and, when he saw that it was bound to pass, he withdrew his support from the Government. Thus, on April 3rd he was given the mandate to carry out elections. He dissolved Parliament and proclaimed elections for May 27th, 1967.

During the nearly two years since the July 1965 crisis began the nation had become almost paralyzed. Greece's reputation for hard work, for the ingenuity of her entrepreneurs, and the tremendous strides she had achieved during the Karamanlis period, had virtually disappeared. In their place came strikes, chaos, anarchy, inflation, slanderous attacks upon institutions, the squandering of public funds, and the demolishing of all sense of hierarchy.

E.D.A. and the Communists were now clamouring for the fulfilment of the promises they had been given by Papandreou during his campaign and in public statements after his fall; promises that the army and the State machinery would be 'democratized.' Strikes followed one another in quick succession, and the police force was completely cowed by terrorists. This situation caused a serious problem of police morale, which, for a while, threatened the whole apparatus with collapse. (The police were to take their revenge for the excesses of the anarchist fringe, and for the lack of protection given them by the politicians, once the military took over.)

Leftist and militant groups, such as the Communist Lambrakis Youth, rioted in the streets, adding muscle to the pressure exerted by E.D.A. and hard-core Andreas supporters. The rioters carried slogans openly attacking both Greece's allies and the Palace. No mass demonstration would have been complete without accusations against the Americans and N.A.T.O.

The situation in the Government and in Parliament was no better. There were daily fist-fights, slanderous attacks by Deputies on their colleagues who, when not fighting, engaged in hurling nationally and morally harmful charges and counter-charges at each other. The only discussions which took place were extremely vituperative and contained allegations of scandal.

Andreas and George Papandreou had indeed taken their grievances to the streets. Andreas went so far as to declare that he would swear in a Government of his choice in Constitution

Square regardless of the outcome of the elections. This was an open call for rebellion.

In the light of the dictatorship which subsequently ruled Greece for seven years many responsible people forgot the statements they had made and their feelings at this time. A false picture has been given to the outside world of the Colonels taking over a nation long steeped in the democratic tradition and used to solving its problems through the principles of discussion and the ballot box.

To illustrate the actual state of the nation just prior to the military coup, here are a few statements which appeared in the press at the time.

Kathimerini, March 2nd, 1967: 'Because Communism, which guides the political activities of the Centre Union, has taken youth as its target, they force our youth into the streets, poison their thoughts and fill their souls with hate.'

Kathimerini, March 14th, 1967: 'The press wonders if the continuing crisis is caused by the confrontation between the King and Mr. Papandreou, or if hidden behind it lies an organized effort by international communism to conquer Greece. Facts proving a well-defined Communist plan to take power through infiltration, using Papandreou as a bridge, are underlined by the press.'

There were similar remarks in other newspapers. One called Greece the 'leader of underdeveloped leadership in the world.' Another called Parliament, 'the most impressive negative phenomenon in the world.'

The leftist press was also using the most vituperative and intemperate language. It quoted—and supported editorially— calls by Andreas Papandreou to throw out the Americans. It also supported his views that Greece was a colony of the United States and that a plot by the Right had the backing of the Americans. The Communist press added fuel to the explosive situation by publicizing the most extravagant accusations made by professional trouble-makers and provocateurs.

But it was Constantine Karamanlis, living in Paris throughout that turbulent period and a victim both of the Palace and of Papandreou's 'unyielding struggle,' who felt most strongly the wrath of the Left and the pettiness and jealousies of the

Right. He has best summed up the situation prevailing in Greece at the time.

In referring to George Papandreou, Karamanlis said what many people believed, but never dared to come out with. 'I blame George Papandreou for the state of the nation because he came into power under the auspices of the Crown, as well as with the advantage of a large parliamentary majority; but he has managed to alienate both, and divide the Greek people through his irresponsible, and almost criminal, behaviour.'

When approached by intermediaries of the King as a possible compromise candidate to extricate the country from its agony, Karamanlis had replied in the negative, saying: 'I cannot be a party to a political situation which means that, if elections take place, the Communists will hold the balance of power. A cleansing is needed before.'

When asked if a Communist danger existed, Karamanlis had written: 'I do not know if such a danger exists. What I do know is that something worse exists—political and moral anarchy. And together they will lead us to civil war.'

Finally, Karamanlis had stated: 'Democracy in Greece is bankrupt. Those responsible are the King, the Members of Parliament of all parties, and the press. If an army takeover is to come, it will merely be the *coup de grâce*. Democracy has long been assassinated in Greece.'

PART IV

Chapter 10

April 21, 1967: The Night of the Colonels

KING Constantine was not displeased with the political situation in the spring of 1967. He had played an important conciliatory role between the leaders of the two major parties, the Centre Union and E.R.E. By invoking the national good he had managed to convince both George Papandreou and Panayotis Canellopoulos that they should put their differences aside and reach a compromise. This, in effect, called for the downplaying of the political differences between the parties, and included co-operation in the event of a parliamentary deadlock after the coming elections.

The King had high hopes that the May 27th poll would clear up the intolerable political climate and move the nation out of its doldrums. By appointing Canellopoulos and E.R.E. as the caretaker Government, he had pleased the army and assured the nationalist electorate that radical and communist pressures would not intimidate the voters. (These pressures and the tactics of intimidation had proliferated during the 1965–67 period.)

Constantine had been persuaded by conservative E.R.E. politicians that Papandreou's irresponsible economic policies had dug the Old Fox's political grave. The same people believed that Andreas's excesses, along with the defection of Papandreou's leading Ministers, excluded a Centre Union landslide.

There were no reliable public opinion polls; the newspapers published misleading figures in order to influence the voters and help the party of their choice. The confidence of the Canellopoulos Government was a delusion. Many of the

163

electorate which traditionally voted for the Right did not admire the E.R.E. leader and his Ministers, nor did they approve of E.R.E.'s royalist stand and sanctimonious behaviour in Parliament.

A disillusionment with politics in general pervaded the country. Liberals were disgusted with the Centre Union because of its contradictory ideology and internal squabbling, while conservatives watched with alarm as élitist politicians, totally out of touch with the people, postured in a quixotic manner as they tried to fill the void left by Karamanlis's absence.

Just as Papandreou's untimely resignation eighteen months before had proved a blessing in disguise for him—because it shifted responsibility for the economic quagmire on to his successors—so the people's disillusion with politics was to work to his advantage once again. The notoriously fickle Greeks had already forgotten how Papandreou brought the nation to the brink of disaster. They saw him now as a martyr.

This fact was not lost on the Communists. Their party cadres around the country were given instructions not to run strong candidates against weak Papandreou ones, but to concentrate solely on defeating E.R.E. aspirants. The Communists played a shrewd game during the troubled period before the elections. They had chosen to show a low profile, concentrating instead on helping the Andreas wing of the Centre Union. But none of these facts seemed to touch the thinking of the leaders of the Canellopoulos Government. With grandiloquent statements they assured the King and party supporters that victory would be theirs.

Then something happened which aroused even the E.R.E. hierarchy from its slumber. Papandreou, contrary to the agreement he had reached with the King and Canellopoulos, suddenly called the naming of the latter as Premier yet another 'royal coup', and once again asked the people to back him with demonstrations.

Political observers at the time attributed this sudden change by Papandreou to his son's influence. Andreas had realized, it seems, that any détente between his father and E.R.E. would lead to a smooth parliamentary solution which left him out of the picture. He therefore decided that, if the elections failed to give any one candidate an absolute majority, he must make sure no deal was struck between the liberal and conservative sectors. It did not take him long to convince his seventy-seven-year-old father that Canellopoulos and the King were out to do him no good.

A mass rally was called for April 23rd in Salonica, the northern metropolis which has traditionally been the starting place for rebel governments. A week before the rally large numbers of militant youth groups, belonging to the Lambrakis and E.D.I.N. organizations, began to move toward the city. Many radicals also were reported to have arrived, as well as known provocateurs. Police reports estimated that the hardcore contingent on the day of the rally would reach 100,000, while the overall crowd was expected to be around half a million.

As if these numbers alone were not enough to alarm the security forces, Andreas was expected to call for open revolt against the palace and to urge his supporters to burn an effigy of the King. How true these rumours were nobody ever found out. But they galvanized the King and his military advisers into action. Contingency plans for an army intervention in case of serious disturbances were drawn up.

It was an open secret in Athens in April 1967 that the King would lead a military takeover should Andreas once again become a dominant force and try to pull the country out of N.A.T.O. and into a pro-Soviet posture. What was not known was that many Generals were pressing for an 'intervention' before the Salonica march and the anticipated violence, while others preferred to wait for the results of the election.

The King, however, excluded both options. He was obsessed with doing things legally, or constitutionally, no matter how contrary to the people's wishes his actions might appear. If this seems a contradiction—how could the King be obsessed with legality while being ready to lead a military takeover?—the answer is simple. Constantine had been assured by many political personalities that a royal coup after the election would somehow be accepted by the people. Besides, there was a precedent in Greek history—that of Constantine's uncle,

George II, who had agreed to the Metaxas dictatorship in the wake of national chaos.

Those who advised the King that a royal coup would be acceptable were politicians, newspaper publishers, high court judges, even senior clergymen. Because they all had something to lose if Papandreou won a landslide victory, they were more than ready to compromise their democratic principles. But they advised the King to wait for the elections, and Constantine consented.

The King was hopelessly caught between contradicting pressures. From one side the army commanders were making threatening noises about the Communist danger which Andreas's anti-N.A.T.O. prejudice was inflicting on the nation, while, on the other side, his political advisers insisted on parliamentary solutions which had already proved bankrupt and divisive.

Most of the King's troubles and his inability to find a solution were to be blamed on his advisers and his immediate entourage. With the exception of his *chef du cabinet*, the jurist Constantine Hoidas, an exceptionally gifted, honest and attractive man, the young King's entourage was made up of 'yes' men, social climbers and dilettantes. They had managed to isolate the King and keep him away from those more suited than themselves to advise a monarch.

The army hierarchy could not penetrate this fence around the King. Even the political and diplomatic leadership were, more or less, in the same position. Constantine was a very loyal person and, because of this quality, coupled with his youth, was unable or unwilling to listen to people who warned him about his advisers.

The King's private life and social environment also suffered from the problem of sycophants. His closest friend was an old schoolfellow whose father was a convicted smuggler. The boy's mother held a position of sorts in Athenian society and had appealed to the royal family to befriend her son, whose father's crimes were no fault of his. The King not only befriended his former classmate, but took him into his confidence.

The King's friend used his position, first to find favour with various shipowners trying to meet the royal family, and later to marry a shipowner's daughter, while pulling off shady deals and running up debts. In spite of all this, the King stuck by him and, even worse, accepted his advice. Another close friend of King Constantine was a sycophantic, vain shirtmaker of the very chic and trendy kind, while still another was nothing more than a rich court-jester, a buffoon who arranged parties and transmitted the latest gossip.

Constantine spent his leisure time mostly with shipowners and industrialists. They, in turn, being of the *nouveau riche* and lacking the traditional dignity of European nobility, flattered the King and grovelled before him. In the jet-set world of mostly uneducated, but rich, people whose only concern, beyond business, was to be seen with the King, no strong-minded person or dissenting opinion was tolerated. The scatterbrained young wives of shipowners, making up for their lack of social background, totally isolated the King from any chance he might have had to hear and understand the mood of the people.

This constant servility affected the inexperienced young King, who found the same syndrome of submissiveness in his military, political and social surroundings. In fact, it would have required a youth of superhuman intellect and strength of mind not to be brainwashed by such an entourage. Constantine would probably have been the perfect monarch in any other European country, with his good looks, athletic ability, intelligence and courage, but in the Byzantine world of Greek politics most of his attributes worked against him.

This, then, was the state of affairs as Papandreou prepared for his triumphal entry into Salonica. The Canellopoulos Government dissolved Parliament, so that deputies could begin their pre-electoral campaigning. And the Supreme Military Council perfected plans for an 'intervention' if the election did not turn out as the Palace, E.R.E. and the nationalist camp were hoping it would.

Thursday, April 20th, dawned unseasonably hot. A heat wave had been scorching Athens all week. The only hotel with a swimming pool, the Hilton, was doing a brisk business as foreign tourists and Athenian jet-setters crowded the pool.

As the noon temperature soared, a few of the beautiful

167

people of Athens recognized the royal couple entering the hotel grounds to lunch under the plane trees. The Queen was expecting her second child, but her beauty was as obvious and refreshing as ever. Queen Anne Marie was rumoured to be unhappy in Greece. Having grown up in the sedate and apolitical atmosphere of royalty in Denmark, she was, in the words of a confidant, '*depassé par les événements*' of the tumultuous Greek scene.

On that day, however, she laughed gaily with her husband, with whom she was thoroughly in love, and his cousin, Prince Michael of Greece. The luncheon finished at 2 p.m. and the King left for his Athens residence, which he used as an office.

As the King left the hotel, which is situated less than a mile from the palace, traffic was stopped to enable him to make the U-turn required. Among the cars that waited for him to pass was a ramshackle old Ford carrying three men. They were dressed in civilian clothes, all of average looks and height, and were headed for Pangrati, a working-class district of Athens near the Hilton.

One of the men inside the car whistled softly as the King passed, while another, a bullet-headed, stocky man said, 'See you later, Sire.'

At Aspasias Street in Pangrati, Colonel George Papado-poulos, deputy director of the operations branch of the army General Staff, Colonel Nikolaos Makarezos of K.Y.P., the Greek intelligence service, and Brigadier Stylianos Pattakos, commander of the armoured forces in the Athens area, piled out of the car and went inside a one-storey house. Waiting for them was Lieutenant-Colonel Michael Roufogalis, also of K.Y.P.

The senior in rank, Pattakos, had a Yul Brynner head which contradicted his ebullient personality, a rollicking sense of humour and deep religious convictions. He had risen from the ranks after having fought bravely against the Italians and, later on, against the Communists. An ardent monarchist, he was fifty-six years old.

Makarezos, forty-eight, was soft-spoken, the best educated man of the group, having attended classes in economics and political science in German universities while posted in Bonn as military attaché. He was an artillery officer during the Second World War and the Communist uprising, but had later been moved to K.Y.P. Makarezos was in charge of the third espionage section of K.Y.P.

Roufogalis, forty-seven, was also quiet and soft-spoken. As deputy director of K.Y.P. he had been trained by the Americans in counter-espionage, had fought during the Communist rebellion, and was the only bachelor of the four. A bit taller than his companions and with a high forehead, Roufogalis was somewhat of a dandy; he was known for his sartorial splendour.

The fourth man, George Papadopoulos, was forty-eight years old and a contemporary of Makarezos in the 1940 class of the Military Academy. Looking rather like a bulldog with receding hairline and a small moustache, Papadopoulos was a small man but his bright eyes had a very penetrating gaze. Trained as an artillery officer, he had fought against the Italians and been decorated for valour. Although he commanded artillery units during the civil war, he had spent most of his subsequent career as an army intelligence officer. On April 20th, as deputy director in the operations branch of the General Staff, he held what was to prove a key position.

The obvious similarities in career, age and rank which bound the four men together were reinforced by their background. All of them came from poor peasant families. The fathers of Pattakos, Makarezos and Roufogalis were farmers: Papadopoulos's father was a village school-teacher.

Although lower in rank than Pattakos, Papadopoulos spoke first. A forceful speaker, he was obviously the leader. 'It is tonight or never, gentlemen,' he said, 'Zoetakis has just confirmed to me that there will be no help from his quarter if we fail.'

Papadopoulos was referring to Lieutenant-General Zoetakis, commander of the élite Third Army Corps stationed in Macedonia. Zoetakis was the only member of the Supreme Military Council who knew what was afoot among the lower-ranking officers. It was he who had confirmed to the conspirators that a Generals' coup was a possibility after the election; a coup which would have the backing both of the king and of some politicians. This was why the four men were meeting in Pangrati.

As the Generals' coup was supposed to install a political government and return to a parliamentary system as soon as possible, it differed radically from Papadopoulos's plan, which called for a complete reversal of the *status quo*. Papadopoulos and his dozen or so fellow conspirators did not trust the politicians, nor did they believe that temporary solutions—as a Generals' coup would be—were the answer.

Their panacea for Greece was a total and radical catharsis based on a more socialist and egalitarian society. In fact Papadopoulos's nickname among his fellow officers was 'Nasser,' as he had often spoken of the Egyptian leader's reforms with great admiration.

The Colonels had met regularly over the years and had frequently discussed the possibility of a radical change for Greece. With the coming of Andreas and the subsequent breakdown of the democratic process, the hardliners began to assert themselves. Every demonstration held, every political deal struck between politicians of different ideologies, every favour handed out by the Palace to the military in return for subservience, helped to make Papadopoulos's idea of a new Greece seem more desirable to his fellow officers. There were about sixteen leaders of the movement, with another forty-five junior officers willing to follow their orders, although not taking part in the actual planning of the coup.

The socialist or egalitarian ideas propagated by Papadopoulos were shared by his fellow plotters, all of whom came from very poor rural backgrounds. The only exception was another Brigadier, Alexander Hadjipetros, who was something of a rarity in the Greek army. Coming from a rich and distinguished family, he had chosen an army career, probably the only man in Greece born to wealth who chose such a profession. He, too, was disgusted by the corruption, privilege and patronage rampant among the politicians and in the army, as well as by the total isolation of the royal family.

Although the plotters should have felt sympethetic toward Andreas's radical policies—after all, both Andreas and the Colonels wanted a new, more egalitarian society—they saw him instead as a mortal enemy. The reason behind this antipathy was their deep anti-communism. Unlike Andreas, all of them had suffered and fought during the civil war, and one leading plotter, in particular, Colonel John Ladas, had seen his whole family of seven butchered in front of his eyes by the communists.

The peasant, puritanical, and strict religious upbringing of the plotters, their admiration and espousal of old-fashioned qualities—such as loyalty, honesty and reliability—clashed with Andreas's lifestyle and socialist ideas, as well as with the communists' anti-religious and cynical attitude.

During the total breakdown of the democratic process in Greece in the middle sixties, and the civil disobedience that followed, the Colonels had decided to intervene. Three times, in fact, they were on the brink of doing so, but were frustrated in their attempts by unforeseen circumstances.

But on April 20th, 1967, a golden opportunity presented itself. The Supreme Military Council, which included nine of the highest ranking Generals in the armed forces, was meeting in Athens to discuss what steps should be taken if and when violence broke out in Salonica on the coming Sunday. The meeting was called by Lieutenant-General Gregorios Spandidakis, the Chief of Staff.

Zoetakis had met Papadopoulos beforehand, told him about the meetings and warned him that any suggestion, within the council, of a possible move by the armed forces was out of the question before the elections and without the approval of the King. He told Papadopoulos: 'You are on your own; I will have to hang you if you fail.'

These exact words were repeated by Papadopoulos to the plotters. 'Gentlemen' he said, 'there is no turning back now. This is our last chance for success in view of the circumstances. They can all be trapped in Athens tonight. "Prometheus" can only work now. By tomorrow it will be too late. By Sunday the nation will be in danger and the armed forces will be on the alert.'

The men shook hands and left for their various destinations. 'Prometheus' was about to go into effect.

The code word 'Prometheus' was the label given to a

contingency plan prepared in the Athens headquarters of the army, the 'Pentagon,' and was an accepted part of N.A.T.O.'s response in the event of war with a communist country. 'Prometheus' involved swiftly rounding up Communist leaders and other security suspects, while securing such key positions as radio stations, communications centres and airfields.

Two things were absolutely necessary if 'Prometheus' was to be used to promote, rather than prevent, a coup d'état. The first was that there should be enough tanks around Athens to ensure a speedy takeover of all key positions. That was Pattakos's responsibility as head of armoured forces in the Attica area.

The second was more difficult and could not be ensured in advance, because it needed the allegiance of a top military leader whose orders would automatically trigger the implementation of the 'Prometheus' plans by all units.

The only person who could give such an order was the Chief of Staff, Spandidakis. Papadopoulos and his fellow plotters had not taken Spandidakis into their confidence. They mistrusted him because he was close to the politicians, the King and the establishment. They even accused him of having employed the usual methods of servility to reach his position.

Nevertheless, Papadopoulos was willing to gamble that Spandidakis was—deep in his heart—committed to a new, uncorrupt Greece, and that when presented with a *fait accompli*—the neutralization of the capital by the plotters—he would come around. Papadopoulos exercised a degree of psychological control over Spandidakis, influencing him through his own strong personality, unending zeal and powerful ideology. He was thus almost certain that he could handle his chief and, as things were to turn out, his calculations were almost perfect.

As night descended upon the ancient city King Constantine left his Athens residence and drove in his Mercedes convertible to Tatoi, fifteen miles north of the capital, where his summer palace was situated. He was accompanied by the Queen and his trusted military adviser and former military instructor, Lieutenant-Colonel Michael Arnaoutis.

Arnaoutis had played a pivotal role in the King's fortunes in the past. He was known to be the one person, besides the Queen Mother, whom the King trusted completely. His opinion was also valued highly. The King treated him like a second father. In view of Constantine's stubborn nature and intense loyalty, this was quite normal. Arnaoutis had taught him war games, and represented the kind of hero all adolescents worship during their school days. Besides, he was the King's immediate link with the army, the one institution which the Greek royalty loved even more than Greece itself.

But the influence of Arnaoutis upon the young King was rather a destructive one. Not that the Colonel was a schemer or tried to undermine him. On the contrary: but Arnaoutis overstepped the boundary of his official duties. Having been elevated to his post of military adviser because of his good war record, his charm, and Constantine's wish to be advised by a friend rather than a stranger, regardless of qualifications, Arnaoutis proceeded to alienate the armed forces with his high-handed way of conducting the King's business.

The Colonel made certain that uncultivated officers were prevented from approaching the King, shielded him too from any strong-minded officer who might have given him frank opinions; in short, exercised the same insidious influence on the King as his social friends.

Inadvertently, Arnaoutis helped to trigger 'Prometheus.' This came about because of his almost insulting manner in dealing with officers of higher rank than himself.

A few months before the fateful spring of 1967, the position of Chief of Staff became vacant. The logical choice at the time was General Leventis, a very able and good officer. One day, however, Arnaoutis had walked into the office of General Leventis unannounced and proceeded to interrupt him as he was talking to a subordinate.

The General saw this as a breach of military discipline and, in no uncertain terms, ushered Arnaoutis to the door. When the time came soon afterwards for the King to approve Leventis's appointment as Chief of Staff—usually automatic—Constantine, at Arnaoutis's suggestion, refused. The army authorities, anxious to please the King, offered Spandidakis's name instead. If Leventis had been Chief of Staff, Papadopoulos might well have thought again before trying to implement 'Prometheus.'

The four men who left Aspasias Street at 10 p.m. that night took with them typed orders to be distributed to the forty or so officers already informed of their plans. The secret papers had been typed by the polio-crippled daughter of Papadopoulos. Zero hour was 2 a.m. on Friday, the hour at which the buses stopped and the consequent decrease of traffic made it possible for tanks to move unhindered. At midnight, the units which were to be led by the plotters would go on the alert. Pattakos, Papadopoulos and Makarezos were to start the operation from Goudhi, where Pattakos's tanks were headquartered. Roufo-galis was to give the alert from his K.Y.P. office to his fellow conspirators of the Third Corps in Salonica.

At midnight parachutists from the Dionysos base near Athens left for the 'Pentagon,' a ten-mile drive. They were under the orders of Lieutenant-Colonel Costas Aslanides, operations chief of the brigade of commando paratroopers, L.O.K., and one of the original conspirators. Leading them was a gentle giant of a man, Major George Constandopoulos. The paratroopers were at company strength, and they split up as they approached the Greek 'Pentagon'—in reality, a square building named after its American counterpart.

The unit led by Constandopoulos was to attack the building from the front, while the rear was to be taken by another group of L.O.K. commandos under Lieutenant-Colonel Michael Balopoulos.

All three officers—Aslanides, Constandopoulos and Balo-poulos—were considered tough men, who had been wounded in past actions and were known to be brave in the face of the enemy. None of the three was by any means an intellectual; they had risen from the ranks, and been picked for this assign-ment because of their steamroller tactics.

Arriving at the main gate, Constandopoulos walked up to the guard alone, asked him to open the gate, and, when he did so, simply disarmed him and shoved him into his sentry box. Then he motioned to the waiting column to advance. The other sentries assumed, from the ease of Constandopoulos's entry that he had been admitted by the guard, and merely watched as the L.O.K. armoured column marched in. They too were disarmed without giving the alarm.

Balopoulos had by now surrounded the rear entrance to the building and was let in by his fellow commandos once the main gate had been breached. All three officers then led the company into the sprawling five-storey army headquarters and proceeded to arrest everyone present. The operation had started exactly at midnight, and the 'Pentagon' had been secured and everyone arrested by 12:50 a.m. without a single shot being fired.

Aslanides then rang the Goudhi barracks, from which Pattakos's armour had left around midnight. He spoke to Papadopoulos, uttering the single word '*eureka*,' before hanging up. This meant that the 'Pentagon' was secured. Papadopoulos joined Makarezos in racing toward their newly-acquired possession.

As the two officers sped from Goudhi to the 'Pentagon'—a mere ten-minute ride by car—the noose was tightening around the city. Pattakos's fifty heavy M-47, and twenty-five lighter M-48, tanks were rolling towards their targets, which were the arterial highways and other strategic points of Athens. Constantine Papadopoulos, George's younger brother and also a Colonel, was commanding an infantry batallion, a unit of specially selected men established in the Athens area to deal with internal revolt. These men were perfectly trained to do the job of surrounding all telecommunications centres, radio stations and post offices.

Colonel John Ladas, the head of the military police in the Athens area and one of the original plotters, had by now given his men their detailed orders. They were to arrest the leading political personalities and many of the King's advisers. They were also to take over some key Ministries with the aid of Pattakos's armour.

By 1 a.m. everybody was at his assigned position; the city was tightly surrounded; individual targets picked out; and Ministries and other strategic centres were fixed in the gun sights of the tank crews standing inconspicuously by.

Back at the 'Pentagon,' however, the scenario of the coup-makers had met a strange obstacle. The Chief of Staff,

Spandidakis, the man who could issue the code word for 'Prometheus,' was nowhere to be found. He was not in the building, nor at his home, nor had he attended the cabinet meeting which had lasted well into the night. Seeing precious time going by, Papadopoulos finally decided himself to give the order to all units that the 'Prometheus' plan should go into immediate effect. He used the King's name falsely, as well as that of Spandidakis.

The chain of command being what it is in the army, Papadopoulos had no trouble at first. His orders were received by all units in Greece, and they all acquiesced. But as Spandidakis had not yet turned up, a terrible suspicion grew upon the plotters. He might have been warned. Papadopoulos, serving in the Chief of Staff's office, knew how to give the code. But he did not know if Spandidakis, hiding out somewhere, could countermand his orders.

The suspense finally ended at 1:45 a.m., when Spandidakis was spotted arriving at his home by the Lieutenant who was waiting for him in front. The Chief of Staff had been playing cards at a friend's house with no notion that anything was wrong. The Lieutenant asked him to come to the 'Pentagon,' because he feared—he said—that a coup was taking place. (The Lieutenant knew absolutely nothing; he had merely been told to bring the general to the 'Pentagon' under the King's orders, but, having seen certain movements, he warned Spandidakis.)

When the Chief of Staff arrived he was brought face to face with Papadopoulos and Pattakos, who were in battle dress and brandishing guns. 'We are about to execute a coup in order to save the nation,' said Papadopoulos. 'This is a revolution which belongs to no political party. Will you join us, or not?'

Spandidakis asked: 'Is the King leading it?'

'We don't know,' was the reply, 'but you have to be clear. Are you with us or against us?'

Spandidakis thought it over for about a minute and then said: 'I cannot do otherwise. I join the revolution.'

From then on, it was simply a matter of time. There was not going to be any fighting between army units. As the Chief of Staff made contact with the various commanders, he confirmed that the King had ordered Prometheus into effect.

Prime Minister Canellopoulos had left the cabinet meeting at the old palace and driven home with three of his Ministers around midnight. He lived in Kolonaki, a fashionable district of Athens, and had seen nothing suspicious during the five-minute ride to his home. Two of the Ministers accompanying him were George Rallis, Minister of Public Order, and P. Papaligouras, Minister of Defence.

Rallis, a gruff, gravel-voiced and somewhat conceited man, had assured the Premier that everything was under control and that the rumours that had gone around about a Colonels' coup were unsubstantiated. Papaligouras agreed. (There had been a leak, it was found out afterwards, but no one has ever been able to trace it.)

After a brief chat with Canellopoulos the Ministers left. Papaligouras headed for a party, while Rallis drove towards Kifissia, a suburb ten miles north of the capital where he lived with his wife and daughter.

At precisely 2 a.m. the plotters struck. First to be arrested was Canellopoulos. Two Lieutenants leading a contingent of ten men knocked on his door. The E.R.E. leader took a pistol from his bedside table, told his wife to go into a room with a second telephone, and went downstairs to open the door. When told that a Communist uprising had taken place and that he was to follow them, he at first refused and stalled for time. Hearing the conversation, his wife called Admiral Spanidis, a close friend. After telling him to signal the navy that something was up, Nitsa Canellopoulos then called her nephew, Dionissis Livanos. She screamed something just as the soldiers ripped out the phone. After that Canellopoulos agreed to follow the Lieutenants, who warned him that every second wasted might cause the shedding of blood among Greeks.

George Papandreou was also a prime target for arrest. He lived in Kastri, a northern suburb which lies on the slopes of Mount Penteli, among pine and cypress trees, twelve miles from Athens. That night he had gone to bed feeling slightly fluish, and had told his faithful servant-bodyguard, Karakos, not to wake him unless there was a revolution.

Two vehicles, a jeep and a troop carrier, pulled up in front of the house at 2 a.m. The guard outside the gate refused them entry and was immediately disarmed. Then Lieutenant Dadiotis and his contingent of five men entered the garden and told the guard inside the house that they must speak to the Premier. When Karambelas, the second guard, came outside to explain that the old man was not to be disturbed, he was overpowered and the Lieutenant went up to Papandreou's bedroom alone.

The 'Old Fox' was sleeping when the officer gently shook him. He opened his feverish eyes, looked at the Lieutenant somewhat blankly for a split second, and then smiled enigmatically. The Lieutenant said that he had orders to place him under arrest.

'Did the King order you,' asked the old man.

'No, sir, the Prime Minister did,' answered Dadiotis.

'You mean Canellopoulos has ordered my arrest?' Papandreou exclaimed incredulously.

'Canellopoulos is no longer Premier, sir,' was the answer.

'Does the King know what you're doing?' insisted Papandreou.

'I cannot tell you, sir, except that I must take you to Goudhi. Please dress at your convenience, but do not try to make any calls as we have cut the lines.'

Papandreou then smiled again. 'You know, son,' he said to the young Lieutenant, 'you are nervous because this is the first time you've done this. For me, it is the fifth.' He then told his maid to bring out a blue suit, rebuked her for fetching a pair of brown shoes instead of black, took a long time over his dressing, and obediently followed the Lieutenant into the jeep.

As the two political opponents were being arrested, all telephone lines were being cut. The telecommunications centre was taken over without trouble, as were the radio stations, the Ministries, and the central police headquarters. There the director of the Athens police, Tasigiorgos, volunteered his help and asked his men to join the revolution.

Andreas Papandreou had been preparing his Salonica speech that evening, and was about to go to bed when he heard cars screeching to a halt in front of his house. His wife and four children were asleep, as were his in-laws who were visiting from America. Andreas, being no fool, immediately understood. He ran upstairs, went out on the roof and hid, lying flat against the reddish brown tiles.

The soldiers were not inclined to accord him the niceties and kid glove treatment reserved for his father and the other politicians. They unceremoniously broke down the door, woke up everyone, and demanded to know where Andreas was. His wife Margaret courageously refused to tell them his whereabouts and insisted on being allowed to call the American Embassy. His older son, George, also refused to say where his father was hiding. The soldiers then systematically searched the house and soon located Andreas up on the roof. They challenged him to come down and he jumped in order to give himself up, cutting his leg slightly upon landing in the garden. His fall was only about ten feet at the most, but it was to be heard around the world. (In Margaret Papandreou's book, which was published after she and her husband were allowed to leave the country, she wrote that the soldiers had threatened to shoot George if he did not tell the whereabouts of Andreas. This is a lie, as the arresting officer treated the children gently and Margaret with great courtesy. There was no question of the soldiers having to find Andreas elsewhere. Their orders were simply to arrest him *if* he was in his house.)

King Constantine, having dined with his wife and Arnaoutis, retired to his bedroom. He did not put out the light until 2 a.m., so he was still awake when the phone rang at 2:10 a.m. It was Arnaoutis. 'Some men are trying to break down my door,' came Arnaoutis's voice over the wire.

'Can you call the police?' asked the King.

'I have, but they said there was nothing they can do,' came the answer, and then the phone went dead in the King's hand.

Constantine at first thought it was Lambrakides trying to intimidate his aide. He ordered the guard to be doubled around his palace, and then called his mother at Psyhico, the Queen Mother's residence located about 500 yards from Andreas Papandreou's house. Constantine told Frederika to gather the royal family around her and to double the guard. Then he called the officers in his Athens Palace to go to Arnaoutis's assistance and to surround his mother's house with a protective cordon. Through a special phone he also ordered all ships to put to sea and to await further orders.

In the meantime, the Minister of Public Order, Rallis, had been informed by the chief of the gendarmerie, Archondoulakis, that tanks were roaming around the city. After trying in vain to get in touch with the Premier and the Defence Minister, he left his house in a gendarmerie car just as armoured cars pulled up in front. Rallis drove to the nearby suburb of Maroussi, where a wireless transmitter was put at his disposal by the gendarmes.

Once he got the transmitter going Rallis learned the bad news. The Prime Minister, the Minister of Defence and the Chief of Police had been arrested. He called the King and told him of the situation. The King and Rallis agreed that the latter would order the 3rd, 2nd, and 1st Army Corps to arrest the coup-makers. Rallis then communicated by radio with the Salonica gendarmerie and asked to speak to the commander of the 3rd Army Corps. This was Lieutenant-General Zoetakis.

Inconceivable though it may sound, Rallis did not know that Zoetakis was in Athens that day, meeting the Supreme Military Council. When informed of this fact, he asked for Brigadier Vidalis, the acting commander of the corps. Rallis was later to reveal that he trusted Vidalis as a very loyal officer, and that his hopes that the coup could be stopped were raised while waiting for Vidalis to come to the phone.

In the meantime he issued a written order for the Third Army to move toward Athens—a 300-mile journey—and sent it off with a messenger. But Vidalis was not about to come to the phone and Rallis waited in the gendarmerie post, hanging on to the transmitter connection throughout the night.

In effect, Vidalis was a loyal officer and was not party to the coup. But he was perplexed when he first received Rallis's signal for the corps to move against Athens, as Spandidakis had, only moments earlier, confirmed the Prometheus signal and told him to ignore all orders except his own. Zoetakis had also spoken to Vidalis and assured him that the King was behind the coup.

Finally, around 5 a.m., Rallis had his last conversation with Constantine. The King told him that the nearby Tatoi airbase had been taken over, that the palace was surrounded, and that no movements against the coup seemed possible. 'What do you suggest?' the King asked his Minister of Public Order.

'Passive resistance, sir,' was Rallis's answer. He then drove back to his home and to the waiting jeep of soldiers.

As dawn broke it was evident that the wildest expectations of the plotters had been fulfilled. The original dozen coup-makers, with the help of some forty junior officers, had managed in a few hours of one night to neutralise a whole city, take over all the strategic points and, most important, confuse the armed forces of a N.A.T.O. country into following their plans.

The key role was played by Spandidakis. The only man within the Supreme Military Council who knew of the plot, Zoetakis, also helped by informing the conspirators about the generals' secret meeting, and, later on, by confusing the orders issued to Vidalis by the King and Rallis.

The coup was a bloodless one, with the few casualties that occurred taking place among civilians on the day after the coup. Not a single shot was fired for or against the coup, so thorough, bold and perfect was its execution. Of course, this achievement was much helped by the King's reluctance to go down fighting or to shed blood among Greek officers and men.

At 8 a.m., Papadopoulos, Pattakos and Makarezos—the architects of the revolution—left the 'Pentagon' and drove to Tatoi. They entered the summer palace, were ushered into the King's private study, and saluted Constantine while standing at strict military attention. The King did not return the salute, something which visibly vexed Papadopoulos.

Of the three coup-makers Constantine recognized only Pattakos, who was a Brigadier and hard to miss with his bald and shaven head. Typically, since the King did not fraternize with Colonels, he had no idea who the other two men were. Standing ten feet away from him, Pattakos spoke first: 'Your Majesty, we have acted to save Greece, and in your name.'

The King, flushed with anger, retorted; 'Who gave you the authority to save the nation? Where are my Premier and my Government?'

Pattakos, standing even more stiffly to attention and trying to appear taller than his five feet five inches, answered, 'Sir, you have no Premier and no Government.'

'I do not consider that an answer,' shouted the King. Then, Pattakos stepped forward and handed him a letter from the Chief of Staff, Spandidakis. This explained that the coup was a necessity in order to head off a Communist plot to seize control of the nation.

After reading this letter the King softened. 'How do I know this is from Spandidakis?' he asked.

'On our military honour, it is authentic,' insisted Pattakos.

Constantine's attitude implied that he was willing to listen if the high command were executing, or at least involved in, the coup. Papadopoulos took this as his cue and, stepping forward, spoke urgently about the feebleness of the Establishment, the Communist danger and the King's duty to support the army.

King Constantine listened without interrupting. He then dismissed the three officers, now returning their salute. His last words before they left were: 'There are to be no executions of political people, Communists or otherwise. If a drop of blood is shed I will hold you responsible.'

The centre of the drama was to return once more to the 'Pentagon.' Early in the afternoon the King drove there in his green open-topped Mercedes. On his way through the almost deserted streets—a curfew had been imposed but, as usual, a few recalcitrant Greeks were ignoring it—he heard over the radio that he himself was to make an announcement to the nation at 4 p.m.

Arriving at the 'Pentagon,' which was the coup's command post, he saw hundreds of officers, heavily armed and in battle dress, as well as many prisoners huddled together. He also saw most of the Chiefs of Staff, although they were not dressed in battle fatigues.

Constantine then demanded that Arnaoutis be brought to him, as well as Canellopoulos and the Chiefs of Staff. Obediently, the officers brought in Arnaoutis, who warned the King that these people meant business. Canellopoulos then told him that he had two choices—either renounce the coup and refuse to sign anything, or play along with the rebels, hoping to persuade them to return the government to civilian hands.

The King then met the Generals of the Supreme Military Council. The Chief of Staff of the air force, Lieutenant-General Antonakos, who had learned about the coup only that morning, was the most doveish. He sympathized with the King's predicament, but, whenever Spandidakis came into the room—he was acting as a liaison between Generals and Colonels—Antonakos would speak of the coup-makers in loud, glowing terms. The navy chief, Admiral Engolfopoulos, however, remained adamant against the King's joining the coup.

Suddenly the scene became comical—or perhaps tragic—as Arnaoutis burst in, screaming that he was being roughed up and about to be kidnapped. Visibly shaken at this and furious, the King issued an ultimatum. Either the Colonels left Arnaoutis alone or he would renounce the coup then and there.

Finally, after four hours of deliberation, King Constantine gave his reluctant approval. He insisted on a civilian Premier, in the person of the chief prosecutor of the Supreme Court, Constantine Kollias, and the swearing-in of a new Government was set for that evening.

After driving to Tatoi and visiting his mother, Constantine returned to Athens. But he refused to speak on the radio or to endorse the coup in any way. When Papadopoulos produced a speech that he wanted the King to deliver, Constantine bridled. 'Stand at attention when you speak to me,' he snapped. 'Who gave you the impression that I was going to take orders from you? Besides, it is badly written.'

His last words after the swearing-in ceremony were words of advice: 'Don't become arrogant! Don't become bullies! Think only of the people and bring back democracy!'

It was obvious that the marriage of convenience between the King and the Colonels was not going to be a long one. Papadopoulos watched the King as he drove away in his shiny Mercedes, and shook his head. 'The Establishment,' the Colonel said, 'is chicken. So is its head. Easter is near. It's a pity we don't have time to kill some chickens.'

Chapter 11
The Colonels' Rule
– The King's Countercoup

REACTION throughout the free world to the military coup in Greece was one of outrage. In fact, the European and American press was far more strident than the Communist and Third World papers in deploring the loss of democracy in the land of its birth.

Significantly, there was much less of a sense of outrage within the country itself. Although dissent was stifled in the press by the censorship imposed and among the populace by the existence of martial law, it remains true that many Greeks sighed with relief at the Colonels' takeover.

With the exception of hardcore radicals, the politicians, the Communists and the intelligentsia, the rest of the country welcomed an end to an intolerable situation. It has been said that the Colonels enjoyed no popular support when they seized power. That is simply not true. A fair and objective guess—it can only be a guess—is that more than 50 per cent of the people welcomed the coup, while perhaps as many as 70 per cent saw the Colonels as a necessary evil brought about by the intolerable squabbling of the politicians.

This fact was hardly recognized outside Greece. And it is obvious why. The people interviewed by the foreign press were almost 100 per cent against the coup. They were generally publishers, intellectuals and politicians. They were not representative of the majority of the people. Although Members of Parliament are supposed to reflect the feelings of their constituents, the Greek people had long ago lost confidence in their representatives and in the system.

Greece is a country made up largely of peasants and poor

urban workers. Along with a growing middle class, they had little in common with the very small, élitist Establishment which ran the country. On the other hand, they did have a lot in common with the unsophisticated Colonels of peasant stock who took over.

The initial accusation levelled against the Colonels was that they were a bunch of illiterate and puritanical officers, lacking the rudimentary requirements to run a country, and that they had used arbitrary means to bring about the downfall of the regime. This was true. In due course the Colonels did fall from power through their own bungling. But in the initial stages of the new regime, the people did not see things that way.

Democracy had become a game of musical chairs played by the various political factions, a fact well understood by the people. The officer corps, on the other hand, was considered the most modern and effective institution in Greek society. It was generally believed by the Greek people that the army was, at least, efficient.

The Colonels who seized power on the night of April 21st were indeed a Spartan band. This, in the eyes of the populace, was hardly a bad thing. The venal politicians and corrupt businessmen had thoroughly alienated the people. They were replaced by a group of officers who promised to clean up the political decay and the decadence of parliamentary life, and to rectify social inequalities. The average Greek, being far removed from socio-political theories about democratic institutions as he struggled to make ends meet, was more than happy to see a thorough house-cleaning. This face was never mentioned by the press, although it was obvious to everyone at the time. Instead the coup was treated as if a country like Switzerland had suddenly been taken over by a bunch of fascist soldiers and its populace kept quiescent by the threat of force.

A powerful key to understanding the initial acceptance of the takeover can be found in the social origins of the coup-makers, in effect of the whole officer corps. They were totally rejected by the Establishment. (The élite beautiful people of the Athenian cocktail circuit—the newspaper publishers, the rich professional politicians and other wealthy professionals—eventually proved correct in their assessment of the Colonels. But this was purely by chance. At the outset they could accuse the plotters of nothing except being puritanical and peasants. The only faction which said they were pawns of the Americans was the Communists—and Andreas Papandreou. The Colonels were their nearest rivals, displaying just those qualities which the leftists preached: concern over social inequality, dedication and discipline.)

Like most peace-loving, hard-working and responsible Greeks, the officer corps has a rural background. Statistical data on the social characteristics of the Greek army show that the officer corps serves as a channel of social mobility, security and prestige in the areas where there is a relative absence of economic opportunity. The recruitment of officers is conducted mainly from the same rural areas, and among groups in humble circumstances. Studies by these same international experts provide evidence that because of the humble origin most officers were essentially denied active participation in their country's social and economic order. Which was not only their link with the populace, but a common denominator in their protest against the Establishment.

It is not the purpose of this book to dwell upon the socio-economic phenomena which produced the country's instability. A thorough study in that field should be done by an expert. Here we are merely concerned with events, but in order to comprehend them, a brief analysis is necessary. That the foreign press, in general, failed to grasp the common links and desires between protesters of the left, the average workers and the Colonels, was—to say the least—an enormous oversight. As was the fact that likening Greece in 1967, with the chaotic political climate prevailing at the time, to an affluent and politically mature European country was like comparing apples and oranges.

The political leadership that the Colonels rejected in 1967 was not only of a different and higher social origin than their own, but was—and still is—an élite group in which economic, political and social power agglomerates. Almost everyone coming from a political background was likely also to possess a high socio-economic status within the framework of Greek society. Even George Papandreou, when imprisoned in a military hospital during the first days of the coup, confessed to his friend, the writer Dimitrios Pournaras, that all the political leaders of his party consistently advanced their heirs into positions of leadership instead of developing democratic methods of selection.

This fact is significant for an understanding of the officers' political behaviour. Because they were denied active participation in the social and economic order and lacked social prestige, frustrations drew professional officers into active political involvement when the opportunity arose. There were similarities between the Egyptian Free Officers' movement and the Greek Colonels. Nasser's men were also of humble origin, coming from families of peasants, minor officials and small landowners.

Colonel Ladas reflected this when he said after the coup, 'We were all so poor that we called Papadopoulos the "rich one" because his father was a school teacher.'

Another accusation levelled at the Colonels from the start of their reign was that they lacked a coherent ideology. That was entirely true. The Colonels came to power with implicit ideological leanings which were at times contradictory. They were first and foremost conspirators, acting secretly to overthrow the established Government; which involved putting themselves in danger. They did not enjoy the comfort of an academic community which could discuss and formulate its ideas and its programme. The political ideology of the coup leaders, as well as of most army officers, was shaped by their social origins, by a heightened social consciousness, and by their own experiences.

The Colonels all spent their formative years, and entered the military academy, during the Metaxas dictatorship. This may have been why their regime placed such heavy emphasis on law and order and rigid anti-communism. The regime also cultivated the religious traditions of the Greek Orthodox church, cherishing visions of a 'third Greek civilization' (the two former civilizations being the classical and the Byzantine).

The bloody civil war in which all of them fought for years had strengthened their anti-communism. Their education, their military experience in various parts of the country, and their post-war contacts with more developed Western systems, all made them aware of the social problems the nation faced. They had seen, too, the inability, or unwillingness, of the Establishment to grapple firmly with these problems. So to their original conservatism and anti-communism a new socialist-populist belief, related to the need for reform, was added.

Many so-called political observers have compared the Colonels with Latin American dictators who periodically take over countries in South and Central America. The slogan 'banana republic' was extensively used by all dissidents to show their disapproval of the Colonels. And although the end of the Colonels' regime certainly resembled that of such a republic, the original motive behind their intervention was one of reform rather than of securing personal power. Indeed, in the speeches of the coup leader, George Papadopoulos, there were repeated tirades against oligarchy, a rejection of favouritism, and calls for advancement through achievement, for talent-oriented methods of recruitment, for national integration, and for the introduction into public life of efficiency, honesty and national loyalty, as well as for the promotion of social and economic reforms, and an attack on waste, backwardness and corruption.

Brave words, one might say. Did not the politicians utter these same words before each and every election in the past? The answer must be 'yes,' but with a difference. The original fulminations of the Colonels rang true to many people because of their strict upbringing and training, their undeniable record of loyalty and honesty, and their unentangled political beliefs, which had only an inherent anti-communism as a precondition.

Needless to say, the ideology of the Colonels brought them only disapproval and ridicule in the press of the developed countries. The simple-minded and religious Pattakos was the first to draw fire. He spoke about a sacred love for one's motherland, belief in Christ, devotion to the family and so on. He was supported by Ladas who, as Secretary-General of Public Order, was responsible, in a moment of puritanical fervour, for closing the Greek frontiers to mini-skirted, bearded or long-haired foreigners. Ladas physically roughed up an editor who wrote in a weekly magazine that many of the famous personalities of ancient Greece had been homosexuals. (Ladas was soon transferred to the Ministry of the Interior where the damage he could inflict upon the image of the revolution became negligible.)

Most foreign journalists, diplomats, and even some social scientists, placed heavy emphasis on the traditional, religious and nationalist aspect of the Colonels' ideology. Using the blunders of Pattakos and Ladas, they heaped scorn and ridicule upon the new regime, not so much for what it had done, but for what it stood for. Countless jokes showing the Colonels' lack of sophistication made the rounds of the diplomatic cocktail circuit, an institution hardly in tune with the blunt and earthy officers. Feeling this hostility, the Colonels responded in kind by being undiplomatic to the diplomats, calling them, off the record, 'a bunch of lazy hypocrites, who just marry rich women and have impeccable manners at the dinner table.'

The articles, essays and expressed opinions of the foreign and Greek intelligentsia about the Colonels' lack of sophistication were not objective. They completely ignored Greek culture. In their haste the Colonels' critics forgot, or simply did not know, that the Greek socialization process uses every possible agent—family, school, mass media, church, even political parties—to transmit values associated with tradition, nationalism and religion.

During the post-war era traditional and modern ideas combined in a confusing and sometimes contradictory manner. This transitional period heightened the problem of the urban masses. Nevertheless—and this should be emphasized—the values and attitudes for which the Colonels stood, and which their critics ridiculed, were shared by most of the Greek population. This was a fact which many left-wing intellectuals and critics of the regime denied; but they were denying something that was as clear cut as the Chinese propensity for gambling, the Latin love of music and romance, or the German proclivity for hard work.

The attitude of the intellectual community towards the Colonels cannot be described as opportunistic. Anything but. The Colonels went out of their way to court this group but were firmly rejected. But criticism can be levelled against the intellectuals for using the traditional values, in which all Greeks believe, as though these were a special weakness of the Colonels. It was as if now, in the post-Vietnam period, the *New York Times* came out against the peasant-soldiers of the North for going around burning copies of *Playboy*, forcing the bar girls of To-Do Street to mend their ways, rounding up pimps and black marketeers, and executing thieves in the market-place. The *Times* and other liberal newspapers will not criticize that sort of regime for wanting to revert to a traditional culture, but were much less tolerant when the Colonels tried to instill the old classical and traditional values into the Greek people.

By the middle Sixties, after the enormous strides the nation had made under the Karamanlis regime, many Greek social scientists had already begun to question the value of 'modernization'. They were sceptical about a phenomenon which persuaded many Greeks to be 'trendy', while ignoring the real wishes of the people. It was especially evident on television, in films and in some publications. The media, in their anxiety to appear modern and European, increasingly abandoned good traditional elements while emphasizing anything foreign, including irresponsible pro-drug films, pornographic books and television serials full of violence.

The more sophisticated societies of Europe and America could perhaps withstand such a phenomenon, but the deeply traditional Greeks found no comfort in it. This at least is what the Colonels strongly believed, as was inevitable in view of their background.

In the regime's initial statement many of the ills which had plagued the nation throughout its turbulent history were pointed out, and a few sacred cows slaughtered. The people who applauded were not, as is now claimed, only wild-eyed rightists, reactionaries and fascist thugs. They were most of the peace-loving, hard-working, patriotic Greeks who, time and time again, had seen the fruits of their labours squandered by an inefficient state, in which only the rich, the shrewd, and the dishonest could climb the ladder to success. The statement, which was delivered by the figurehead civilian Premier Kollias, had been drafted by George Papadopoulos and indicated the military regime's ideological orientation, or to be more accurate, its objectives.

It began by giving the immediate reasons for the intervention as 'political decadence and moral decline'. It continued: 'For a long while we have been witnesses to a crime which has been committed against our nation and our society as a whole: the shameless and wretched horse-trading of the parties, the decay of a great part of the press, the methodical attack against all institutions . . . the paralysis of the state machine, the complete lack of understanding of the burning problem of youth . . . moral decline, confusion and uncertainty, secret and open cooperation with conscienceless demagogues who have destroyed the calm of the country, creating a climate of anarchy, chaos, hatred and division, and have led us to the brink of national catastrophy. There remained no other means of salvation than for the army to intervene.'

This statement was as badly written as it was true. It typified the simplistic peasant outlook of the Colonels, their straightforward language, their fears and their basic antipathy toward the politicians. The second part of the statement called for political and national unity; it associated the army with the lower classes and set the objectives of social and political reform. 'We do not belong to a particular party, and do not plan to give advantage to any political group at the expense of another. We do not belong to the economic oligarchy . . . but to the class of toil. We seek to abolish corruption . . . and to create a healthy basis for the rapid return of the nation to orthodox parliamentary life. We proclaim brotherhood. From this moment on there are no rightists, leftists, or centrists. We will march forward towards a radical change. Our basic objective is social justice, the just distribution of national income, the material and moral improvement of society as a whole, and especially of peasants and workers, and of the poorer classes.'

These were certainly brave words, and the people who

professed them and vowed to make them come true seemed brave in trying. Greeks scattered throughout the world heard them and cheered. Perhaps, they thought, these peasant Colonels will make our country one to go back to instead of one to leave.

Christos Mavrogeorgos, for example, an associate professor at the University of California at Berkeley, was a liberal and saw in the Colonels' programme a ray of hope for the disenfranchized and the poor. He decided to leave teaching and return to his native land to work for a new Greece. There were many others like him. Seven years later, when the regime had degenerated into a Gestapo-style terror, with the whole of the population against it, Mavrogeorgos recalled to Papadopoulos that initial statement. 'What a pity you and the rest of the Colonels turned out to be chicken,' said the professor. 'You had the chance of a lifetime really to change Greece for the better.' The fallen idol only shook his head and blamed the people and the politicians for his failure; but this time no-one was listening.

During the night of the coup and throughout the following day some 6,800 people were arrested by the gendarmerie, from lists supplied by K.Y.P. The detainees were herded into sports stadiums, the Athens hippodrome and a few hotels. Some forty top political and military personalities were also arrested, thus depriving the opposition of any effective leadership. After a day the politicians were moved to a hotel in the Athenian suburb of Pikermi. According to their written statements, they were all treated with politeness and provided with reasonably comfortable quarters.

The large group of detainees held in the soccer stadiums and hippodrome consisted mostly of Communists and extreme leftists. After a few days they were all removed to the bare and inhospitable island of Yaros in the Aegean. Among them were journalists, municipal councillors and left-wing party officials. The 6,000 soon dwindled to about 1,000 and, at a later date, there were only about 400 political prisoners. This number was far below that of the political prisoners held under both the Karamanlis and Papandreou regimes. Nevertheless, the arbitrary arrest of dissidents continued throughout the seven-year rule of the Colonels, rising sharply in numbers during the terrible last days of Ioannides's reign.

There was no overt opposition or resistance of any kind to the takeover. Many rumours circulated, and were fueled by broadcasts from foreign stations, about mass executions of political leaders and dissidents. The fact is, however, that only one or possibly two people lost their lives during the forty-eight hours between the start of the coup and its consolidation. A forty-five-year-old man, Panayotis Elis, was shot dead by army Lieutenant George Kotsaris while allegedly trying to escape from the racecourse where Communist suspects were being held. The Lieutenant was not charged until after the final collapse of the Colonels. He claimed that he was only trying to scare the victim by firing towards his feet; nevertheless, he was convicted of unpremeditated murder. There was also the alleged shooting of a woman from an armoured vehicle in downtown Athens on the day of the coup, but the incident has never been substantiated. Thus, despite efforts by both foreign and domestic media to prove otherwise, the coup and its immediate aftermath were virtually bloodless.

The only place where a voice of protest was raised was Candia, in Crete. In that largest of Greek islands, renowned as a bastion of democracy, the people succumbed to the military junta as easily as in the rest of the country. But they managed to protest about it. Small groups, consisting mainly of youths, gathered in the town square and taunted the police and soldiers with shouts of '*Zito Papandreou* (Long live Papandreou).' They also shouted their disapproval of the King, and it was only through the restraint shown by the security forces that violence and bloodshed were prevented. The protesters soon tired and by nightfall things had returned to normal. Military dictatorship or not, on the following Sunday the people of Candia flocked to the army barracks to eat and drink with the soldiers and to crack Easter eggs in the customary manner. On this holiest of Greek holidays the people and the soldiers always feast together, and 1967 was certainly no exception.

This incident was typical of the apathy shown toward the coup, just as it is also indicative of the bond which binds soldiers and citizens together. The officer corps in Greece, which does not derive from a nobility, nor from the upper classes, has never had to face the kind of hostility which has been provoked in other European countries.

On the morning of April 21st, the military regime issued a decree, allegedly signed by the King, declaring a state of martial law. Special military courts were created with power to try whatever cases they saw fit. Assemblies of more than five people were forbidden, as was the right to strike and the right to criticize the Government. A strict censorship was also imposed.

With martial law imposed and a complete lack of resistance, the regime felt secure enough to begin freeing political leaders. After only one day in detention, the Premier of the last government appointed by the King, Canellopoulos, was sent home. He was only kept under surveillance, although he began to posture militantly, called impromptu press conferences to heap scorn upon the Colonels, and tried his best to be re-arrested. The Colonels, however, left him alone. They were after bigger fish, men with die-hard followers and international connections.

George Papandreau was moved to a military hospital because of his failing health. He was apparently resigned to his loss of power and was much less militant than Canellopoulos. At times he spoke almost with kindness of the Colonels and of their altruistic, radical plans.

As always, Andreas presented the biggest problem, although not by his attitude. He had lost all his militancy and aggressiveness as soon as he was arrested, cowering with fear for his life. He was convinced that he was going to be shot, and told his relatives and close associates that the Americans wanted him killed. C. L. Sulzberger, the *New York Times* columnist, visited him at the Pikermi Hotel where he was held, and reported that he did indeed blame the Americans for the coup but, at the same time, expected them now to save his skin by putting pressure on the Colonels.

The new regime was not eager to stop the judicial investigation of Andreas in connection with the Aspida conspiracy, but did not want to make him a martyr. The wheels of justice had begun to roll, and Andreas had already been named as a conspirator: but, after the success of the coup, the Colonels felt that the Aspida trial would only be probing old wounds.

Andreas, nevertheless, was publicly accused of high treason by the prosecutor and moved to Averoff prison on May 10th. Many American personalities asked for leniency on his behalf; even President Johnson intervened. (Johnson had been caught completely unaware on April 21st. He was told of the coup by Dean Rusk early in the morning. Jumping out of bed, he yelled into the phone: 'Tell those Greek bastards not to shoot that son-of-a-bitch Papa-what's his name.')

Pattakos then visited Andreas and had a long avuncular talk with him. After his release and voluntary exile Andreas wrote of the stupid, bald-headed tank commander, who parroted the Bible and asked him to mend his wicked, wicked ways. But he was less ironic with the Brigadier when in prison. He told Pattakos that he totally agreed with the principles of Christian-Hellenism, and spoke of his distrust of politicians and of the nation's need for change. Honest and not very bright, Pattakos fell under Andreas's charm. He rescinded the order which Andreas had agreed to obey, calling for him to purge himself and his colleagues in writing. (It is one thing to be scared to death when in jail, but quite another to betray one's principles and one's associates. Andreas had done both and had not been tortured; neither had he endured any psychological pressure.)

With Pattakos and the American Embassy pushing for his release, the regime found a way out of the Andreas obfuscation. A few days before Christmas 1967, an amnesty was announced for all political prisoners. On December 24th Andreas was driven to his home in Psyhico. After discussing with his father his future plans, and after a long talk with U.S. Ambassador Talbot and an even longer one with Pattakos, he decided to leave Greece and oppose the Colonels from abroad.

Nevertheless, the damage that Andreas had managed to inflict on Greek politics before the coup was minimal compared with the harm he did to U.S.-Greek relations afterwards. Although there had been no response by youth groups and labour unions to his pleas for resistance—as Andreas himself admitted immediately after his arrest—his allegation that the

C.I.A. was involved in the coup became imbedded in the minds of the people. Later, when the Colonels' popularity was transformed into disgust, Andreas's charges were used by the press and the politicians to fire anti-American sentiment among the masses.

Undoubtedly the reaction of foreign governments, and of the United States in particular, was of the greatest importance for the coup leaders. Seeking to establish a new political system with socialist undertones, but with their inherent anti-communism forcing them away from a non-aligned or pro-Soviet position, the Colonels saw America and her classless society as a model. The ingredients were to be free enterprise, a strong army and social reform. So they were especially anxious to cultivate America's friendship and to have her continuous support.

The American Government had been taken by surprise. Ambassador Philip Talbot learned of the coup from Canellopoulos's nephew, who telephoned him, asking for help. Although American officials had been worried about the deteriorating political climate, they had high hopes that the King, who was strongly pro-American, would somehow straighten things out. To the disillusionment of most Greek politicians who had hoped for some intervention by the United States after the coup, America's official position became one of temporary support and acceptance. After all, the legitimate head of state, the King, had not only remained but had sworn in the new regime.

After the bitter experiences of Santo Domingo and Vietnam, it would have been folly for the United States to get mixed up in the Greek political situation, especially as the new Government promised a quick return to parliamentary life. But although the administration did not wish to take any measures against the new regime, Congress sided with the dissidents. American military assistance was interrupted, although only formally. Greek political exiles continued to press Congress for a yearly re-examination of this military assistance over the next seven years and managed to curtail enough heavy weaponry to force the Greeks to go shopping elsewhere. But as C. L. Sulzberger pointed out, one must distinguish between military policy toward a fellow N.A.T.O. ally and political policy toward Greece as a nation. As a key component of N.A.T.O.'s South-Eastern Command Greece deserved the weapons available to other allies, including modern tanks, guns and aircraft, which were being held back by Congress. An M-48 tank is no more useful against hostile crowds than an M-47, but is certainly more useful against a potential external enemy.

Since American aid was minimal by the end of the 1960s— only $17 million in a direct grant, the rest of the $111 million in obsolescent military hardware or given as a long-term loan— there was very little pressure which the United States could exert on the Colonels. Senator Fulbright tried time and time again, but in view of the circumstances Papadopoulos merely ignored him.

The official American attitude was that the United States was in no way involved in a coup which had been the result of Greek internal politics and poor administration; that N.A.T.O. needed Greece and that the United States was, therefore, in no position to intervene against the Colonels; that Papadopoulos was a moderate and a shrewd political personality, strongly attached to the idea of a return to democracy; that a withdrawal of America's moral support and the complete cutting off of military aid could jeopardize his position and bring to power extremists like Ladas and Ioannides; therefore, to sum up, American support for, and good relations with, the regime were the only way to bring about a return to parliamentary government.

But because the United States did not take a stronger stand against the regime or send in the marines as Andreas wanted, even the eventual degeneration of the Colonels, with all their faults and injustices, was blamed on the Americans.

During the first days after the coup and throughout that first year the policy of the Colonels toward the King was one of benign neglect. They treated him as an understanding father might treat a child not quite right in the head. The King, in turn, brooded like Achilles in his tent, wishing them to go away; hating them at times, feeling betrayed by them, but hoping that he could talk some sense into them. He cooperated by signing Bills and, in effect, legitimizing the regime: but he knew, deep in his heart, that they were dangerous to his prerogatives and to his throne.

He had become cautious after his July 1965 experience. He would bide his time, build up support on his own, and eventually move against what he considered to be the usurpers of his beloved army. On the day after the coup, when the American ambassador had visited him in Tatoi, Constantine confided: 'I will put them to sleep, and after that I will surprise them the same way they surprised me.'

A game of cat and mouse began, with the young King trying to gather support inside and outside the country, and the Colonels maintaining an artificial cordiality towards his person but removing his men from the centres of power. In June, Constantine expressed a desire to visit the military units in northern Greece. He had a good excuse as Greece and Turkey were once again at the brink over Cyprus.

The King could count on the undying support of General George Perides, commander of the powerful Third Corps. Another unswerving royalist was Brigadier Andreas Erselman, who commanded the 20th Armoured Division of the Third Corps. Constantine also managed to install General Apostolos Zalachoris as head of the 91st military command of the Third Corps. Perides's Chief of Staff was Brigadier Orestis Vidalis, another close friend of the King.

The Colonels did nothing about these appointments. They knew that most of the higher Generals would remain loyal to the King, and allowed him to mix freely with them. Once again Constantine had misjudged the mood of the army, as well as of the people. He listened to his trusted Generals, who assured him of their support, but he did not examine all the factors closely to see if their support alone would be enough. When he finally let the Generals know that he was planning a coup, they were enthusiastic. But Papadopoulos meanwhile had not been idle.

A widespread network of officers loyal to the junta had been organized to cover every unit like a blanket. The overwhelming majority of officers were Papadopoulos's friends and admirers. Constantine they knew only as a symbol, and the commanding Generals were almost as far removed from them and their problems. Nearly every regimental, batallion and company commander was a keen supporter of the Colonels—a fact which the King's civilian and military advisers had again failed to report.

In the meantime, the ruling triumvirate went out of their way to please the King. They drummed up support for every one of his visits to the front, and mobilized crowds at airports and stadiums to welcome him wherever he went. It was as if Papadopoulos, the master puppeteer, was pulling the strings and putting the puppet king complacently to sleep through the cheering of the crowds.

In August the King paid an unofficial visit to America, to attend the America Cup races off Newport. He also visited Washington and met President Johnson. It was later revealed that the President told the King that, if he could handle the Colonels, America would be more than pleased and would increase her military and economic aid. But, Johnson warned, for obvious reasons the United States could not become involved in pushing the Colonels out. Constantine reportedly winked and said: 'Don't worry. I can handle those people myself.'

By summer's end the King's intention was no longer a secret in Athens. The socialites who knew him talked openly about a coup, playing guessing games aboard their yachts about the date of it. Several politicians pressed the King to hurry and do away with the Colonels. Most of these politicians were afraid that they would soon be forgotten; others missed their parliamentary privileges; all of them objected to crude Colonels bathing in the spotlight which had been reserved for them.

George Mavros, a leading Centre Union politician, actually threatened the King that his party would symbolically depose him if he did not move against the Colonels. When an old General, Thrassyvoulos Tsakalotos, a hero of the wars against the Axis powers and the Communists, reminded Mavros that the Colonels would be difficult to topple, Mavros assured him that 'these peasants will run like rabbits when the people and the army turn against them.'

The King worked out his plan with General Constantine Dovas, the chief of his military retinue. Others who assisted him were General Ioannis Manetas, Inspector General of the army at the time; General Constantine Kollias, chief of the First Army Group in Larissa; General Perides of the Third Corps in Salonica, and some of his commanders, such as the giant Brigadier Erselman. The plan was as follows: Constantine would fly to Salonica and take personal charge of the Third Army. General Kollias of the First Army would cut communications between the north and south of the country. Mobile units would then move towards the capital, after the King's men there had destroyed the two radio stations and taken over the Armed Forces Headquarters.

The weakness of the plan lay in its choice of priorities. Athens—the nerve centre of the country, the capital from which almost all successful uprisings had taken place in the past—was not programmed for capture. Moreover, because of rampant rumours about the impending coup, the element of surprise was minimal. Once again the King and his advisers were extraordinarily naive. They seemed impervious to the reality of the situation. Worse still, the rigidity of their thinking made them stick to the original date, December 13th, even though the imminence of a Greco-Turkish war had forced the headquarters of Perides's Third Corps to move to the small town of Komotini, close to the eastern frontier. This meant that the King would have to begin his action in the town of Kavalla or Komotini, and only then move toward Salonica with much precious time having been lost.

Several Generals, including Kollias (no relation to the Premier) and Manetas, warned the King that he should wait until the military situation had cooled down sufficiently for Perides's headquarters to return to Salonica. There the powerful radio station would be at his disposal, as well as control of Greece's second largest city. But Constantine was adamant. The coup was set for the respectable hour of 11 a.m. on December 13th.

As the time approached, Kollias, Perides and Manetas continued discreetly to press the King to change his plans. They wanted to have his message to the people ready for release just as the King flew to Kavalla. Constantine did not even give it to them until the last day. Kollias kept insisting on a better organized plan and Salonica as the start of the coup, but to no avail. On December 12th, Constantine happened to meet Ambassador Talbot at a friend's house. He asked the envoy to visit him at 9 a.m. the next day in Tatoi. When Talbot arrived there, the King cheerfully announced that he was about to kick the Colonels out. 'We shall probably have dinner together here in Athens tonight,' said Constantine. Talbot was speechless, but recovered enough to wish good luck to the King. Constantine in his naive way was probably hedging his bets. Feeling sure of success, he was trying to earn some credit with America by informing the Ambassador beforehand. If he failed, he could count on American sympathy and support. In making his move, he conld say that he had kept the United States fully informed.

The King's coup turned out to be as much of a tragicomedy as his encounter with Talbot. While Constantine was speaking to the American envoy, his pregnant wife was collecting her possessions after sending the servants away. Family jewels and plenty of clothes for the royal couple and their children were all packed in numerous suitcases and trunks. General Dovas arrived, followed by Prime Minister Kollias, who had been informed of the plan only the day before. Then came the Queen Mother, Frederika, accompanied by her beloved dog, and the King's younger sister, Princess Irene. Air Force chief Andonakos had been summoned and told of the plan at the last minute. Finally came the Queen's obstetrician, Dr. Koutifaris, who was to accompany the royal couple in case the Queen felt ill. The Archbishop of Greece, Ieronimos, was also summoned but he never arrived. No one could locate him. Doubtless the wily prelate had perceived what was going on and made himself unavailable, thus ensuring that he could safely bless the eventual winner.

At Tatoi, Constantine's private Grumman Gulfstream took off from the small military airport with the royal couple and their entourage, while a Dakota C-47 left for Larissa with Andonakos aboard. There the tactical Air Force Group was located. Both planes took off at 10:30 a.m. Precisely at the same time Papadopoulos left his office in the Old Palace and drove to the 'Pentagon.' Before leaving he stationed an armoured car—just one—before the Old Palace as a security measure.

Upon arriving at the 'Pentagon' Papadopoulos was greeted by Pattakos and Makarezos as well as the other original coup-makers. It was like a reunion. Then they began to trace the King's movements, and to issue orders to junior officers in the north of Greece. At one moment a Major asked over the phone what was happening, and Papadopoulos gave him a precise, up-to-the-minute account of what was due to occur in a few hours. The Major stuttered, said goodbye, and hung up.

The coolness shown by Papadopoulos in face of the King's threat was a result of his having kept all the high-ranking royalist officers under surveillance from the beginning. He had also tapped many phones, including Constantine's private one. So he knew every move of the King in advance, and had alerted all units and the military police.

The first indication of trouble was picked up by General Kollias in Larissa. Waiting in his office for the King to land in the north and for the signal to start the coup, he answered his telephone and heard a familiar authoritarian voice on the wire. It was General Anghelis, the army chief and a pro-Papadopoulos man. 'What the hell is the matter with you?' exclaimed Anghelis to Kollias. 'We know about the coup and the King's departure from Athens. If I were you, General, I wouldn't do anything foolish.'

Surprised and angered at the bungled state of affairs, Kollias then tried to talk Anghelis into joining them: 'The King is adamant; he will not retreat. I appeal to your patriotism. Don't respond by shedding the blood of your brothers.' Kollias proposed a meeting between the King's men and the junta, with Anghelis as intermediary. But Anghelis simply hung up, then ordered all lines of communication cut between north and south.

The fleet, meanwhile, was supporting the King whole-heartedly. Under Admiral Dedes, the commanders of the two naval units, Vice-Admiral Rozahis of the Ionian Cretan fleet and Vice-Admiral Panas of the fleet in the Salamis bay area, had agreed to steam north and join the King. But Dedes was arrested by Papadopoulo himself and held in the 'Pentagon' under guard, leaving the two Vice-Admirals without further orders from their chief. Constantine could not be contacted by phone, nor did the Salonica naval command know where he was. As a result, the fleet just steamed aimlessly about, while its commanders debated alternative courses of action.

The King landed in Kavalla around noon. Rooms had been prepared for him and his entourage at the Astir Hotel. But his plans started to fall apart almost immediately. Brigadier-General Erselman called in the unit commanders of the 20th Armoured Division, told them of the coup and gave them orders for action. Lieutenant-Colonel Petanis, commander of the Second Armoured Batallion based outside Komotini and near the all-important Third Army Headquarters, said he had trouble with some of his officers and could not move his unit. He then suggested that General Erselman drive over and help put things in order. The brave, but naive, Erselman, jumped into his staff car and dashed into the wolf's mouth, being immediately placed under arrest. The 20th Armoured Division, and the Second Batallion in particular, were to have been the units which moved on Salonica.

At 3:30 p.m. the King landed by helicopter at the headquarters of the Third Corps in Komotini. Generals Perides and Vidalis told Constantine that the situation was good. Neither of them was aware that Erselman had been arrested or of the fact that nothing and nobody had even begun to advance towards Salonica.

Inside that city, at 1:45 p.m., General Liarakos, commander of the war college, had received the King's message and ordered it broadcast from the radio station. But the building had already been taken over by an infantry batallion under Lieutenant-Colonel Tassiopoulos, who had just secured the airport. There was nothing for Liarakos to do but send a messenger to Perides in the north, telling him of the disaster. Meanwhile, he waited for his last hope, Colonel Kokkas of the Second Armoured Command, to arrive.

The Minister for Northern Greece, General Patilis, was hospitalized that day. When he heard that something was happening, he jumped out of bed, put on battledress, and went to the Salonica Army Corps headquarters. He ordered the radio station to begin broadcasting the regime's messages, arrested all suspect officers, and ordered units to move against

Perides and the King, who was still waiting in Komotini. When heavy armoured units drove up to his headquarters, Perides mistook them for armour rolling on to Salonica. He went outside in pouring rain to salute them and was arrested instead. Not a shot was fired.

Perides did, however, break away for a moment and managed to call Kavalla. He shouted over the line to General Kehagias, the commander of the 2nd Division: 'Tell the King I am under arrest and unable to help further.'

In the centre of the country, at Larissa, General Kollias was in the same predicament as his fellow conspirators. He ordered his units to move north and capture Salonica, but the junior commanders refused to obey. Kollias was then placed under arrest.

When the King and his trusted Dovas finally realized the gravity of the situation it was late in the afternoon. Nevertheless, they decided on one last move. Constantine ordered General Despiris to go to the furthermost eastern units and tell the 10th Division commander stationed there to organize armour and infantry and march on Salonica. This gesture proved as fruitless as the rest. The King's envoy was arrested by junior commanders of the 10th as soon as they reached divisional headquarters.

Finally, young Lieutenant-Colonel Petros Gillas organized an armoured unit and moved against the King at Kavalla. Thus, instead of gaining support, the monarch now had units moving against him. His last option was the Tactical Air Force base in Larissa. But by now he had lost his nerve. Quickly rounding up his family and belongings from the hotel, and wearing his Marshall's uniform, he left in his private plane for Rome. While in the air he was intercepted by two F-104's, piloted by pro-regime men. One of them shouted over the intercom that he was going to bring the plane down. But orders from Athens forced the pilot away, leaving Constantine's silver plane among the clouds in its lonely flight toward Rome.

Basically the King erred because he thought that the junta did not command the loyalty of the army, and that his presence among the troops would turn all the armed forces against the usurpers. Furthermore, he was reluctant to use the units loyal to him—and there were many under very good commanders, including much of the air force—to fight the junta supporters. He was known to be against letting any blood be shed.

Chapter 12
Papadocracy

DESPITE the fiasco of the royal countercoup in December 1967 King Constantine did not lose his throne. A compromise solution was sought by the Colonels which resulted in the appointment of the senior in rank among the original plotters, General Zoetakis, as regent. Thus Greece remained a kingdom although the man who occupied the throne had to accept a low-profile, mainly social, existence in Rome.

The Colonels did not abolish the monarchy because the repercussions would have been counter-productive. The 35 per cent or so of the Greek people who were royalists would have turned against the revolutionary regime; the army itself would have experienced internal convulsions, since king and country were linked in the minds of many soldiers. Besides, Constantine was the fig leaf of legality which allowed most nations—especially America—to maintain diplomatic relations with the junta. The Colonels also realized that, while they continued the King's stipend and kept Greece a monarchy, Constantine would not join the growing number of political dissidents in exile who were plotting against their regime.

Immediately after the attempted countercoup major changes in the Government took place. Papadopoulos became Prime Minister and also took over the Ministry of Defence. Pattakos was named Deputy Premier as well as Minister of the Interior, while Makarezos retained the powerful Ministry of Co-ordination. Power was shifted toward this triumvirate with Papadopoulos as its undeniable head.

Now the way was clear for the objectives of the revolution to be sought without interference from such leftover institutions as the monarchy. The regime was even encouraged from some unexpected quarters—by Dean Acheson, a former American Secretary of State, and the present Secretary, Dean Rusk. Both men argued that the Colonels and their promised reforms were what Greece needed. Rusk promised support while, at the same time, reminding the Colonels that a quick return to democracy was imperative. And Great Britain, Canada, and Italy, which had previously withheld diplomatic relations, now officially recognized the regime.

These favourable reactions came as a result of Papadopoulos's handling of the King's countercoup and of the Cyprus crisis which preceded it. In both cases he had shown restraint and wisdom and no blood was spilled either among brother Greeks or fellow N.A.T.O. allies.

Cyprus had once again become the focus of conflict in the late summer of 1967. Soon after the April 21st takeover it became obvious that a spectacular result, such as the union of Cyprus with mainland Greece, would lead to increased popular support; an objective which suited the chauvinistic nationalism of the military leadership.

George Papadopoulos had visited Cyprus and had allegedly agreed with Makarios on a defence policy for the island and on a common bargaining position about what Turkey could be given in return for union, or 'enosis'. In effect, Papadopoulos was willing to accept the Acheson plan, which called for a large Turkish base on the island. Simultaneously, Papadopoulos was cultivating Greco-Turkish relations and an agreement seemed near. Then Makarios demurred, and, despite later efforts by the Colonels and a historic meeting with the Turks at Evros, negotiations fell through.

But events in Cyprus would not allow the situation to remain static. In November, a clash between Greek-Cypriot police and Turkish-Cypriots holding the village of Kofinou, astride the Nicosia-Larnaca road, soon developed into a major crisis. From time to time, the Turks used their strategically-located position to harass traffic on this main highway. Greek-Cypriot police failed to dislodge them. It was then decided, at the insistence of Makarios himself, that Greek troops on the island should be used to capture the position. During the operation about twenty Turkish Cypriots were killed. Further bloodshed was halted by the United Nations peacekeeping force, but, by that time, mainland Turkey was up in arms, threatening to invade Cyprus and asking for the withdrawal from the island of 10,000 Greek troops which had been there clandestinely since 1965.

President Johnson sent his trusted envoy, Cyrus Vance, in a desperate attempt to avert hostilities. Although Vance found the Turkish demands very stiff—they asked for Grivas's departure from the island, indemnities for the Turkish victims of the fighting that had already taken place, and the removal of the 10,000 Greek troops—to his surprise he also found Papadopoulos extremely understanding and anxious to avoid war.

Although Papadopoulos recalled both the troops and Grivas only after arguing with his fellow officers that they could be re-infiltrated into Cyprus at a later and more propitious date, his position looked like a sell-out. Nevertheless, it convinced foreign statesmen that here was a Greek leader who could be counted on for responsible action, however unpopular, rather than emotional outbursts. It did not convince Greek public opinion, however, nor many of his fellow officers, whose high opinion of their leader began a steady decline from then until his fall from power.

Although the prime concern of Papadopoulos in avoiding war at that time was his wish to consolidate his regime and to begin a radical reconstruction unhampered by debilitating outside factors, he was indelibly marked as a foreign puppet in the minds of many people from that moment on. When the regime finally collapsed, Papadopoulos's behaviour during the November 1967 Cyprus crisis was offered as proof that he was a paid agent of the C.I.A.

With the coming of the new year, the Colonels stood unchallenged and could proceed unhindered toward their revolutionary objectives. The regime had cast itself in the roles of leader, father and teacher. But, from the beginning, there was also a desperate desire to be liked. Perhaps because of their simple background, the Colonels believed that, if one filled the pockets of the people, they would remain quiescent and content.

Even critics of the regime were to admit that during the seven-year reign of the Colonels Greece could boast one of the most enviable economic performances anywhere. A fantastic 10.5 per cent annual growth rate was achieved, combined with a low 4.4 per cent rate of inflation. The rate of increase of the national product was almost 50 per cent higher than during the Karamanlis years. It was the best performance of any country except Japan and Taiwan. People's real income doubled in seven years; in 1973 it was above $1,700 per capita, making Greece—according to the conventional economic criteria—a developed nation rather than a developing one.

The annual rate of increase in the volume of industrial production during 1956–1963 was 9 per cent. During the 1968–1972 period it reached 13 per cent. Industry during the junta period became, for the first time, the sector on which the total economic activity of the country depended. What Karamanlis had started, the Colonels expanded. Not only were large numbers of new industrial units built, but old ones were modernised. Parallel to that working conditions in most factories were greatly improved.

For the first time the products of many Greek industries began to compete with foreign products in both the domestic and foreign markets. Industrial exports represented only 15 per cent of total national exports in 1966, but by 1974 they had reached 45 per cent—a tremendous achievement. The total value of exports was $1,220.5 millions in 1973, which meant that they had tripled in seven years. Industrial exports, which reached a level of $523.5 millions in 1973, showed a tenfold increase.

The heavy emphasis on industrialization during the first three years of the military regime produced a slowdown in agriculture—a phenomenon present in every industrial country. This emphasis carried with it the twin problems of rapid urbanization in Greece and emigration from the rural areas to Western Europe. But after 1970, programmes of regional development and a decentralization of governmental authority were initiated for the first time in Greek history, with the purpose of lessening the difference between rural and urban standards of living.

Great strides also took place in the shipping industry. By convincing the enterprising Greek shipowners that the state would protect them from strikes and high taxation, the government persuaded the wandering modern Ulysses to invest in his country by such promotional schemes as making the Greek flag one of convenience. Millions of shipping tons were transferred to the Greek flag and the state profited handsomely. A similar confidence was created in the business sector, while a government campaign convinced the people they should invest their money in local banks instead of hiding it under the mattress, as was the custom, or smuggling it out to safe foreign havens.

Foreign exchange controls, which had always existed nominally but had effectively applied only to the poor and uninfluential, finally prevented the rich from depositing their money abroad. The drachma improved by leaps and bounds. The families of workers outside the country and of seamen, the workers at home and the small businessmen, chose to put their money in local banks. This, in turn, enabled the banks to finance development. There was also a heavy demand for bond and share issues.

One of the Colonels' most conspicuous successes was in the tourist sector. After an initial setback during the 1967–68 period—when anti-junta propaganda kept many people away—tourism flowered again in Greece as never before. The number of visitors rose from 315,000 in 1960 to 966,900 in 1966, 1,047,800 in 1971 and a fantastic 2,620,100 in 1973.

In order to accommodate these millions of tourists who suddenly descended upon Greek shores, a building boom turned Athens, and the entire countryside, into a noisy inferno. But the Greeks—long used to a pastoral life without fringe benefits—did not seem to mind, perhaps because of their new-found affluence. It was ironic when, later on, Communist and other leftist leaders attacked the regime for destroying Greece by allowing cheap hotels to be built, as well as roads, hydroelectric plants, shipyards and oil refineries. These very people had previously criticized conservative governments for not building enough new industry so that they could keep people back on the farm, quiescent and controllable. In fact, the leader of E.D.A., the Communist front party, owned one of the most lucrative pieces of real estate in downtown Athens and profited handsomely from the enormous edifice that was erected upon it.

A large number of new roads, commercial airports, fishing ports and marinas for yachts were constructed. One of the most significant achievements of the regime, however, was the improved telecommunication network. With the impetus of the European Games, held in Athens in August 1969, Greek telecommunications were completely modernized and considerably expanded, thus providing businessmen with much needed facilities. The ratio of telephones per inhabitant and the degree of automation equalled that of other European nations.

The incredible economic strides made during the late sixties and early seventies were a direct result of the people's confidence in a government free of political upheaval. However, that chronic failing of the Greek economy in the past—the gap in the balance of payments—was never eradicated. By 1972 the Government's expansionary policies coupled with imported inflation signalled danger ahead for the drachma. The first anti-inflationary measures were taken in December 1972, but were not severe enough. In 1973, when the first democratic experiment by Papadopoulos went into effect with an all-civilian government being appointed and parliamentary elections called for, specific anti-inflationary measures had been agreed upon but were forestalled by the Ioannides coup. But, by then, the oil crisis had already engulfed Europe and the free world; the measures—had they been put into effect—would not have made much difference.

In the area of social policy the regime was much less successful than in the economic field. It did, however, raise social security benefits for the nation's farmers. It also cancelled once and for all their debts to the agricultural bank. (These debts had been used as a pawn by the politicians; successive governments would promise to remit them, and then rescind their promise, to suit the timing of elections.) Price supports for wheat, dried fruit, tobacco and cotton were established in 1968, and then replaced with a system of minimum prices for agricultural products. These measures would have greatly benefited the farmers if there had been parallel encouragement for the opening of new markets and a larger role for producers' cooperatives.

Increased social security coverage and health insurance, with larger benefits for almost all the population, was also a credit to the Colonels' regime, but the benefits and health services provided never matched the country's capabilities.

The original promise of a unification of social welfare institutions, with a simultaneous reform of benefits and services, did not materialize because of the Colonels' lack of commitment to the idea. Professor Patras, the Minister of Social Services, insisted upon this programme but was overruled by the Colonels.

The labour market, too, benefited significantly from the political stability which the Colonels imposed upon the nation. For the period of 1968–1972, income from employment at current prices increased by 30 per cent and over, and this increase was coupled with the relative stability of price levels. More important, the industrial and agricultural sectors of the economy offered new opportunities for employment which rapidly expanded the number of working people, including women, thus raising total family income.

Employment opportunities, which had been somewhat static between 1963 and 1969, took off between 1969 and 1973. By 1971 the demand for labour was so great—partly due to the emigration of unskilled workers to Germany during the Fifties and Sixties—that the Government, under pressure from the productive sectors, faced the problem by importing a number of foreign workers from Asia and Africa. In order to avoid social and racial problems these foreigners were allowed to work only in the merchant marine or in secondary tourist jobs.

All in all, one can safely say that economic affluence and growth during the seven-year period was unprecedented in Greek history. There was hardly a village or a hamlet, however small, in which some kind of development did not take place. As the political sector was moribund, newsreels of the time showed an unending series of Government representatives.

usually led by Pattakos, cutting ribbons and commemorating new bridges, plants, schools, hospitals, refineries, factories or communications centres. Slogans praising the revolution were everywhere and could be seen on public buildings, on any government edifice and in schools and playgrounds.

Greece had become a bustling, modern, industrial nation; young men had gone 'mod,' young women were partly liberated. The sidewalk cafés were now surrounded by thousands of cars spewing out fumes; advertisements covered the once ivy-green walls near the Acropolis; the beaches were bursting with bikini-clad foreigners; tourist complexes dotted and even obscured the craggy and picturesque shores. Greek businessmen resembled their American counterparts, sweating, hustling, even having nervous breakdowns. Money was being spent everywhere and everyone—according to the Government communiqués—was happy and enjoyed equal opportunities. But somehow, beneath the glorious facade of a modern developed society, there was a malaise. Greece and her people were getting rich, but the fat around the middle did not make up for the loss of her soul.

Every dictator believes he has the right to impose his will on a people because he knows what is best for them and for the nation. Otherwise he wouldn't be there. Papadopoulos and his colleagues had a vision, however misty, of the sort of Greece they were trying to create, but they never managed to convey this vision to the people, nor to inspire them in any way.

Another extraordinary thing about Papadopoulos was that the longer he stayed in his position of undisputed strongman, the more he acted like a politician about to stand for election. Because of this phenomenon—and his attempt to please as many people as possible—certain contradictions developed. And certain areas needing radical reform were neglected.

Late in 1968 Papadopoulos had overcome the last hurdle standing in the way of his inexorable march toward a new society. A referendum was called to let the people vote for or against the new constitution which had been drafted by his legal experts and was geared to what Papadopoulos considered the special needs of the country. The constitution was a legal framework for the everyday running of the country and it reenforced the power of the executive—something long desired by Karamanlis in the past, and finally put into effect by him after his return to power in 1974.

This constitution, although ratified by the 1968 referendum, was never fully implemented, since many of its articles were restricted by the existence of martial law. Although carefully policed by many foreign observers, the referendum could hardly be called a free one. There was some tampering with the results, but, because of press censorship and the nature of the Greek voting habits in the countryside, no proof of ballot-rigging was ever seriously examined.

This was the first attempt by Papadopoulos to legitimize the revolution. The overwhelming ratification of the new constitution by the people probably influenced him to drift slowly towards parliamentarism, wrongly believing that he could have both the army and the politicians under him.

The regime swept a number of other problems under the carpet, not realizing that their neglect would be disastrous in the long run.

One of the most backward sectors of Greek society was—and still is—education. Papadopoulos was cognizant of this, having been warned by some of his advisers responsible for government planning that, without basic reforms at all levels of education and an educational budget comparable to that of Western European countries, Greece would face insurmountable problems in the decade 1975–1985, as the need for skilled personnel could not be met.

Under the brief tenure of George Papandreou a good start had been made in the educational field. The raising of the school leaving age to fifteen years, assigning major status to modern languages, and making university education free—these innovations were kept by the Colonels. But, unfortunately, such basic reforms as increased emphasis on the physical sciences and mathematics, and the introduction of new subjects like economics and sociology, were proposed and then scrapped. This was due to the Colonels' irrational distaste for anything smacking of Papandreou's influence and, perhaps more importantly, to the unfortunate appointment of traditionalist

Theofylaktos Papakonstantinou as the first Minister of Education.

Here once again the humble origins of the Colonels, their love for traditional things like ancient Greek instead of economics, their distrust of anything progressive, undermined their efforts to move the nation ahead. The revolution's failure in the educational sector reflected its lack of success in other fields as well. The problems were inter-connected. Papadopoulos knew that overnight results were impossible, that educational success could not be put on display as his economic successes had been. So he hesitated when hard decisions had to be made, preferring to take the easy way out, favouring his industrial, rather than his educational, adviser.

Papadopoulos had some of the best brains in the country working for him; better, in fact, than most other Premiers had commanded. This he was able to achieve by bringing back Greeks who had studied and worked abroad. Many Greek-born professors, mostly in the United States, had responded to his appeal to return and help their native land turn a new page in its history. With the assistance of these people, significant five- and ten-year programmes were evolved for education and the civil service. These technocrats included the brilliant Elias Balopoulos, Takis Pavlopoulos, Professor Christos Mavrogeorgos from Berkeley, Anthony Kefalas and others.

They all pushed for reforms that would crystalize in the long term and for which they found Frangatos, who was later appointed Minister of Education, pleading as well—but to no effect. Papadopoulos wanted immediate results and compromise with the traditionalists who intended to keep their seats of power.

The educational reform programme drawn up by Papadopoulos's advisers and Frangatos covered every aspect of education at all levels. With freedom of thought as a central theme it paid primary attention to the development of a critical mind, rather than to the accumulation of facts and figures. It provided for new curricula with subjects which would enable the country to adapt to the needs of an industrial state. It proposed new schools offering vocational education, plus an increase in the years of compulsory schooling.

This programme, although never implemented, is still significant in that it indicates what is lacking in the Greek educational system. Although the antiquated buildings were modernized by the Colonels, the professors' antiquated way of thinking and the antiquated curricula were not. Nor was any attempt made to relieve crowded classes in the universities, since most of the Government's attention was directed toward rural primary schools.

By 1972 Papadopoulos had lost most of his revolutionary fervour, was avoiding the advice of the progressives, loathing Frangatos, and listening to the traditionalists who accused the Minister of Education of being a Communist for wanting to curb their prerogatives.

In the civil service exactly the same syndrome could be found. In fact the problem was more acute there, because implementing a radical solution would have brought to a halt the entire machinery of government. After an initial exposure of corruption, the chronically ill civil service returned to its traditional ways. Its problems derive from its very nature, being a hybrid between Ottoman and European influences, with the former overshadowing the latter. Rigid centralization of authority, the low quality of personnel, a confusion of responsibility among departments and bureaux, complicated and costly procedures, and a disregard of the citizen, were some of its outstanding weaknesses. Nevertheless, during the first two years some progress was made. Fear of the authoritarian regime had a lot to do with it. Afterwards, the traditional inertia returned, despite a brilliantly conceived five-year programme which called for new methods of forecasting social needs. But the blocking element here was the low quality of civil service personnel.

With the industrial sector booming, increased economic opportunities drew most of Greece's talented young people into the private sector. Recruitment of able people for the civil service became almost impossible, and some of those already there were dismissed in witch hunts started by their less talented colleagues.

Papadopoulos was aware of this weakness. Most of his programmes for reform wound up in the waste basket because totally inefficient cadres below the ministerial level were unable or unwilling to cope with them. In a state of utter disillusionment the Premier turned more and more toward the private sector where the enterprising Greek entrepreneur did not fail him.

This, in turn, had a backlash effect, since many officers saw his growing attachment to shipowners, industrialists and businessmen as a sign of corruption. But Papadopoulos and his close associates were not corrupt. The dictator's close relations with banker, shipowner, industrialist Stathis Andreadis was one example. An unscrupulous man throughout his career, Andreadis had funded all political parties including the Communists, and was enormously successful. He and other sharp operators, such as Vardinoyiannis and Onassis, convinced Papadopoulos that Greece could be pulled up by its boot-straps if only they were allowed to work without state interference. An exception was Stavros Niarchos. Unlike most of them, he had always been prepared to invest his foreign-earned millions in his native country.

(It was interesting to see how the Greek businessmen slowly, but surely, brought the ascetic Colonels 'around to their way of thinking.' First came discreet invitations to their homes at which the humble colonels gazed with awe. Then yachts and private planes were made available as the ingenious Athenian business community pursued its prey. One man who approached many of the unsuspecting Colonels was Nikos Livas, a middle-man, who through charm and the time-honoured principle of boot-licking managed to introduce many ministers to the houses of entrepreneurs. The officers turned politicians were plainly impressed by the sophistication, material possessions and cleverness of the business world. That the bourgeoisie were laughing behind their backs and ridiculing their peasant ways was something they discovered only after their fall from power, when the business community denounced them, with one voice, as oppressors and fascist beasts. Particularly loud in these denunciations were, of course, Andreadis, Vardinoyiannis and Livas.)

The revolution's failure to reform that chronically ill and most divisive of Greek institutions, the press, was another example of the Colonels' short-term thinking. Control of information in radio and television had always existed, since both were state-run. But after the army takeover the media came under the strict control of officers. This brought the cultural and intellectual level down, and because of the infantile propaganda put out, the effect of their message was frequently counter-productive.

The press was a different matter. After the Colonels came to power only one chain closed its doors, that of Helen Vlachos, the powerful conservative publisher. Although she had gone as far as the junta in signalling the Communist danger during Andreas's heyday and in hinting that the army might be called upon to intervene, she found the Colonels not to her liking. A royal intervention with the Generals leading it was more what she had been hoping for. Therefore she decided to close her newspapers and, after being placed under house arrest for having made a number of statements defying the regime, she was able to escape to London, where she continued to heap abuse on the Colonels.

As for the rest of the publishers, they stayed on and dutifully put out the junta's propaganda. The Lambrakis papers, which had militated in favour of Papandreou and were the power behind him throughout his career, were the only ones—with the exception of *Eleftheros Kosmos*, an extreme right-wing paper—which praised the Colonels in editorials. Lambrakis received enormous amounts of money from the banks under a deal he struck with Papadopoulos, as did the Botsis chain. After the fall of Papadopoulos it was rumoured that the closing by Ioannides of *Vradyni*, a conservative afternoon paper, was instigated by Lambrakis, who wanted to eliminate competition in return for his backing of the military.

Censorship of the press was most severe during the first two years of the Colonels' rule, but continued throughout the seven years. *Ethnos*, a liberal afternoon paper, was closed in 1970 and *Vradyni* in 1973. Letters from politicians critical of the regime had appeared in both papers, *Vradyni* having published one from Karamanlis. The inexperience of the Colonels in such matters was evident, because most foreign publications were permitted to circulate freely throughout their reign and the extensive criticism of the regime found in the foreign press was then spread by word of mouth.

The revolution's failure primarily was that it did not try radically to change Greece's yellow press. Papadopoulos did no more than limit it, using the press laws as a bludgeon and martial law as a straightjacket. No attempt was ever made to create a new and healthy press or to uproot the old one, nor to reduce the power of the five or six most prominent publishers who, throughout the post-war period, had made or brought down governments. It was a well known secret that Ministers had been symbolically 'sworn in' at various newspaper offices before taking the oath before the sovereign. So the yellow press reappeared, yellower than ever as soon as the Colonels fell.

Many able and honest journalists had quit in disgust when censorship was imposed. The publishers replaced these men—most of whom left the profession—with well-known Communists and low-level incompetents, knowing full well that these people would be easier to handle and would also demand lower wages. After democracy was restored, these inefficient and basically dishonest men remained in their jobs, while trying to disguise their collaboration during the previous seven years by putting out divisive and scurrilous stories.

Acts of open resistance during the Colonels rule were few and far between. Some politicians fought the regime courageously with speeches and with the pen. Some of them were imprisoned, although the important ones, like Kanellopoulos, Zigdis and Mylonas, were only placed under house arrest, or alternatively exiled for brief periods.

Some clandestine groups were formed but never managed to bother the regime in any serious way, their resistance consisting mainly of putting out pamphlets and exploding an occasional plastic bomb. Foremost resisters among the intelligentsia were Professor Dionyssios Karayiorgas, who had his hand blown off while preparing a bomb, Professor George Mangakis and the man who tried to assassinate Papadopoulos, Alexander Panagoulis.

Resistance against the Colonels received most of its publicity through such dissidents abroad as Andreas Papandreou, Melina Mercouri, Lady Fleming and Mikis Theodorakis.

Papandreou received large amounts of money from socialist movements in European countries, while Melina Mercouri's career skyrocketed in Paris, London and New York largely because of her political attitude. Mostly independent and ideologically divided, these people were given a lot of mileage in the press but contributed little to the Colonels' downfall.

The thorn in Papadopoulos's side was always the refusal by the Greek intellectual community to share his vision and help build a new Greece. After the first two or three years, when incompetence and corruption started to creep back in, prospective politicians and young technocrats began to shy away. And the initial welcome by the people as a whole turned to complete apathy. A Paris-based roving reporter for a large English daily was correct when he wrote in 1972: 'Apathy even more resounding than order reigns in Greece.' The pre-coup failure of the politicians had a lot to do with it. The people had been split ideologically, were never organized and, therefore, throughout the seven years were never able to unite against the Colonels.

The only politician of stature was Karamanlis, but he stayed brooding in Paris. Inside Greece Papadopoulos reigned supreme; even his worst enemies admitted that he was a political heavyweight.

Domestically and abroad the politicians continued their old ways. They were divided and disorganized. The Communists, ridden by internal differences, were grouped around three movements: the pro-Russian Greek Communist party, which took orders directly from Moscow and had its headquarters in Eastern Europe; the Communist Party of the Interior, which did not subscribe to Moscow's will and followed an independent course; and a third communist splinter group which considered the two previous ones responsible for the sad state of the Party in Greece, and rejected the traditional forms of political organization within the Communist movement.

The Centre Union was also split, especially after the death of George Papandreou in 1968. Most of the leadership had been expelled from the Union after the apostasy in 1965. The mediocre George Mavros had inherited the coalition's mantle. The radicals of the Centre Union were again headed by

Andreas Papandreou, who from his safe haven abroad continued to demand action against the Colonels, but, on the other hand, was unwilling to enter into a common front with the moderates and conservatives of the party.

The best effort to unify the opposition forces was conducted by the composer-politician Mikis Theodorakis. After his release from prison in 1970, he proposed the creation of a National Resistance Council for all exiled dissidents. His effort was torpedoed by Andreas, who claimed that 'liberation struggles need to provide a future for those who fight them.'

As usual, Andreas clouded the issue by excessive rhetoric and a fundamental error. His aim of radicalizing the masses against the junta was a pipe dream; first, because his voice was a distant whisper to the Greek people; second, because one should not talk like the Viet Cong without commanding soldiers like the Viet Cong. One should not indulge in verbal extremism much greater than the actual forces one can mobilize.

Andreas, nevertheless, was successful in raising considerable sums of money from Greeks abroad, thus amply financing his extensive and luxurious travels around the globe. His ideology had by now turned more to the left, combining elements from Marx, European socialism, anarchism, and the kind of national socialism practised by totalitarian leaders of underdeveloped countries who place a heavy emphasis on xenophobia.

The conservatives were also split. Canellopoulos, their leader, led a brave fight against the Colonels on the home front, but his efforts were always overshadowed by the imposing figure of Karamanlis in Paris. People had not forgotten Canellopoulos's efforts to keep the leadership of E.R.E. at the expense of losing the election to the Centre Union. Many E.R.E. leaders, such as Evangelos Averoff-Tositsas, the historian-politician, advocated a 'bridge' with Papadopoulos. They recognized the necessity of the April 21st revolution, although they had neither condoned it nor suffered under it. Being honest men, they accepted reality and Papadopoulos's undisputed qualities of leadership. By bridging their differences they hoped to prod the Colonels into lifting martial law and bringing an early return to parliamentary life. Nevertheless, politicians like Averoff were few, most of them preferring to play the role of martyrs rather than admit that it was their own folly which had brought the Colonels to power in the first place.

By the end of 1971 the regime felt secure enough to close the detention camps and release all but fifty dangerous Communists. Papadopoulos had never been in better shape domestically or internationally. With the passage of time, his regime had been recognized by all foreign governments. He was openly supported by the United States which believed in his sincerity as an ally, and also in his intention of returning to a democratic system. All European Governments cooperated with the Colonels, despite protests from some of them about the lack of elections.

Papadopoulos was the first post-war Greek leader to establish an independent foreign policy by increasing contacts with Eastern bloc Governments and with those of Asian and African countries. Without any politicians to embarrass him in parliament or to call him 'soft on Communism,' he even opened diplomatic relations with Greece's arch-enemy, Albania, sending the incredibly handsome and dashing Denny Karayiannis to Tirana as the nation's first Ambassador. The Foreign Office was run by the shrewd and capable Panayotis Pipinelis, who wangled an invitation from Red China for Makarezos. Greece's relations with Turkey were as good as possible, and both Papadopoulos and Pipinelis enjoyed a working relationship with Makarios.

From the beginning Papadopoulos claimed that his regime was a 'parenthesis' between the old politics and a new system of democratic life. An ironic, if tragic, sidelight was the hounding and arrest of most right-wing officers who remained loyal to the king. Most of the deportees to Aegean islands or mountain villages were politicians of the right and centre or royalist officers, such as Generals Perides, Kollias, Erselman, Koumanakos and Colonels Opropolos, Papathanasiou and Papaterpos.

Five political trials took place during the Papadopoulos regime under Law 509 of 1947. The most celebrated accusation against the Colonels was that political prisoners were tortured. At the beginning only a few people accused the Papadopoulos regime of torture; but the charges have increased since the restoration of democracy. By the time this book was written, sixty-four officers and men of E.S.A. and the security police had been indicted. Over 120 individuals detained during the Colonels' regime were scheduled to testify against their alleged torturers. Just a few police officers, however, and three military police majors—Theophyloyianakos, Spanos and Hatzizisis—were the main culprits.

Undoubtedly, such inhuman and brutal practices were not in accordance with the Colonels' thinking. When I confronted Papadopoulos with the torture charge in 1970, he reacted with genuine surprise and indignation. His regime did not condone such methods, although lower officers in security positions certainly did. Police brutality had always been a way of life in Greece, and a suspect's rights have never been protected by habeas corpus laws.

By 1972 foreign observers and knowledgable Athenians were speculating that Papadopoulos would arrange elections after forming his own political party. Few people realized that he had already missed the boat. The people's initial welcome, followed by apathy, had begun to turn to hate. If Papadopoulos had stood for election in 1970, he would probably have won by a landslide, especially after three years of uninterrupted political peace, economic progress and social harmony. The puritanical Colonels had not, as yet, begun turning bourgeois themselves, and the army was still enjoying its new-found affluence without being greedy.

However, the Greeks are volatile, freedom-loving people, and their benefactors had begun to remind them of past political leadership. The populace was unable to do anything about changing the colonels, but the junta itself—being Greek after all—did it for them.

Chapter 13

The Fall of Papadopoulos

THROUGHOUT the rule of the junta the West was presented with a terrible dilemma. It was one thing for the U.S.S.R. to crush Czechoslovak liberals. That was deplorable but understandable, and could not be prevented. It was something altogether different for a clique of faceless Colonels to establish a dictatorship in a Western European country—particularly in the place which freedom-loving people all over the world considered the cradle of democracy.

The agonizing 'Greek problem' was especially poignant for America as, throughout the post-war era, there had been a very special relationship between Washington and Athens.

Since Greece emerged as a small state, she had never been able to afford the luxury of an independent foreign policy, and was compelled by economic and military weakness to look to various super-powers for protection. After 1947 and the application of the Truman Doctrine to Greece (which spelled out that America would not tolerate aggression by subversion), the Greeks came under the American protective umbrella. In return, America has used that umbrella as a stick to bully various governments into following her policies. The Colonels were not exempt. The heaviest cross Papadopoulos had to bear (in his own words) was the constant American prodding that he must return to parliamentary rule. Despite the encouragement given to him and his revolutionary council by visiting Pentagon and Government officials, America's policy was one of benign neglect as long as the Colonels continued to rule by decree.

It is typical of our times that the fabrications of a few people like Andreas Papandreou and the Communist exiles could convince the Greeks—including, in the end, the Colonels themselves—that the junta survived purely because the United States wished it to. Papadopoulos, the brilliant juggler and schemer, realized that an eventual return to parliamentary rule was unavoidable: it was also a potential matchstick that could set off fires beyond his control. His dilemma was solved— as usual in Greece—by a compromise.

Papadopoulos had been constantly pressed by the hawks within his cabinet—Aslanides, Ladas, Ioannides and others— not to revert to parliamentary rule: but was also aware that many army people were disenchanted with the existing situation. By 1972 there were hundreds of jokes going around about the Colonels. One of them implied that Despina Papadopoulos was promiscuous because she shared her bed with the Regent, Prime Minister, Minister of Foreign Affairs, Minister of Defence and Education—all of whom were actually Papadopoulos, who had found it increasingly difficult to get capable people for sensitive posts. He had dismissed Zoetakis as Regent in early 1972, and assumed even that ceremonial office himself. (By sometimes refusing to sign Bills or because he wished to discuss them further with Papadopoulos, Zoetakis had held up legislation. This peasant General, turned Regent, took his duties seriously, but Papadopoulos had no time for such scruples and fired him outright.)

The army, with its new-found power, did not look kindly upon Papadopoulos's close associates nor on the members of his cabinet, who had begun to behave in a manner all too reminiscent of politicians in the past, appointing relatives and friends to influential jobs. This was known to Papadopoulos, but he was unwilling to break with his old colleagues. Charges of nepotism and corruption abounded by early 1973, most of them put out by disgruntled army officers.

So in the autumn of that year Papadopoulos decided to ease out the revolutionary council by first installing a civilian regime and then proceeding to elections. Although everyone looked upon him as the undisputed leader of the junta, he in turn counted upon Ioannides of the dreaded military police, as well as on Athens-area units of the Marines and Rangers, in case any junior officers got the same ideas as he had had in 1967. These units were commanded by trusted officers and were in close contact with his brother.

In an earlier reorganization of the Government he had promoted Makarezos and Pattakos to be Deputy Premiers, thus removing Makarezos from the powerful Ministry of Co-ordination. Other Colonels-turned-Ministers—like Balopoulos of Tourism and Aslanides the Secretary of Sport—were kicked upstairs, along with Ladas, Lekkas, Karydas and Kotselis: they were put in charge of regional administrations, well away from the centre of power in Athens.

If democracy was to function well Papadopoulos knew that fresh faces and younger, more rational, political leadership were needed. In his annual address to the nation on December 14th, 1972, he had vowed a move toward democracy during the year ahead. Like Karamanlis before and after him, he thought that a system of guided democracy was necessary. He realized too that the Greek people were not prone to accept a dictatorship for long. And above all, he knew that his overriding, Utopian reason for taking power in 1967—to secure a radical change, including the development of more viable democratic institutions—had not been achieved.

This failure must be attributed to Papadopoulos himself as the leader of the revolution, although it was not he alone who was responsible. Papadopoulos had tried to renew the political leadership but had been frustrated by people like Pattakos and Ladas, who had heaped abuse on anybody who collaborated with the regime. At the same time, the Colonels' excessive fear of any progressive idea, plus their feeling that the revolution was their own property, a kind of irrevocable privilege, had systematically obstructed participation by the politically minded, educated and active individuals who believed in the revolution. This general atmosphere had thwarted the creation of an ideology or of any real programme, thus isolating the revolution from the masses and particularly from the young.

The goals of the revolution were therefore frustrated, since it was impossible for a radical change to take place with young people excluded from participation. Again a contradiction appears, for Papadopoulos himself stated that they should concern themselves *exclusively* with their studies. Lacking any political orientation, they were simply not prepared to take up their duties as useful citizens when they came of age. They were even more disoriented than the previous generation.

Papadopoulos had his own personal weaknesses and contradictions. Instead of changing the Greek establishement, he tried to get it to accept him. Although clever in many ways, and cognizant of the problems facing the revolution, he lacked the determination to do what was needed. Although well informed, he became isolated from the sources of information. Although he uncovered corruption, he was unable or unwilling to curtail it. Constantly seeking the brilliant and extraordinary among men, he nevertheless accepted the amorphous and invisible ones.

Believing that he could get the best civilians into the forthcoming provisional government, he eased out the military. His plan was for a 'guided' democracy with himself as watchdog. In 1969 he had asked for a basic analysis of how the people could be educated for democracy and the assumption of their responsibilities as citizens: but, after the first steps had been taken in the schools, the teaching, instead of seeking to transmit democratic ideas and behaviour, reverted to the old emphasis on anti-communism and glorification of the revolution's birth.

If Papadopoulos had not been so slow to rid himself of his colleagues and had therefore been able to get his programme moving, he would probably still be ruling today. But by the time he decided to make his move, events had overtaken him. The economy had run into severe inflation and the students were on a rampage, as were some naval officers.

In May 1973, a conspiracy by Averoff, Garoufalias and a few naval officers was discovered. Although this was never proved, the King and Karamanlis were probably involved in it also. Their attempted coup was a total disaster. Everybody involved was arrested, with the exception of Captain Pappas, who sailed his cruiser *Velos* into Italian waters.

The conspirators had planned to restore Constantine to the throne. Instead, they lost it for him. Papadopoulos decided the time had come to renounce the King and declare a Republic. After acting like a lion in 1965 and like a hawk in

1967, Constantine turned into a lamb in 1973. He took no clear position over the coup, did not encourage or discourage dissidents, but finally spoke out against the Colonels when his royal stipend was about to be cut off by Papadopoulos.

As usual, the King was catastrophically advised. By keeping all his options open, he lost his influence through inactivity and indecision. Andreas was partly responsible since he made sure that no exiles threw in their lot with the King.

Six years having passed since the King had left the country, the abolition of the monarchy did not cause the reverberations it might have done if it had occurred earlier. On June 1st, 1973, the monarchy was formally abolished. A referendum was called, on July 30th, to ratify, not the abolition of the monarchy, but a new constitution eradicating all trace of it from the law of the land.

In this new constitution Papadopoulos included his own election as President of the Republic with extraordinary powers. This quite naturally raised an uproar, since his opponents regarded it as merely a ploy for one-man rule in the guise of democracy. The excessive constitutional authority assigned to the President also brought under his control vital sectors of national policy, including foreign policy and defence.

The 1973 constitutional referendum took place under strict surveillance by the foreign press corps and diplomatic observers. Ex-politicians visited their old constituencies and openly campaigned against Papadopoulos's presidency. In the rural areas many of them were told: 'We are tired of you politicians. We don't trust you. You only come around when you need our vote.'

The constitution abolishing the monarchy and electing Papadopoulos President and the retired General Anghelis Vice-President for a seven-year term was ratified by 78.4 per cent of the people. Although the voting in Athens against Papadopoulos reached 49 per cent, the rural areas were overwhelmingly for him. Despite the usual cries by the politicians that fraud had taken place, the referendum was probably one of the most honest ever held—by Greek standards.

Why did Papadopoulos win so handsomely? Because the Greeks always vote for the favourite, and no one seriously considered that a change could come about for a long time.

The result of the referendum buoyed him up. His secret information was that the ballot boxes had not been tampered with, and that the vote was a true indication of the people's mood. Whether or not this was correct or whether his informants were merely acting as sycophants remains a subject for discussion. Anyway, he accepted the outcome and acted accordingly.

The first all-civilian government, headed by the brilliant economist, Spyros Markezinis, was then named and told to prepare the country for elections within six months. As the head of a small conservative party Markezinis's fame was established through his ingenious fiscal policies, which had started Greece's post-war economic recovery. He is also a very successful historian and a great raconteur.

Before accepting the mandate Markezinis had requested Papadopoulos that a general amnesty should be granted. This was done by an extraordinary presidential order, under which amnesty was offered even to Alexander Panagoulis, the man who had tried to kill the junta leader in 1968. All other political and non-political persons who had been courtmartialed (under martial law all political offenses were brought before military tribunals for trial) for crimes against the regime whether inside the country or abroad were allowed to go free or to return as equal citizens. These included publishers Helen Vlachos and Panos Kokkas, Andreas Papandreou, Melina Mercouri and many more.

This was the high point of the Papadopoulos era. He had reverted to civilian rule against the opposition of his fellow officers, some of whom, like Ladas and Aslanides, objected violently to his retaining all the privileges while they were pensioned off.

But, despite this intricate and dangerous manoeuvre by Papadopoulos, despite the liberalization measures and the announcement of free elections within six months, the former politicians refused to participate in this first step towards a return to normality. Most of them were hostile to the Markezinis solution, seeing themselves left out, their positions of influence gone and their automatic election a thing of the past.

A few agreed that, in the circumstances, Markezinis should be welcomed. Elias Eliou, leader of the Communist front party, was one. So were Athanasiades Novas, an ex-Premier, and S. Stephanopoulos. George Rallis, the Minister of Public Order who had been caught unawares by the Colonels, concurred but with reservations. He was known to echo Karamanlis's wishes. These people all pressed Markezinis to persuade Papadopoulos to relinquish some of his extraordinary presidential powers, especially control of foreign policy and public order. As this was to be an 'informal' transfer, Papadopoulos agreed. He also pledged himself not to interfere with any of the workings of government or with a future revision of the constitution.

Papadopoulos's efforts toward normalization and a smooth transition to democracy were real and substantial. Trying hard not to alarm the army by his concessions to the politicians, he found himself caught between the Scylla of the politicians headed by Canellopoulos and Mavros, and the Charybdis of the hawks within the armed forces, who watched his balancing act with increasing disillusionment.

The dreams of many people who had believed in the revolution, and the hopes of others who saw in the Markezinis government a way out of military rule, were soon shattered. On November 25th, 1973, the forces of intolerance and authoritarianism, controlled by the ascetic Ioannides, were unleashed.

Under the pretext of memorial services for the late George Papandreou, called on November 11th, student political groups assembled inside the central cemetery of Athens. With martial law recently lifted and the right of free assembly restored, every ex-political leader attended. The Government had sent flowers. The speeches, however, were not memorial orations. They were straightforward political attacks on the Markezinis-Papadopoulos experiment, which was stigmatized as a fascist plot.

The police were kept at a discreet distance from the cemetery, with orders only to stop the crowds from demonstrating in downtown Athens. Many of the so-called 'mourners' were carrying clubs and were armed with stones. When they were ordered by the police to disperse peacefully after the service, a pitched battle began. The student groups were led by experienced provocateurs who immediately attacked the outnumbered police force with predictable results. The police overreacted, both sides were bloodied, and the new Government was embarrassed as pictures of police brutality were displayed in the recently uncensored press.

Markezinis, meanwhile, was preparing for a nation-wide televised press conference during which he intended to pledge himself to carry out really free elections with the participation of such hostile personalities as Andreas Papandreou, Melina Mercouri and Mikis Theodorakis. As this event was scheduled for November 17th it was a most inopportune moment for the demonstration. Worse still, perhaps, was the reaction of two veteran politicians, Canellopoulos and Mavros. Both of these supposedly honest and responsible political figures attacked the Markezinis government, while at the same time showing their approval of the student excesses and acting as if these were the spontaneous gestures of an enslaved people. They totally ignored the presence of provocateurs and the fact that both Papadopoulos and Markezinis were bending over backwards to satisfy the people.

Once again a historic opportunity was lost, and catastrophic consequences were to follow from this irresponsible behaviour by the ex-politicians. If a climate of understanding had prevailed then, democracy would have returned to Greece without a heavy price being paid, and probably with the same people who are now in the seats of power. Instead, democracy returned eight months later at the cost of thousands of dead and hundreds of thousands of homeless in Cyprus—developments which traumatized the Greek body politic for generations to come.

On Monday the 12th, students began to assemble at the Athens Polytechnic demanding, at first, certain freedoms connected with university life and going on to cries against the 'fascist' Government of Markezinis. By Tuesday and Wednesday the school had been taken over and the student body infiltrated by Maoist and other radical elements—and by military police, under the orders of Ioannides, who acted as provocateurs.

A small radio station went on the air from somewhere on the university campus demanding the resignation of the Government, and especially of Papadopoulos. The head of the Athens police force, Daskalopoulos, an intelligent and cultivated man, prevented his men from entering the school grounds and urged them not to react to provocation. But when a bus full of military officers crossed the avenue adjoining the campus, it was immediately encircled by the students; officers were spat upon and their families terrorized. Finally, the whole avenue was taken over by the youthful demonstrators.

The Government throughout acted with patience. Although it could have silenced the radio station by jamming and starved out the students by isolating the area without infringing upon the inviolability of the university grounds, it chose to wait. By Thursday, even the Athenian middle classes had begun to turn against the students, who increased their demands every time a glimpse of a rapprochement appeared. Some of the students understood what was happening in their midst, and approached professors and politicians for advice. They were told either to purge their committees of radical elements or to leave the school instead of supporting the extremist demands by their presence. On the other hand, Canellopoulos advised just the opposite. He said that the demonstrations should continue, and so should the escalation of demands.

By Friday the 16th, student mobs were rampaging in the streets of Athens, beating up officers, overturning cars, setting fire to buses and commandeering private vehicles. They eventually succeeded in entering the building which housed the Ministry of Public Order.

By midnight Athens was a shambles, with store windows broken, overturned buses serving as barricades, ambulances taken over by the mob, fires burning on the central avenues. Police units reporting from various parts of the city claimed that they could not control the situation. (Tapes of these calls are available and were submitted to the public prosecutor, who later investigated the uprising and the ensuing battle.)

Around 11 p.m. on Friday, Chief of Police Daskalopoulos called General Mavroides, commander of A.S.D.E.N. (High Military Command of Athens), asking for army assistance. Mavroides communicated with the Joint Chief of Staff, General Zagorianakos, who approved but requested a written application.

Upon receiving the request Zagorianakos called Papadopoulos at his villa outside Athens, and secured his approval as well. Markezinis was then told of the police demand, and he too reluctantly approved.

Since Tuesday there had been contingency plans for a possible intervention. Armoured units from Goudhi and rangers from Megalo Pefko, under the command of Lieutenant-Colonels Makrigeorgos and Misailides, were made ready and moved toward the city. The lead tank from Goudhi under Captain Stathakis reached the school just after midnight. It stopped facing the main gate with other armour alongside it. The students were then ordered to disperse with a promise that safe conduct would be given to all, but this they did not believe. They shouted back: 'Fascists down, freedom for the people!' After waiting for two hours, one tank advanced toward the main gate, spun swiftly around and, in reverse, backed up into the gate, crushing it beneath its treads. Then the commandos rushed in.

I was one of five newsmen who went in behind the tank. I mention this fact because the wildest and most misleading rumours followed that incident. Some members of the foreign press corps described the assault on the polytechnic as a massacre; but the truth is different. For the two hours during which the tanks lay waiting in front of the school, U.P.I., A.P., Reuters and Japan Television correspondents, plus an Italian journalist, took cover behind them. Scattered shots were directed at the tanks but no one could tell for sure where they were coming from. Many times the foreign pressmen had to duck for cover. After the gate was breached, the commandos cleared out the campus with no brutality, without even roughing up a student.

What did occur was that the police who were waiting outside attacked and beat up many students. No one was killed or injured inside the walls of the school, and the twenty-five dead were mostly innocent victims of random shooting in the air by troops and police, and also by provocateurs from various extremist organizations, including the military police, who wanted to create a bloody and chaotic situation. (The Government claimed that only thirteen people died. All in all, twenty-five dead have been accounted for. Most of them had gunshot wounds entering the upper parts of their bodies and exiting in an upward arc, proving that they were shot from below. This was because the unfortunate victims had been outside, on terraces or at windows, trying to see the demonstration and the pitched battles below in the centre of the crowded city. The constant firing in the air produced probably 75 per cent of the victims, the other 25 per cent occurring when provocateurs and army troops fired into crowds.)

Not a single polytechnic student died, although rumours swept Athens that hundreds had been buried in mass graves inside the university campus. Throughout Saturday and Sunday isolated incidents took place, but the reimposition of martial law and a dusk-to-dawn curfew kept people off the streets. Cleverly circulated rumours, however, continued to spread, increasing the number of dead in mass graves all around Athens. It is true that the exhausted and outnumbered police did rough up many youths in the ensuing two days, as hundreds were arrested or pulled in for questioning. But after routine checks they were all allowed to go free.

Although not responsible for Public Order at the time, Markezinis assumed full responsibility in a nation-wide address on the following Wednesday. He later testified that his efforts to put down the Polytechnic uprising had only one goal in mind—not to allow the army's hawks and hardliners to exploit the situation and topple his regime before the elections. He was right. The students had played straight into the hands of Ioannides, who looked upon the coming elections with a jaundiced eye. So had the irresponsible statements of Canellopoulos and Mavros, two vain self-seeking men. So did the accounts in most of the Greek and foreign press, which backed the students' demands as if they were the normal, everyday complaints of students everywhere. No-one except Markezinis realized the consequences until too late; least of all Papadopoulos, who assured Markezinis that martial law would be lifted soon, and then the elections could take place as if nothing had happened. History will probably be kind to Markezinis, because no-one tried harder to serve his country at a historic moment. Having stood accused of high treason, he was exonerated by the Supreme Court, as were the members of his Government; a landmark decision.

On Sunday November 25th, Papadopoulos was awakened before dawn by a call from his personal guard, who told him that tanks were reported approaching Lagonissi. He lived in a villa rented from Aristotle Onassis on the easternmost shores of the Attic peninsula, near the temple of Sounion.

Soon afterwards Papadopoulos found that his lines of communication had been cut. He was simultaneously informed by his special guard post, situated ten kilometres away along the road leading to the villa, that armour was advancing towards the nearest village. Preparing for battle, his guards and his private chauffeur advised him to escape. The President demurred. He dressed quietly, told his wife not to worry, and instructed a guard to take care of her children, who were staying with them at the time.

In a few minutes the first tank appeared, from which descended Lieutenant-Colonel Douzepis, who saluted him and announced: 'Your Government has resigned. I have orders to keep you under house arrest, as the armed forces have decided to intervene.'

Papadopoulos smiled at the obviously embarrassed Douzepis. 'Is Ioannides behind all this?' he asked.

'You will be informed through the television network, sir,' was the reply.

Throughout Athens similar scenes were taking place. Joint Chief of Staff Zagorianakos, roused from his bed, was furious and called the arresting officer a traitor. Markezinis simply smiled, perhaps remembering the elder Papandreou's enigmatic gesture eight years earlier. Anghelis, the Vice-President, an austere and honest soldier, asked no questions and with a look of disgust, returned to bed.

One more bloodless coup had taken place. Once again, in the dead of night, tanks had rumbled into the streets of Athens, and soldiers with fixed bayonets had surrounded strategic government buildings. The coup had been fast and efficient. The first indication Athenians had that anything out of the ordinary had taken place was when they picked up their telephones on Sunday morning. People who ventured into the streets were politely told to go home. No newspapers circulated. Finally, around 11 a.m. an announcement came over the radio. 'Papadopoulos betrayed the ideals of the 1967 revolution,' it said, 'by dragging the country into an electoral adventure. Since conditions are not yet ripe for such a move, the armed forces, obeying the supreme law of the land and desiring to save the country, have decided to intervene.'

In a televised ceremony from the old parliament building, the new President, General Phaidon Gizikis, was sworn in by Archbishop Seraphim of Ioannina. Gizikis, an austere, honest-to-the-bone, aristocratic-looking officer, was fifty-five years old and commanding the First Army Corps when he was summoned by Ioannides to accept this position. He was assured that the country's affairs would be put in order and honest elections held within two years.

Incredibly, most of the politicians rejoiced. Canellopoulos, Rallis, Mavros, even Averoff, put out statements praising the armed forces' intervention. So did Andreas Papandreou and Helen Vlachos. These approving statements were proof of the unrealistic, self-seeking attitude of the people who made them, of their hate for Papadopoulos, and their fear of him, because, even under a democratic system, he could expose them to the public as the political midgets they really were. Their resentment at having been excluded from positions of privilege and power blinded them to such an extent that they saw Ioannides as a saviour.

They were soon to be bitterly disappointed. In fact, the moment the new cabinet was sworn in, under the premiership of the nonentity, Amandios Androutsopoulos, most people understood.

From that moment on, Greece's fortunes began an inexorable decline to culminate in July of the following year with the Cyprus débâcle. The economic crisis which had begun with the Yom Kippur War hit the Greek balance of payments very severely. Suddenly the boom was over, and a grey and amorphous government could do nothing to calm the people's fears. Opponents of the regime trembled under a new reign of terror, with the military police cracking down on every possible liberal institution. Torture became an everyday occurrence; hundreds of people were arrested and thousands deported to Aegean islands.

American support for the regime quickly turned to hostility, particularly after all efforts by the American Ambassador to lead Ioannides towards a more liberal attitude had come to nothing. Just before the Cyprus coup, two C.I.A. men met Ioannides. In his capacity as head of the military police, he was unavailable to the American Ambassador and other dignitaries, whose contacts with the regime were confined to his puppets. The C.I.A. men confronted Ioannides with reports which had filtered out that something was being prepared in Cyprus.

'We ought to warn you, Brigadier, that if anything should happen in Cyprus which provoked Turkish intervention, our Government will not only remain neutral, but will take an extremely unsympathetic view of your position,' they told him.

'I understand,' he replied, 'and I assure you that nothing is going to happen.'

Papadopoulos's dream of a new Greece had collapsed as ignominiously as his rule. People today blame his fall on his continued faith in Ioannides, his willingness to let Ioannides encourage spartan, puritanical and extremist views inside the army. That is probably correct, but the problem goes much deeper.

By the time Papadopoulos had consolidated his power in early 1968, his contacts with the army had gradually diminished. In a sense, he chose to ignore the army, correctly relegating the officers to a position outside that of policy-making. With General Anghelis as his second-in-command he felt secure. But, below the top echelons, middle-rank officers at corps and divisional level were coming together under the ideological umbrella of the hard-eyed ascetic Ioannides. Like King Constantine before him, Papadopoulos became a remote figure to them. Officers heard of his dining with industrialists and shipowners, but were themselves unable to obtain even a five-minute interview. Like the politicians he replaced, he had become a typical member of the Establishment, that hated institution.

Ioannides, however, never changed. Throughout the junta period, and even during his own brief reign, he continued to associate only with brother officers. He secured their promotions, cared for their families, seemed void of personal ambition and shunned all publicity.

Another reason why Papadopoulos was overthrown appeared in the case of the Polytechnic. The army saw its role of policemen as a shameful one, a disgrace, causing it to lose prestige among the people. Although the Ioannides group included no more than forty officers, the army followed these new leaders wholeheartedly after Papadopoulos was overthrown.

It is a paradox of democratic life that the measures Papadopoulos took to liberalize and democratize his regime precipitated his fall. In particular, the granting of political amnesty—and with it the possibility that Andreas and others like him could return to power—alienated many officers. Many of these purists had begun, during the last years, to consider Papadopoulos himself and his Ministers corrupt, because of what the purists saw as their extravagant way of living. Under the Ioannides regime attempts were made to expose corruption, and some trials took place, but without any convincing result.

The Polytechnic 'revolt' was magnified by the Left; understandably, since this was the only overt act of mass resistance in seven years. It should be noted, however, that the 'revolt' took place under conditions of constitutional freedom, after the lifting of martial law, and with the assistance both of Maoists and of Ioannides's secret agents.

How will history judge Papadopoulos? Probably he will be forgotten. Since the junta came to power through force of arms, invoking high principles for the good of the country, its failure must be judged harshly.

This failure had crucial implications for many people. For those who saw the Colonels as agents of a rapid socio-economic transformation, it meant disillusionment, which resulted eventually in the withdrawal of their support. For the politicians, it confirmed their belief that they alone were capable of ruling the nation, and that the army should confine itself to barracks. The politicians had learned nothing. They reappeared waging the same political feuds, making the same irresponsible speeches, forgetful of past excesses, eager once more to dominate, divide, and rule.

There were implications, too, for historians and political observers. For them, the revolution never established its legitimacy because it did not succeed. Had the Colonels managed to implement their original objectives, the regime's place in history would have been secure.

Why did Papadopoulos fail? Because he was reluctant to dismantle the political system, to root out old ideas and a corrupt mentality. How could he have done so? Perhaps by creating a political party which opened its doors to the young, those with new ideas, the politically active, irrespective of past beliefs; and then proceeding to parliamentary elections, which he would easily have won. Once legitimized, his regime would then have attracted the educated and talented men whose support he tried so hard, but failed, to gain; failed because they were afraid of being associated with a dictatorial regime. As Papadopoulos had always insisted, the creation of its own party by the regime smacked too much of the totalitarian Third World or the one-party system of Communist countries.

This reluctance of the Colonels, in the beginning, to decide on the exact nature of their regime prevented the people from participating. Stressing rather its temporary, provisional character, the revolution thus alienated an important segment of the population, who preferred to wait and see. Then, after a few years in power, Papadopoulos and his colleagues lost their commitment to change, and preferred to compromise instead.

Finally, the Colonels succumbed to the old Greek habit of nepotism. Favouritism became rampant, and many able professional people and politicians were excluded, because of their past beliefs, in favour of incompetent persons, known to be reliable and close to the Colonels. By 1972 the same climate of boot-licking and patronage as had existed before once again imbued the life of the nation.

The military assumed power without having any clear programme of economic and social reform. They ruled for seven years without ever formulating one. Their firm belief was that love of country, honesty, and fear of God were enough for success. Every great period in a nation's history has depended on some spiritual awakening, rather than an economic miracle: but Papadopoulos and the Colonels thought that by lining the pockets of the people with money they would gain the respect they wanted and mass support for the 'revolution'. It was not enough. The spiritual revolution never took place, because the Colonels lacked the nerve to try.

PART V

Chapter 14

Epilogue

IT would have taken a Hollywood screenwriter to conjure up as triumphal a return as the one Karamanlis and democracy staged together when the junta disintegrated. The audience would then have been left to believe that the tortured nation afterwards proceeded steadily toward a better life, with a smooth-running, viable democracy brought forth and cherished by the people because of the lessons they had learned.

Greece's fortunes, it is true, took a turn for the better, but Cyprus came once again into the forefront of the news, overshadowing Karamanlis's return and the restoration of democracy. After forming a Government of National Unity which encompassed most of the political personalities of the past, Karamanlis sent his Foreign Minister and Deputy Premier, George Mavros, to Geneva for talks with the Turkish and British Foreign Ministers.

There Mavros failed miserably. Basking in the limelight of publicity, full of importance and blind to reality, Mavros fell for a Turkish trap. Having rejected outright the acceptable terms offered at first—as the Turks knew he would—Mavros then watched helplessly as they left the conference table and proceeded to overrun 40 per cent of the island with their armour and troops.

Thus 200,000 Greek-Cypriots became refugees and are now living in squalid camps in the south, while the richest and most developed part of the island fell into the hands of 40,000 Turkish soldiers. Citrus fields in the north, producing the island's main export and wealth, came under Attila's boot, while tourism, the second industry, was suddenly extinguished.

Hundreds of new hotels, tourist complexes and resorts were taken over by Turkish soldiers; homes were ransacked for any articles of value and properties confiscated. It was an unprecedented disaster. An island with one of the highest standards of living in the area was turned into a huge refugee camp overnight.

Nonetheless, Greece could not help her Cypriot brothers. Her only reaction was to leave N.A.T.O., charging it with responsibility for the Turkish excesses. (Greece left the military arm of N.A.T.O.; she remained within the alliance, in the French mould.) Karamanlis had vowed not to go to war over Cyprus and when, in August, the second Turkish attack came, he had barely set up a Government and was still trying to consolidate his power over the army.

Karamanlis headed a newly-formed party called the New Democracy. Its political orientation was Centre-Right and it encompasses many new faces from the progressive wing of the Right, as well as many old ones. The Centre Union, led by George Mavros, was joined within its ranks by a left-of-centre group calling itself New Political Forces. Andreas Papandreou, who has caused more controversy and aroused more passion than any other man in modern Greek history, returned triumphantly to head the Panhellenic Socialist Movement, whose ideology at times was to the left even of the Communists.

The Communist Party was legalized and, although split into three factions, presented a common front in the elections that occurred in October of 1974. Under the reinforced proportional system Karamanlis and his New Democracy Party scored the greatest victory ever, by winning 54 per cent of the vote in a landslide which gave him 220 deputies out of 300. The election will undoubtedly go down in history as the fairest poll since Greek independence.

In November of that year a referendum was held concerning the monarchy. Again it was probably the fairest one ever held in the country. Constantine was soundly defeated, receiving only 31 per cent of the vote. Although no ballot-tampering took place for or against the King, a psychological atmosphere of terror was created by the Left against his return. Constantine himself had to campaign through television tapes which he sent from London. Despite the abolition of the monarchy, one-third of the population remain hard-core royalists, so the King cannot be totally excluded from the nation's future.

Two months after having been invited by the army to take up the reins of government Karamanlis had dismantled the main junta apparatus and brought the armed forces under political control again.

Moreover, he had dismissed some 125,000 local government officials appointed during the seven-year period and suspended hundreds of professors and judges, pending investigation of their activities under the junta.

Life does not always produce a screenwriter's happy ending. Despite the enormous social, political and economic problems facing the country after the restoration of democracy and the Cyprus débâcle, the business of retribution—rather than reconstruction—dominated its everyday life.

Given the fact that the army handed over power voluntarily, and considering the Government's absolute majority in Parliament, the administration inexplicably allowed a most disruptive and divisive campaign to rake the nation's institutions once again. The entire country was split into juntists and anti-juntists.

At the centre of the drive to purge everyone and anyone who had come into contact with the junta was, naturally, Andreas Papandreou, whose party came in third after the Centre Union (20 per cent) with 13 per cent of the vote. The Communists got 9 per cent.

The press, too, had not mended its ways. It came back after censorship as bad as it was before. As the Minister of Information, Panayotis Lambrias, put it, 'The Greek press is once again the yellowest in the world.' Lambrias was not exaggerating. Under the banner of freedom of expression it denied the right of free speech to anyone who didn't agree with the witch-hunts which charged thousands of people with collaboration. Press reports dealing with collaboration distorted facts and trampled upon the rights of citizens who had not even been accused in the courts.

What constituted collaboration was never clearly defined. Many individuals took advantage of the spirit of the times to accuse their political or business opponents. Anyone who had collaborated with the Greek officers was compared by Andreas and the Communists with those who had worked for the invading German hordes during the occupation.

Harilaos Florakis, a notorious Communist guerrilla accused of several killings, sat in Parliament as an elected member while many patriotic Greeks were about to be excluded from the centre of power and influence for having believed the Colonels.

A better solution to the problem of a national cleansing would have been for the courts to decide. But the Government gave in to the Opposition and acted in an unconstitutional manner by infringing upon the rights of the judiciary, which had appointed a committee to study the facts of collaboration. A parliamentary decision pre-empted the judiciary's findings and declared the April 21st coup illegal, that it had never established or created legality, and that it was a regime of oppression. (No-one doubted the first and last propositions, but what about having established legality? Were the children born during that period illegitimate? Were pensioners illegal recipients? Were civil servants and jurists, professors and diplomats, promoted during the seven year period, supposed to be demoted?) Therefore, under this act, the amnesty of July 26th, 1974, became null and void. Every person who had come into contact with the 1967–1974 regime in any way was liable to persecution.

Many of the thousands dismissed from their jobs because of charges of collaboration obviously felt that they were being unfairly dealt with.

'If every baker stopped selling bread, every shopkeeper closed his shop, every pensioner refused his pension, then we would have been wrong in working with the Colonels,' was their point of view. 'But they did not. How were we to sur-vive—we who deal with the Government or work for it?' Others went even further. 'The politicians are mostly rich, or at least well-off. They could afford to do nothing for seven years. The Communist Party took care of its own; Papandreou did not starve when in exile, journalists worked and then had the excuse that censorship had been imposed. But who was supposed to take care of us?'

It is undoubtedly and tragically true that most of the charges of collaboration came from hypocritical people hoping to profit from them. Many professors who left their positions during the junta period for reasons of age or inability were now charging those who were appointed on merit. The same happened in the business sector. Businesses are being deprived of loans already agreed upon by the Bank of Greece because charges of gift-loans by the junta are being investigated.

All this has merely shaken the confidence of the people even more. 'The old system of "to the victor belong the spoils" is back again,' was the way some people put it. Others ask: 'How can we believe in our country when, no matter what happens and which Government comes in, past agreements and contracts can be declared null and void?'

Karamanlis probably did not intend to pursue such a policy; but, oversensitive to criticism that he had previously governed with an iron fist, he is now bending over backwards to avoid arbitrariness in government. Andreas, the Communists and the leftist press have all understood this, and are taking maximum advantage of the situation by spreading the most vicious, scurrilous and untrue rumours against anyone or anything that stands in their way.

To avoid being called a Fascist the best tactic is to denounce someone else in louder terms. Skeletons in closets remain, however, and most of the Members of Parliament who demanded a national cleansing, and much of the press too, have ample skeletons of their own lying around.

When anybody charged with corruption during the junta period, or of collaboration—as in the case of Markezinis, was found to be innocent, the howls by the anti-juntist group turned the public's attention away from the verdict and against the courts. The opposition newspapers, claiming to be defenders of democracy and the rule of law, actually trampled on such principles by accusing justice itself of being fraudulent, and have thus established a dangerous precedent.

Greece's good fortune in moving from a dictatorship to a democracy without bloodshed is being squandered by the extremists, who are trying to prevent Karamanlis from implementing his programmes. The purging process became a unique opportunity to advance schemes, or serve interests and ambitions, which had nothing to do with the ostensible purpose. One might say that a new Establishment was created, that of the anti-juntists, a group with essentially negative motives.

Papadopoulos, Pattakos, Makarezos and Ioannides were accused of high treason because of the April 21st coup and jailed, as were many of their collaborators. Ioannides was also charged with responsibility for the Cyprus débâcle. Both charges carried the death penalty.

The epilogue to a dictatorship was written in a hall of the women's section of Greece's showpiece jail, the Athens Korydallos Prison. In all, some 300 top men, officers and civilians, were to be tried on various charges. Top billing in a cast of fallen stars went to Papadopoulos and Ioannides.

The trial was held before the Athens five-member Court of Appeals, presided over by Judge Deyannis.

Papadopoulos set the tone of the defence. His once jet-black hair now streaked with grey, his face disfigured by boils, the fallen dictator said that, while he assumed 'full responsibility' for the April 21st revolution, he refused to defend himself. Following suit, Pattakos, Makarezos, Ioannides and the rest declared that they would not participate in the trial either. They all accepted responsibility for their actions. They all declared they were proud to have taken part in the coup.

Defence lawyers justified their clients' attitude on the grounds that the Karamanlis Government had prejudged the case by retroactively declaring the 1967 coup to have been a criminal offence. They said too that the trial was being conducted in a climate of terror and violence.

Whether there was terror and violence may be debatable. What is certain is that the Colonels' unpopularity rendered a fair trial impossible. Extremely bellicose press reports concerning defence witnesses made sure that none of these witnesses could feel safe. Editorials even warned jurists that any penalty less than the maximum would be unacceptable.

That the Colonels were railroaded, their case prejudged, the amnesty granted to them ignored, is undisputable, even if there was poetic justice in seeing Papadopoulos and his colleagues in the dock after having sent so many of their fellow countrymen to trial and prison.

The moral problem arises: should a democratically elected government use methods and ukases like those of the dictatorship it replaced, no matter how well deserved by the dictators? Is excess in defence of liberty no vice? Should a sovereign government compromise the rights of citizens, no matter how unpopular, in order to appease the majority—or rather to appease a vociferous faction? Are political trials ever fair? Have they ever stood the test of time?

When the trial of the Colonels was first announced, democratic and freedom-loving people inside and outside the country applauded. But, as usual in Greece, a positive action was compromised by the instinct of expediency.

The legal ball was set rolling when a lawyer with a sharp eye for publicity sued Papadopoulos and the others for high treason. His action was emulated and soon snowballed into countless suits by lawyers, doctors, professors, civil servants, military personnel and ordinary citizens with past grievances against anyone remotely connected with the Colonels' government. The press gave unlimited coverage to these legal actions, and encouraged the ploy.

Seven major trials, and countless smaller ones, were scheduled. They involved charges of torture and of responsibility for the Cyprus débâcle, for the Polytechnic 'massacre,' for the conspiracy to revolt by thirty-five officers in February 1975, for a variety of unsubstantiated economic scandals, and, finally, for a long list of suspected killings and disappearances which had occurred during the seven years.

The trials began in July 1975 and were still continuing in the autumn of 1976. A Statute of Limitations declared by the Government raised an immediate howl of protest from the press. In the forefront of the people who clamoured for retribution rather than unity, forgiveness and reconstruction were the Communists and Papandreou.

Karamanlis was known to be against the trials, mainly because of their political nature. Having eradicated all junta influence within the nation's institutions, he favoured a 'let bygones be bygones' solution—which would not, however, include charges of torture and economic scandal. But, despite his popularity and power, he did nothing to stem the avalanche of demands for retribution which came from individuals trying to further their own political interests. To have done so would have been politically unwise, but courageous and necessary.

The Greek Nuremberg, as the trial of the twenty-eight principals in the 1967 coup was dubbed, was the first to begin.

Deyannis, the presiding judge, got rave notices from the press when he treated the accused with scorn while conducting himself in an imperious manner. He also allowed the publicity-seeking actress Melina Mercouri to assault Ioannides, spit on him and insult him, to the delight of the audience. Deyannis had risen to his present position during the junta period through the mass firing of judges by Papadopoulos when they refused to obey his orders and condemn certain liberal dissenters. After the trial Deyannis said that he hoped the exemplary punishment would discourage future coups by the military. That theory, however, is debatable. Out of some thirty-two coups which have taken place in Greece during her modern history, all except the 1967 one were ordered either by politicians who had come second in an election or by Generals for or against the King. If this pattern is not to continue, Greeks should perhaps take a closer look at England or the United States, where a defeated politician either goes quietly to the back-benches and provides loyal opposition, or retires from public life without trying to wreck the system which threw him out of office.

The main issue of the trial was whether or not the Colonels had in fact seized power illegally in 1967. Although the accused refused to defend themselves, and did not co-operate with the court-appointed lawyers, defence counsel reminded the judges that the Colonels' superior officer, the Joint Chief of Staff, Spandidakis, had approved and even joined the coup. Evidence that the Colonels had set up a legal government was unexpectedly reinforced by the testimony of a prosecution witness.

Panayotis Canellopoulos, the Premier from whom the Colonels took power by force, stated at the trial that no less a figure than King Constantine had legitimized the Colonels' rule. Canellopoulos, a man who had grovelled in front of the King in the past, expertly and conveniently forgot his former relationship by presenting Constantine as a weakling and a coward. The fact that the King acted as he did in order to avoid bloodshed went unappreciated. And Constantine's plan at the time—to rid himself of the Colonels at a more propitious moment—was never mentioned. The opposition press had a field day, pillorying the King and hinting that he was a fellow-conspirator with the Colonels. (Editorial writers, especially in the Lambrakis chain, could claim immunity for collaboration because of the knife-at-the-throat menace. The King was allowed no such excuse.)

Canellopoulos's testimony undermined the charge of insurrection. Moreover, during the prosecution evidence, it became clear that Premier Karamanlis himself had tacitly accepted the junta's legitimacy. It was the junta which summoned Karamanlis back to Greece to form a government, and it was a President appointed by the hardliners of the Ioannides faction which swore Karamanlis in as Premier.

Thus the charges of insurrection were discredited despite the testimony of many high-ranking Generals who held important posts just prior to the 1967 coup. They told of being arrested at gun-point and kept in the 'Pentagon' against their will.

But the accusation of high treason—for acting against the national interest—was strengthened when Andreas Papandreou's turn came to testify. Andreas claimed irrefutable proof that the Colonels took direct orders from the C.I.A. and the American Ambassador. His proof was his word. The press had another field day.

Most of the politicians who testified claimed that the nation was sailing along on calm waters when the Colonels interfered. It became obvious, however, that the Right had been preparing a coup of its own, although a broad coalition of personalities and factions—in other words the Establishment—was alleged to have been in favour of it.

What also became obvious was that the Colonels were the offspring of a tightly spun fabric of vested insterests, which had controlled the nation since the end of the Communist revolt by brandishing the threat of an impending Red takeover.

The prosecution accused the junta of having plotted for a long time to seize power by means of violence and fraud. The very people who accused them, however, were the ones who had encouraged them, in fact brainwashed them, for decades; people like Helen Vlachos, Canellopoulos, Karamanlis, Papagos, the industrialists, the Palace and the press lords. The trial ended at 1:30 p.m. on Saturday, August 23rd, 1975. The verdicts were read before a crowd that listened with bated breath. 'Death, cashiering, life imprisonment—Death, cashiering, life imprisonment—Death, cashiering, life imprisonment—.' The same sentence, the supreme penalty, for each of the three leaders. The three men heard their death sentences imperturbably and with remarkable *sang froid*.

Papadopoulos tightened the grip of his hands on the arms of his chair. Ioannides heard his life sentence with an enigmatic half-smile, Spandidakis with visible emotion. The patrician General Hadjipetros was acquitted, along with ex-Colonel Karydas, but neither man showed any emotion, perhaps in deference to the others.

Judge Deyannis asked the prisoners to stand and, if they wished, to address the court. No-one spoke. The trial ended in total silence.

Almost immediately the Government commuted their sentences. 'In a democracy,' the communiqué said, 'justice is an independent and constitutionally protected function. However, the constitution allows the Government to commute the sentences. In the final analysis, what must prevail is a feeling of high political responsibility.'

This vague statement underlined the general feeling that the court had been heavily swayed by a hysterical press and by the self-serving testimony of dubious witnesses with political futures to protect.

Beside the three principals, eight defendants were sentenced to life imprisonment: Ioannides, Spandidakis, Zoetakis, Ladas, Costas Papadopoulos, Roufogalis, Lekkas and Balopoulos. The court imposed jail sentences ranging from five to twenty years on the rest. Two went free. The giant Constandopoulos, who had stormed the 'Pentagon' with his paratroopers, got twelve. He sneered at the sentence. 'I fought three wars for this country,' he said afterwards, 'and it took Greeks to call me a traitor.'

Two of the convicted Colonels, Aslanides and Kotselis, were tried *in absentia*. They had read the writing on the wall and left the country once democracy was restored. (Aslanides was being held in prison in Genoa. The Italians finally had to release him because there was no evidence for the accusations of fraud.)

At a separate torture trial it was proved beyond reasonable doubt that there had been maltreatment of prisoners. Beatings, threats, deprivations and humiliations took place. But it was also proved that torture was not a policy originating from the top. It was practised by stupid, bestial and ignorant officers who allowed the lowest human traits to get the better of them. But, once again, the horror of their deeds was compromised by the many false statements of prosecution witnesses. People who had been seen walking around normally two days later claimed to have been tortured, testifying, for example, that 'one hundred soldiers beat me for twenty hours non-stop with metal sticks.' And a few, under cross-examination by the defence, admitted that the leaders of dissident organizations had ordered them to testify and told them what to say.

In the main torture trial, which took place in August 1975, the leaders of the dreaded military police, as well as a few ordinary police officers, were tried. Of thirty-one men accused sixteen were convicted. Sentences ranged from twenty-eight years to eighteen months. Theophyloyianakos, Hadzizisis and Spanos were the main culprits and received the heaviest sentences.

Other torture trials followed, in Salonica, Halkis, Patras, Athens and Crete. So far 120 people have been charged, of whom seventy-six were convicted and thirty acquitted.

These figures are only approximate. In listing all the torture charges, I found sixty-four people accused, seventy-six convictions and thirty acquitals. This is because many E.S.A.—that is, military police—officers were tried two or three times on different charges. Juggling the figures in order to suit any particular purpose thus becomes easy.

So how many people were in fact tortured? The answer can

only be a guess. Many never came forward to testify, fearing reprisals if the junta returned. On the other hand, just as many made bogus claims. In order to reach even an approximate number, one has to settle for the number of prosecution witnesses who claimed torture and whose testimony stood up. This is 120.

In order to examine properly the 'torture in Greece' issue, which preoccupied the foreign press, the Council of Europe and Amnesty International so intensely, two elements must be separated—the actual cases of torture, and the exaggerations about torture during and after the Colonels' regime. There was undoubtedly a certain amount of torture—but probably no more and no less than that had been used previously by Greek security services on criminals, and, in some cases, on Communists. (The behaviour of the E.S.A. is a different matter, which will be discussed presently.) The Greek police have always applied brutal tactics, more so than other European security services. In particular they roughed up young Communists before 1967, hoping to bring some of them 'back to their senses'. Paradoxically they never used beatings or any kind of torture on hardened convicts, for the simple reason that such men were either collaborating with the authorities or were too tough to break.

During the dictatorship a number of bourgeois or non-communist politicians were arrested and treated as 'enemies of society'. Hardly any of them were mistreated but the shock of being put into a dirty police cell along with real criminals, and of being made to give information about other people, was such that they eagerly seized any opportunity to revenge themselves on the men who had humiliated them. (The guilt of having given away fellow-resisters without actually having been tortured seems to be the main reason for exaggeration.)

During the trials that followed the fall of the junta, the only people who spoke of bad treatment and torture were those involved in bomb explosions. Only three of them bore scars.

Where the military police was concerned it was a different story. People under interrogation were first given a systematic dose of terror, and if that didn't work (in nine cases out of ten it did), beatings followed. For example, Demitrios Tsatsos, a respected professor and now a Member of Parliament for the Centre Union, a man in his middle thirties, testified about the conditions of his arrest. He called the E.S.A. headquarters where he was held a 'Greek Dachau'—which earned banner headlines in foreign newspapers, especially the *The Guardian.* He described how he was ordered to stand at attention, and how, after twenty minutes of that, he heard screams coming from the next room. Weeping, Tsatsos admitted that he then spilled everything he knew. Horrible as this treatment may be, applied to a civilized and intelligent person like Tsatsos, it was not exactly vintage Dachau.

In some cases, however, people were indeed given a very tough time. The heroic Alexander Panagoulis, Anastasios Minis and the unfortunate Moustaklis were three genuine resisters, who did not embellish the story of their sufferings. They were tortured, beaten and mistreated, but never broke. Typically, Panagoulis understated his role both as a resister and as the recipient of inhuman treatment. The same is true of Minis, a courageous officer. Moustaklis developed a blood-clot while being beaten, and is partially paralyzed as well as having a speech impediment.

Most victims of E.S.A. torture were military officers plotting against the regime or setting off bombs, although the publicity has concentrated on the tribulations of dissident politicians and intellectuals.

Exaggerations about the use of torture were partly an excuse for the fact that there was very little organized resistance to the Colonels' regime, and that almost none of the organizers escaped arrest, imprisonment or collaboration in the end. Greeks are now busy re-writing history, with countless serials in the press telling heroic tales of the resistance. But wishful thinking does not change the facts.

That torture was not institutionalized during the Papadopoulos regime became obvious during the trials. The worst excesses took place from the winter of 1973 onwards, and even those were perpetuated by only a few sadistic officers. The sentences meted out were mostly for having 'struck, abused or mistreated superiors', not for any systematic use of torture.

Countless other trials were held simultaneously, on charges of conspiracy, police brutality and on individual complaints. During the Polytechnic trial, foreign journalists who had covered the uprising from the beginning were never called to testify: Andreas Papandreou, however, who had been touring the Western Hemisphere at the time, was.

Andreas used this platform to attack the Government for being soft on the junta, and to attack the United States for causing all the ills that have ever befallen Greece. He charged the Americans with having plotted and assisted both the April 21st coup and the July 15th Cyprus coup. His accusation that Papadopoulos and the Colonels were paid members of the C.I.A. was echoed by the press and soon believed by the majority of Greeks.

A self-confessed Communist millionaire publisher began an afternoon daily paper, which quickly captured the people's imagination with its virulent anti-American line. Along with the Lambrakis chain of papers and the two Communist dailies that serve as mouthpieces for the Greek Communist Parties, it not only echoed Andreas's charges but depicted the United States as an imperialist, cynical giant endlessly plotting to keep Greece under its influence through a succession of Quising regimes. (Greeks are notorious for their lack of realism about themselves. In ancient times the gods were to blame for their self-induced disasters. Now, it is the United States and the C.I.A. Humiliation over Cyprus and guilt feelings over the junta period were easily wiped away by the belief that America had supported the Colonels—and later the Turks. The Watergate story was unfolding as democracy returned to Greece; the search for scapegoats coincided with the exposure of dirty tricks by the C.I.A.; the pieces fitted neatly.)

The left-wing press was not alone in its condemnation of America. Even traditional pro-westerners like Helen Vlachos joined the anti-American bandwagon. Mrs. Vlachos returned from exile and re-opened her morning newspaper. During her exile she had been an outspoken critic of the Colonels and an ally of the exiled King. She wrote a book about her house arrest in which she described Karamanlis as a respected politician, admired by the Greeks who saw him fleetingly and from afar. 'But he had come to be disliked by his colleagues for his conceit and mounting stubbornness. He was completely self-centred, and unburdened by any feeling of gratitude towards anybody. He demanded flattery, held a certain disdain for friends and resented the slightest criticism.' Mrs. Vlachos had been instrumental in bringing down Karamanlis through her alliance with the Palace. During her exile she resented the fact that Karamanlis did not oppose the Colonels more actively. When she re-opened her paper, she strongly backed the King. Once Karamanlis was elected in a landslide, however, and the King had lost in the referendum, she turned anti-monarchist and pro-Karamanlis. The Premier nominated her to Parliament as one of the twelve non-elected deputies. Having lost her natural constituency, which was the affluent, right-wing Establishment, Mrs. Vlachos has concentrated her fire against America. Readers, however, remain unimpressed. Her circulation figures hover around 20,000 daily.

Despite Premier Karamanlis's efforts to reduce friction between the two countries, the anti-Americanism of the Greek press has become so strident that it threatens to damage relations for years to come. The items listed below were picked at random. They cannot begin to convey the intensity of the campaign being conducted in Greece against the United States. This is kept alive by the daily publication of fiery editorials and political analyses 'proving' that America is the most fascist, oppressive and imperialist power on earth. Here are a few examples: U.S. military personnel in Greece are described as an 'occupation army' (*Athinaiki*, December 1975), visiting U.S. bankers and businessmen as C.I.A. agents (*Avghi*, October 1975), U.S. diplomats attending a Greek party as 'Fascists preparing a plot against Greece' (*Ta Nea*, December 1975), and a marine seismic data map drawn by an American consultant firm as a 'plot by the C.I.A. to turn over our oil to Turkey' (*Ta Nea*, April 1976). There have also been headlines announcing that definite proof has been discovered that America ordered Turkey's invasion of Cyprus.

Foreign journalists who reported the excesses of the Greek press and its poisonous anti-Americanism were immediately 'exposed' as C.I.A. agents and their characters assassinated by insinuation, half-truths, distortion of what they wrote, and out-and-out smears.

Such press practices were indirectly responsible for the murder of C.I.A. station chief Richard Welch on Christmas Eve 1975. Far from propitiating anti-American feelings, the assassination served only to intensify them. The press went so far as to suggest that Welch was murdered by his own colleagues. In fact he was not, nor was he killed on the orders of the K.G.B. because of his previous work against Communist infiltration in South America, as was originally thought. He was murdered by three Cypriots who are rumoured to be members of E.O.K.A.-B. The ring has been apprehended by the Greek intelligence service, working together with the C.I.A. So far, however, all the necessary proof has not been obtained.

It is typical of Greece's instinct for self-destruction, irresponsible press and opportunistic politicians that two years after the return of democracy the country is still racked by divisions.

Karamanlis and his Government have dismantled the junta apparatus, reorganized the civil service and are preparing the country for admission to the European Common Market some time in 1979. Yet when the majority passes a law in Parliament which does not please Andreas Papandreou's Socialists or the Communists, the tiny minority does not hesitate to walk out of Parliament and take their grievances to the street. Athens has already endured three bloody riots by a small group of provocateurs, with hundreds of people injured and some dead. American warships visiting the Greek islands on courtesy visits have been chased out. The opposition press—which means most newspapers—applauds such actions.

Karamanlis has bent over backwards to appease the Opposition. The more he gives in, however, the more the minority demands. After the press had manipulated a tragic car accident into a political issue, the Minister of Information, an ex-journalist who had left Greece because of the Colonels' regime, issued the following statement: 'A situation prevails in the Greek press which is detrimental to the country's democratic institutions. Newspapers sensationalize with the aim of causing unrest. The common denominator is disrespect for the truth, for the law, and for the citizens. Abuse of democratic freedom is a daily occurrence in the Greek press.'

The Minister, Takis Lambrias, then attacked Papandreou as the man behind both the riots and the general malaise. His words went unheeded, as did the lessons of the past. Further demands for purges, and the virulent anti-American campaign, are inhibiting the Government's programme and polarizing the people.

Unfortunately, throughout the ages, revenge has always been a stronger force in the Greek culture than compassion, and retribution more important than reconstruction, and divisiveness more conspicuous than unity. Karamanlis is the only man who can save the country from another adventure into dictatorship. Will Andreas, the Communists, and the press allow him to? This writer doubts it, although praying fervently that they will; because next time the military intervenes it may not be with a bunch of chicken-hearted Colonels.

Index